THE
GREATEST
COMEBACK

THE
GREATEST
COMEBACK

How Richard Nixon Rose from Defeat
to Create the New Majority

PATRICK J. BUCHANAN

CROWN
FORUM
NEW YORK

Library of Congress Cataloging-in-Publication Data
Buchanan, Patrick J. (Patrick Joseph), 1938–
The greatest comeback / Patrick J. Buchanan. — First edition.
pages   cm
Includes index.
1. Presidents—United States—Election—1968.   2. Nixon,
Richard M. (Richard Milhous), 1913–1994.   3. United States—
Politics and government—1963–1969.   4. Republican Party
(U.S. : 1854–)—History—20th century.   I. Title.
E851.B83 2014
324.973'0904—dc23   2014007614

ISBN 978-0-553-41863-7
eBook ISBN 978-0-553-41864-4

Printed in the United States of America

Unless otherwise designated, all photographs
are from the author's collection.

Book design by Lauren Dong
Jacket design by Jess Morphew
Jacket (front) photograph by Dick Halstead/Getty Images

10 9 8 7 6 5 4 3 2 1

First Edition

To Shelley,
my wife of forty-three years
who was there—right from the beginning

Contents

The Resurrection of Richard Nixon

BARRING A MIRACLE his political career ended
last week.
—*Time* ON NIXON (NOVEMBER 16, 1962)

B UCHANAN, WAS THAT you throwing the eggs?" were the
first words I heard from the 37th President of the United
States.

His limousine rolling up Pennsylvania Avenue after his inaugural had been showered with debris. As my future wife, Shelley, and I were entering the reviewing stand for the inaugural parade, the Secret Service directed us to step off the planks onto the muddy White House lawn. The President was right behind us. As he passed by, Richard Nixon looked over, grinned broadly, and made the crack about the eggs.

It was a sign of the times and the hostile city in which he had taken up residence. He had won with 43 percent of the vote. A shift of 112,000 votes from Nixon to Vice President Humphrey in California would have left him with 261 electoral votes, nine short, and thrown the election into a House of Representatives controlled by the Democratic Party. In the final five weeks, Humphrey had closed a 15-point gap and almost put himself into the history books alongside Truman—and Nixon alongside Dewey. But the question that puzzled friend and enemy alike that January morning in 1969 was:

How did he get here?

In *The Making of the President 1968*, Theodore H. White, chronicler of presidential campaigns, begins with a passage from Dickens's *A Christmas Carol*: "Marley was dead to begin with. There is no doubt whatever about that. The register of his burial was signed by the clergyman, the clerk, the undertaker and the chief mourner. . . . Old Marley was dead as a door-nail."

That Richard Nixon would be delivering his inaugural address from the East Front of the Capitol on January 20, 1969, would have been mind-boggling a few years before. This is not to say that Nixon was not a man of broad knowledge, high intellectual capacity, or consummate political skill. He had been seen in the 1950s as the likely successor to Dwight Eisenhower. As vice president, he had traveled the world, comported himself with dignity during Ike's illnesses, survived a mob attack in Caracas, and come off well in his Kitchen Debate with Soviet dictator Nikita Khrushchev. In 1960, no one had challenged him for the Republican nomination.

Yet Nixon had lost. While the election was among the closest in U.S. history, and there was the aroma of vote fraud in Texas and Chicago, Nixon was seen as a loser. He had not won an election in his own right in ten years. He had twice ridden Eisenhower's coattails into the vice presidency. In the off-year elections of 1954 and 1958, where he had been the standard-bearer, the party had sustained crushing defeats. By the day of Kennedy's inaugural, conservatives were shouldering aside Eisenhower Republicans to engage the Eastern Establishment of Dewey and Rockefeller in a war for the soul of the party. As Democrats had moved beyond Adlai Stevenson to a new dynamic leader, so had we—to Barry Goldwater.

Back home in California, Nixon plotted his comeback. He would challenge Governor Pat Brown in 1962, go to Sacramento, and be available should the party turn again to him. Should the GOP look to a new face in '64, a likely reelection year for JFK, he would finish one term as governor and pursue the presidential nomination in

1968. California was replacing New York as first state and the governor's chair in the Golden State was an ideal launching pad for a second presidential run.

But in 1962 Nixon had lost again. He had begun the campaign behind, but had been gaining ground when the Cuban missile crisis aborted his surge. Kennedy's perceived triumph over Khrushchev had given a boost to every Democrat. Then came the "last press conference," where Nixon berated his tormentors and declared himself finished with politics. "It had seemed the absolute end of a political career," wrote Norman Mailer. "Self-pity in public was as irreversible as suicide." Career over, Nixon packed up his family and moved to New York, the city of his old antagonist Nelson Aldrich Rockefeller.

So it was that Nixon began the sixties losing to Kennedy, losing to Pat Brown, quitting politics, and moving east to practice law. He had lost his political base and seemed to have no political future. How did this politician of the forties and fifties, an Eisenhower Republican of moderate views and middle-class values, a two-time loser, emerge from a decade of assassinations, riots, sexual revolution and social upheaval, and the rise of a radical New Left and a militant New Right to win the presidency?

In "The Snows of Kilimanjaro," Hemingway writes of a mystery on the mountain. "Close to the western summit there is the dried and frozen carcass of a leopard. No one has explained what the leopard was seeking at that altitude." This book is an effort of the aide closest to Nixon in his now-legendary comeback to explain how he maneuvered through the conflicts and chaos of that most turbulent decade of the twentieth century to reach the "western summit"—and become President of the United States.

CHAPTER I

A Loser—in a Party of Losers

SOMETIMES NOTHING is a real cool hand.
—PAUL NEWMAN, *Cool Hand Luke* (1967)

T HE RISE OF Richard Nixon was spectacular.

First elected in 1946, he entered the Republican-controlled 80th Congress with another young veteran, John F. Kennedy, and was put on the House Un-American Activities Committee investigating Communists in the Roosevelt and Truman administrations. Nixon swiftly made a name for himself and became a national hero for standing by ex-Communist Whittaker Chambers and helping expose the wartime treason of Alger Hiss, an icon of the liberal establishment. As the best-known freshman congressman in the country, Nixon won the nominations of both parties in his Orange County district in 1948. For this bipartisan young member of Congress was no Robert Taft conservative. He supported the Marshall Plan, endorsed Dewey at the GOP convention in 1948, and backed NATO in 1949 and military aid to Turkey and Greece, then battling Soviet subversion. Nixon was a Cold Warrior in tune with his times whose anti-Communism paid dividends. Running for the Senate in 1950 against Helen Gahagan Douglas, the ultraliberal wife of actor Melvyn Douglas, Nixon amassed more votes than any candidate in the history of California. Early in that campaign, Jack Kennedy, his colleague and friend, came over to Nixon's Senate office with a $1,000 check from Joe Kennedy for Nixon's campaign against Douglas, whom neither JFK nor his father could stand.

In the battle for the nomination in 1952, Nixon again went against his majority leader, Senator Taft, Mr. Conservative, to support Ike. The Eisenhower-Taft battle was the test of loyalty for conservatives of that era. But Nixon had made the right call. Eisenhower won and put him on the ticket. On January 20, 1953, Richard Nixon, forty years old, six years into his political career, was inaugurated as the second-youngest vice president in U.S. history. Only John C. Breckenridge of Kentucky, James Buchanan's vice president at thirty-seven, had been younger.

By 1956, because of the rough campaigns he had conducted in '46 and '50, and his attack role as number two on the ticket in 1952 and as bayonet of the party in 1954, Nixon was now seen as deeply partisan. In a stunning gesture, President Eisenhower, who had been ready to dump Nixon from the ticket during the "fund scandal" of 1952, which Nixon brilliantly countered with his "Checkers speech," urged Nixon to "chart his own course." Ike offered Nixon any Cabinet post he wanted in a second term save State, which was reserved for John Foster Dulles. With Ike showing a new willingness to drop him from the ticket and move him out of the line of succession, Nixon, wrote biographers Earl Mazo and Stephen Hess, "planned to quit public life in disgust." A source close to Nixon called this "one of the greatest hurts of his . . . career." Nixon fought to hold on to his vice presidency. And Ike relented. But Nixon never forgot.

1960: NIXON VS. KENNEDY

As 1960 approached, Nixon was not only the favorite for the GOP nomination, he was without opposition. Nelson Rockefeller had been elected governor of New York in 1958 and had assumed the leadership of the Eastern Establishment. But only a year in office, in January 1960, he could not take a sabbatical to challenge Nixon in New Hampshire. Had he done so, Rockefeller would have been crushed. Nixon had solidified his party base. The Republican delegation in Congress and the Republican National Committee were behind him, as were the Republican county chairmen. Nixon was Mr. Republican and a household name after having survived a Castroite mob attack in Caracas in 1958, and having debated Soviet dictator Nikita Khrushchev in the model kitchen at the American exhibit in Moscow in 1959. And given the popularity of Eisenhower, who had twice routed Adlai Stevenson and would have been easily reelected to a third term, Nixon was considered a strong favorite to succeed the retiring Ike.

On the Democratic side, Senate Majority Leader Lyndon Johnson and Senator Stuart Symington of Missouri were looking at the nomination, as were their younger colleagues, Hubert Humphrey and John F. Kennedy, who had made a bid to become Adlai's running mate in 1956, when he threw the vice presidential nomination open to the convention floor. But Kennedy had lost to Senator Estes Kefauver of Tennessee.

In 1960, however, beginning in New Hampshire, Kennedy ran in ten primaries, sweeping them all and decisively defeating Humphrey in the two most fiercely contested: Wisconsin, where the Catholic vote came out strong, and West Virginia, the crucial test for a Catholic candidate. Joe Kennedy's money, Jack's dramatized war record, and the glamorous Kennedy family proved decisive. And Humphrey's lack of military service—exploited by JFK surrogate Franklin Roosevelt, Jr., son of the president beloved in the Mountain State for all the New Deal had done—turned it into a rout. Humphrey was finished.

Kennedy won on the first ballot at the Los Angeles convention, and in a bold and brilliant move to hold Texas and the South, put Lyndon Johnson on the ticket. From mid-August to election day, it was one of the closest races in U.S. history. No more than 4 points separated the candidates in the Gallup polls. And among the reasons for the tightness of the race was the public perception that Nixon and Kennedy did not really disagree.

Both men were veterans of World War II, in their forties, and strong anti-Communists, with Kennedy taking a harder line on Cuba than Nixon, who was aware of Eisenhower's plan to support an exile invasion of the island. Nixon took a tougher stance on the use of force to defend Nationalist China's offshore islands of Quemoy and Matsu from the People's Republic of Mao Tse-tung. So alarmed were Democrats that Americans saw the two candidates as almost identical on the issues that Arthur Schlesinger churned out a book titled *Kennedy or Nixon: Does It Make Any Difference?*

It was a rough campaign. Kennedy alleged that the Eisenhower-Nixon administration had allowed a "missile gap" to develop with the Soviet Union. Yet the Cuban missile crisis, two years later, would reveal that the gap was massively in favor of the United States, with tens of thousands of nuclear weapons. Nixon was portrayed by Democrats as a savage and sinister figure, "Tricky Dick," with huge photographs of him with a shifty look carrying the caption "Would You Buy a Used Car from This Man?"

While Nixon was portrayed as a "white-collar McCarthy," it was the Kennedys who had been closer to Joe. Father Joe Kennedy had been a friend, admirer, and supporter of the Wisconsin senator, the Kennedy girls dated Joe, Bobby had worked for him, Teddy played football with him at Hyannis Port, and JFK absented himself on the Senate vote to censure McCarthy. At a Harvard dinner in 1954, when a speaker expressed satisfaction that the college had never produced an Alger Hiss or a Joe McCarthy, JFK roared, "How dare you compare the name of a great American patriot with that of a traitor!" and walked out.

Kennedy had other advantages. The Democratic Party was far larger, measured by its relative strength in the House, the Senate, and state legislatures. And Kennedy—rich, charismatic, charming, and a war hero—was the favorite of a national press that had never taken to Nixon. Many loathed Nixon for having been right on Hiss and for his anti-Communist campaigns of the late '40s and early '50s. And JFK's slogan, "Let's get this country moving again," fit the temper of the times and the mindset of many in the Silent Generation after eight years of the grandfatherly Ike.

Nixon was better known than Kennedy and had experience at the apex of American power as vice president to a successful president who had ended one war in Korea and kept us out of any others. But while Ike had routed Stevenson by 11 points in 1952 and 19 points in 1956, he had presided over a dramatic decline of the Republican Party. When Ike took the oath in 1953, the GOP had majorities in both houses of Congress. By 1960, the GOP was outnumbered 64–34 in the Senate and 283–153 in the House. From the time I first spoke with Nixon he would harp on this shrunken base, in House and Senate seats and state legislators, as a near-fatal weakness. Before we can even think about 1968, he told me many times, we must restore the party base. Otherwise the nomination is almost not worth having.

Kennedy had predicted he would win the election in the debates, and Nixon had agreed to four. And while Nixon held his own or prevailed on the issues in the four, the first debate may have cost him the election.

Not only did Kennedy come off as personable and self-assured, Nixon looked wan and tired and seemed to echo JFK. Weeks earlier, Nixon, while campaigning, had banged his knee on a car door and it had become infected, hospitalizing him and costing him two weeks of his 50-state campaign. He had come to Chicago the night before the debate, continued campaigning that night and the next morning, then arrived at the studio and declined to put on makeup, though he was ten pounds underweight and looked even more so. On substance it was a stand-off. Those hearing the debate on radio thought Nixon had won. But on appearances, Kennedy won hands down. After mid-September, Nixon never led in a Gallup poll, though on election night it was a dead heat.

Despite the allegations of vote fraud, not only in Chicago but Texas, Nixon refused to demand an investigation, and Kennedy was President. "Victory has a thousand fathers, while defeat is an orphan," JFK would say. And Nixon was castigated by Republicans for having blown the election with an uninspiring "me too" campaign.

Nixon, it was assumed, was a loser. He had not won an election in his own right since 1950. He had been carried into the vice presidency twice by Ike. In the off-year elections of 1954 and 1958, when Ike remained aloof and Nixon had been the standard-bearer, the GOP had gone down to defeat. In 1954, with the Army-McCarthy hearings and a Republican Senate moving to censure its most famous and controversial member, Joe McCarthy, who had begun the year with a 50–29 approval rating, the GOP lost both houses.

In 1958, with the Soviets having won the race into space with Sputnik, the GOP dropped 13 Senate seats, the largest loss of any party in history, falling to 34. Democrats picked up 15 seats, including both from the new 49th state of Alaska. In that recession year, where the unions made right-to-work laws a national issue, the GOP also lost 48 House seats, falling to 153. Nixon then lost to Kennedy in 1960 in an election, critics said, he should have won. Though with Nixon at the top of the ticket the GOP had taken back 20 House seats from the Democrats, many Republicans concluded that he had had his shot. We need someone new, they said, we need to find our JFK.

CALIFORNIA DREAMING

Having lost in the closest race of the century, still a young man in presidential politics at forty-eight, Nixon returned to California, his home state, and began to plot his future. Having served six years in the House and Senate and eight as vice president, he had been a leg-islator and adviser to a president. He knew the Congress and knew the White House. What he lacked was executive experience and a political base, if he were again to seek the Republican nomination.

Against the advice of many close associates, Nixon decided to run for governor of California, which was replacing New York as America's most populous state. Victory would provide him with an unrivaled political base. As governor, he could be a kingmaker at the 1964 convention, be drafted for the nomination should the GOP's liberal and conservative wings deadlock, or sit out the prob-able reelection of JFK and seek the nomination in 1968.

The governorship of California perfectly fit the political needs of the ex–vice president. He had never lost in California, had won in a record vote in 1950 for Senate, and had carried the state against JFK. What Nixon did not fully appreciate, however, was the depth, breadth, and intensity of the rebellion rising in his own party against the Eisenhower Republicanism he represented and the centrist campaign he had just conducted. To the New Right, the Eisenhower-Nixon administration had failed to make good on John Foster Dulles's pledge to "roll back" Communism and had failed to roll back the New Deal. It had permitted the establishment of a Communist base camp "90 miles from Key West." The Right did not want to see Nixon back as party leader in 1964. As early as April 1961, I had told a college friend that Barry Goldwater was the man to take on JFK, who was even then wiping the egg off his face for the fiasco at the Bay of Pigs. Thus when Nixon declared for governor of California, he found he already had stiff competition.

A STAR OF the "Thundering Herd," the USC Rose Bowl teams in 1939 and 1940, and a wartime Navy pilot, Joe Shell was the minority leader in the state assembly. He had declared for governor before Nixon. Shell painted Nixon as an opportunist who wanted the governorship as a base from which to plan a second run for the presidency. Shell's right-wing backers portrayed Nixon as a card-carrying member of that suspect sanctum sanctorum of the Eastern Liberal Establishment, the Council on Foreign Relations.

The John Birch Society, whose founder and leader, Robert Welch, in his privately circulated book, *The Politician*, had described Ike as a "dedicated, conscious agent of the communist conspiracy," became a major issue. Nixon had denounced the Birchers. But the state party platform, though it condemned the society's leaders, did not condemn the society itself. Shell argued that the Birchers should be allowed to remain active in the GOP.

After Nixon rolled up a 2–1 victory in the primary, Shell began to make demands as the price of his endorsement. Liberal Republican Tom Kuchel, who had been named by Governor Earl Warren to fill Nixon's Senate seat when he became vice president, refused to endorse Nixon. Governor Pat Brown said Nixon wanted to "double-park in Sacramento" before running again for president. Buffeted from left and right, his momentum halted by the Cuban missile crisis, Nixon lost. His defeat became the stuff of legend when, exhausted and bitter the morning after, he told the press this was the end of his political career and fired a virtual 12-gauge blast into the faces of his tormentors: "Think of all the fun you'll be missing. . . . You don't have Nixon to kick around anymore because, gentlemen, this is my last press conference." Even admirers agreed that Nixon's hour at the apex of American politics was over.

ABC'S "OBITUARY"

The following Sunday, November 11, Howard K. Smith anchored ABC's "The Political Obituary of Richard M. Nixon," an hour-long hatchet job. In the opening, Smith introduced Jerry Voorhis, who called Nixon "a ruthless opponent." Voorhis was followed by Alger

Hiss, who had been convicted of perjury for lying under oath about being a wartime spy for Stalin, and whose treason Nixon had helped to expose. Implying that he had been railroaded, Hiss said Nixon had seemed "less interested in developing facts than in presenting some kind of preconceived case." Smith twice called Nixon a "savage political fighter," who had "accused great and patriotic Americans like Adlai Stevenson of things they and others cannot forgive." Smith added that Nixon possessed an "un-subtle mind, a two plus two equals four mind, someone called it—agile but not deep."

The "obituary" seemed to confirm everything Nixon had said about a hostile and vindictive press. Tens of thousands of telegrams poured in to ABC. Four ABC stations refused to carry the program. The Schick Safety Razor Company, Kemper Insurance, and Pacific Hawaiian Company, makers of Hawaiian Punch, sought to cancel their advertising with ABC.

Among the many newspapers that condemned ABC was the *Los Angeles Times*. In an editorial, "The Inning of the Anti-Nixon Liberals," the *Times* called the use of Hiss the "central obscenity":

> For years the liberals have been panting for the Walpurgis Night when they would all dance on the grave of Richard Nixon. They performed the first of their ghoulish revels on Sunday night and it was so thoroughly in the medieval crossroads-and-gibbet spirit that even some seasoned Nixon haters must have hurried away to be sick.
>
> It was done with television (ABC, Howard K. Smith as witch-master) and Alger Hiss held the position of chief gloater.

Ayn Rand wrote that giving national television time to a Soviet spy "to pass judgment" on a former vice president of the United States was a "national disgrace . . . typical of the hooligan extremes to which certain 'liberals' permit themselves to go." Democratic senator Tom Dodd, professing his "personal disgust," called on the FCC to investigate ABC's use of the Stalinist spy who had spent three years in federal prison for lying under oath.

"Reprehensible Hiss Incident" was the title of the *St. Louis Globe-Democrat*'s lead editorial that accused ABC of "wretchedly bad taste," a "disgraceful attack" on a statesman. When ABC, in retreat, offered Nixon equal time, and Nixon's staff dismissed it as an "atrocious, pathetic gesture," the *Globe-Democrat* landed on the network again. Jim Hagerty, Ike's press secretary and now president of ABC, defended Smith's editorial judgment on First Amendment grounds. In the paper's third editorial, which I wrote, we said of ABC, "If patriotism is the last refuge of the scoundrel, so has freedom of the press been used to cover a multitude of sins committed in its name."

Declared dead after his defeat, Nixon was now a figure of sympathy. And if his career was marked by a malevolent view of the press, he had not reached the verdict without a preponderance of evidence. "They hate me and I welcome their hatred," FDR had said of those he called the "money changers in the temple of our civilization."

About the press Nixon felt the same. "The press is the enemy," he would tell me when I suggested they might be a composite of the good, the bad, and the ugly. Early in our White House years, I would come around to Nixon's view: It was us or them. And I would author, with Nixon's own editing, Vice President Spiro T. Agnew's attack on the networks.

Jack Kennedy, too, felt that the press had been merciless on Nixon. Early in the 1960 campaign, when his neighbor Joan Gardner attended a party at his Georgetown home and referred to Nixon as "dreadful," JFK shot back, "You have no idea what he's been through. Dick Nixon is the victim of the worst press that ever hit a politician in this country. What they did to him in the Helen Gahagan Douglas race was disgusting."

In 1966, Nixon, who did not read many novels, instructed me to read *Capable of Honor*, the new novel by Allen Drury, who had won a Pulitzer for *Advise and Consent* in 1960. Drury lacerated America's TV commentators and liberal columnists as systematic distorters of the truth for political ends. Nixon loved the satirical novel and would carry it back and forth to work. Drury's book made up in bile what it lacked in subtlety.

THE SURVIVOR OF '64

Nixon sat out the Goldwater-Rockefeller battle of 1964, though in New Hampshire and other primary states he received thousands of write-in votes. Theodore H. White, however, depicts Nixon as maneuvering offstage at the Cleveland Governors' Conference in June to block Goldwater's nomination. After meeting with Nixon, Governor George Romney told the press Nixon had urged him to get in. Nixon denied it. To the press it appeared that Nixon wanted to derail the Goldwater express by pushing Romney out onto the tracks, anticipating that, should the convention deadlock, he would emerge as the compromise candidate.

At a press conference the morning after his meeting with Romney, Nixon said that "it would be a tragedy if Senator Goldwater's views, as previously stated, were not challenged and repudiated." The dispatches out of Cleveland "made it seem obvious that Nixon was trying to deadlock the nomination against him, using Romney as the pawn," wrote White. "Nixon's posture of neutrality and party-healer was now shattered." In an editorial, "Comedy of Cleveland," the *Globe-Democrat* said Nixon's "political sagacity" had "badly sagged." Goldwater was brutally dismissive: "Nixon sounds more and more like Harold Stassen [the perennial GOP candidate] every day." Perhaps with the Cleveland debacle in mind, Nixon told me: "Buchanan, if you ever hear of a group forming up to 'Stop X,' put your money on X."

After Cleveland, Nixon awoke to reality. The party was going with Goldwater, even if it meant going over the cliff. Nixon then volunteered to speak at the convention and introduce Goldwater. Cleveland was forgotten when Nixon took the podium at the San Francisco Cow Palace to deliver his call for party unity:

> Before this convention we were Goldwater Republicans, Rockefeller Republicans, Scranton Republicans, Lodge Republicans, but now that this convention has met and made its decision, we are Republicans, period, working for Barry Goldwater.
>
> And to those few, if there are some, who say that they are going to sit it out or take a walk, or even go on a boat ride, I have to answer; in the words of Barry Goldwater in 1960, "Let's grow up, Republicans, let's go to work—and we shall win in November."

Nixon introduced as the party's nominee "Mr. Conservative" and "Mr. Republican . . . the man who, after the greatest campaign in history, will be Mr. President—Barry Goldwater."

Goldwater, however, was not in a conciliatory frame of mind. Burned and bitter over the rule-or-ruin tactics of Romney, Rockefeller, and Scranton, who had demanded the Republican platform denounce the Birch Society for being equally repellent as the Communist Party and the Ku Klux Klan, Goldwater cast aside considerations of party unity and, as "Cactus Jack" Garner used to say, gave "it to 'em with the bark on."

> Anyone who joins us in all sincerity, we welcome. Those who do not care for our cause, we don't expect to enter our ranks, in any case. And let our Republicanism . . . not be made fuzzy and futile by unthinking and stupid labels.
>
> I would remind you that extremism in the defense of liberty is no vice! And let me remind you also that moderation in the pursuit of justice is no virtue!

Goldwater had told the unreconciled Republicans he did not expect or want their support. In the limousine carrying Nixon away from the Cow Palace the air was blue. He had brought the convention together in one of his finest speeches, and Barry had proceeded to tear it apart again.

In that summer of '64, after driving from St. Louis to Philadelphia, Mississippi, where the civil rights workers had just gone missing, then to Meridian, and Birmingham and Anniston, Alabama, I had gone to Stone Harbor, New Jersey, to view the Cow Palace convention with my parents. I watched the crowd shaking its fists at the press table when Ike denounced "sensation-seeking columnists and commentators," the jeering and hooting as a smirking Rockefeller goaded the convention to put the Birch Society into the same box as the Communist Party and the KKK, and then Nixon's call for unity.

When Goldwater delivered his most memorable line, about extremism, my father got up and said, "He's finished!" I did not disagree. With these words Goldwater had gained nothing, but had persuaded millions, like my father, who were taking their first long look at the conservative nominee, that he just might be what his enemies said he was. Eisenhower reacted as my father did. Goldwater's bitterness was understandable, but he was now the nominee. Nixon was trying to bury the convention's rancor and look to the future race against LBJ. Barry had used the most important speech he would ever deliver to let his enemies know what he thought of them. Nixon was trying to build a bridge for moderates to cross over and come home. Barry was speaking to and for his followers, and giving his liberal tormentors a taste of his contempt. Hearing him, I knew the cause in which I believed and the movement to which I belonged were headed for a crushing defeat.

Goldwater lost all but 5 states of the Deep South and Arizona, as the GOP lost 2 more Senate seats, reducing its number to 32. And the party lost 36 House seats, cutting its number to 140. The GOP had been chopped to less than one-third of each house of Congress. Republican governorships had been cut to 17. The slaughter of state legislators—529 seats were lost—left the GOP outnumbered 5,071 to 2,520 in the 50 legislatures. In only 6 states did Republicans still control both houses. While Nixon had been the principal surrogate in the Goldwater defeat, campaigning harder for him than did the nominee himself, no one blamed him. Nixon was credited for having put himself on the line to save as many Republicans as he was able to save in that Pickett's Charge of the American Right.

Romney and Rockefeller had lit out for the tall grass. Nixon would be standing beside Mr. Conservative as the party went down to its worst defeat since Alf Landon was the nominee in 1936. His campaigning in 36 states for Goldwater and every Republican who asked for his help accorded with Nixon's instincts—and his interests. When good times return, we remember who was there in the bad times, and who was not. "From the coming disaster," wrote Tom Wicker of '64, "like Ishmael floating on his coffin, Richard Nixon only 'would escape alone to tell thee'—not, in his case, of past tragedy, but of future triumph." But few saw it that way then.

Standing amid the ruins, Nixon ripped into Rockefeller as a "party divider" who had forfeited any right to lead by deserting his post in the hour of battle. Columnist Murray Kempton wrote that Nixon, who had called for a time of healing, seemed to want to "bind up the wounds of the Republican Party with a tourniquet around the neck of Nelson Rockefeller."

Goldwater thanked Nixon profusely and publicly pledged his support for a second Nixon run for the presidency. The bitterness toward Rockefeller and Romney ran deep. Better to fail in a cause that will one day triumph than succeed in a cause that will one day fail, we conservatives said in our humiliation. Nixon's stand, beside Barry Goldwater in that cause, was a classic case of the right thing being the smart thing to do.

Yet, as 1965 opened, with Lyndon Johnson prepared to launch

his Great Society, with 295 Democrats in the House and 68 in the Senate, the Republican Party was at its nadir. In the twelve years since Ike had first taken the oath of office with Republicans in control of both houses, party strength in Congress had been cut to less than one-half that of the Democratic Party.

"Will the GOP Survive?" was a common theme in those middle years of the sixties, when liberalism and the Democratic Party held sway over all. And Nixon was now written off as a chronic loser in what the columnists and authors were calling "The Party That Lost Its Head."

CHAPTER 2

Rapprochement with the Right

YOU GO HUNTING where the ducks are.
—BARRY GOLDWATER

THIS, THEN, WAS how Nixon was seen from various vantage points when I arrived at Nixon, Mudge, Rose, Guthrie & Alexander, next door to the New York Stock Exchange at the corner of Wall and Broad, in December 1965. From Harvard to Hollywood, liberals viewed Nixon with derision and contempt. To them he had been a Red-baiter in the days of Joe McCarthy and the Hollywood blacklist, a savage partisan who impugned the patriotism of every liberal against whom he had run, from Jerry Voorhis in 1946, to Helen Gahagan Douglas in 1950, to Truman and Stevenson. Liberals had reveled in his defeats, humiliation, and departure from politics. Said writer-editor Victor Navasky, "You can't have voted for Richard Nixon and be a member of the New York intellectual establishment."

The Republican establishment had never taken to him. After Nixon moved to New York in 1963 and entered what he called his "wilderness years," Rockefeller, Senator Jacob Javits, and the Empire State Republican Party shunned him. The national party, however, liked and respected Nixon, and many revered him. To these folks he was a tireless campaigner, a brilliant strategist, a statesman, and a figure of history welcome in their precincts.

And he had two qualities few denied: Nixon was a loyalist and Nixon was a fighter. Even his enemies said of him that Nixon had a unique ability to decapitate a man while leaving the skull on the shoulders. Every poll of Republican county chairmen revealed Nixon to be their favorite for 1968. Their hesitancy in supporting him could be summed up in three words: "He can't win." We love him, the rank and file would say, we just can't elect him. "Nixon is a loser."

And the conservatives? Those on the Right who respected Nixon did so for the reasons the Left reviled him. He had exposed Hiss. He was an anti-Communist who had laid the wood on Truman and Adlai Stevenson for his "Ph.D. from Dean Acheson's college of cowardly communist containment." Most critically, he had stood with Goldwater when the establishment abandoned him. For the Right in the 1960s, the preeminent issue was Communism and the Cold War. And here Nixon's credentials were unimpeachable and unrivaled. It was his experience and his views on foreign policy that had drawn me to Nixon.

Nixon's troubles with conservatives were rooted in a belief that, at heart, "he is not one of us." He had vaulted to national prominence before the birth of our movement. In college he had been "a liberal" but "not a flaming liberal." In law school his heroes were Justices Brandeis, Cardozo, and Charles Evans Hughes. He had, early on, denounced the Birch Society. In his 1962 primary race against state assemblyman Joe Shell, Nixon had called himself a "progressive conservative." He was seen by many as a moderate they did not trust but might have to accept as the alternative to a Rockefeller or a Romney, or one of the others who had gone over the hill in 1964. On the hard right many could not abide Nixon (nor he them). Yet there was a cold pragmatic argument for Nixon on the right: What other potential nominee is out there who is preferable? For many on the right, a Nixon candidacy was the fallback position to which we had to retreat after the Little Bighorn.

"THE MUNICH OF THE REPUBLICAN PARTY"

Most damaging to Nixon's reputation with the Right was the Pact of Fifth Avenue, back in the summer of 1960. On the eve of the Chicago convention, Nixon had flown to New York to negotiate with Governor Nelson Rockefeller at his apartment on Fifth Avenue. He wanted Rockefeller's endorsement and perhaps to persuade him to take second spot on a Nixon ticket, which might ensure victory. To smooth the negotiations, Nixon signed on to some of Rockefeller's ideas and phoned the platform committee to insist that they be incorporated.

The changes in the platform were insignificant. But that Nixon had requested the meeting, flown to New York, agreed to Rockefeller's changes, and phoned them in to a platform committee more conservative than Nixon was, let alone Rockefeller, and that Rockefeller had announced the deal—proved explosive.

"The Munich of the Republican Party!" roared Senator Barry Goldwater. "Sellout!" echoed the Right. The Pact of Fifth Avenue resurrected a latent distrust of Nixon and ignited a revolt to seize the nomination and confer it on the Arizonan. Goldwater had to take the podium to quash the insurgency.

"Let's grow up, conservatives," Goldwater told the convention. "If we want to take this party back, and I think we can, let's get to work." This was a seminal movement in the history of the Right. When Rockefeller arrived in Chicago, he introduced the nominee as a "man of courage . . . of vision and of judgment . . . Richard E. Nixon."

When Nixon lost to Kennedy, conservatives who thought he had run a "me too" campaign turned to the man who now wore the mantle of Mr. Conservative. A Draft Goldwater Committee was formed without any commitment from the senator to run in 1964. The issues that drove the conservative movement were America's perceived retreat in the world, the size and power of government, and law and order. Books like Goldwater's *The Conscience of a Conservative* and *Why Not Victory?*, Phyllis Schlafly's *A Choice, Not an Echo*, and John Stormer's *None Dare Call It Treason* sold in the millions. Symbolically, Schlafly and Stormer lived in the American heartland—the St. Louis area.

AMERICA, 1965

After Goldwater's crushing defeat, Lyndon Johnson had majorities in both houses unseen since the high tide of the New Deal after FDR's 46-state landslide in 1936. He swiftly exploited them to lay the foundations of his Great Society. By early 1965, construction had begun: Medicare, Medicaid, the Elementary and Secondary Education Act, the Higher Education Act, the national endowments for arts and humanities. The Immigration Act of 1965, whose floor manager was Senator Edward Kennedy, was signed into law and Executive Order 11246 was issued, mandating affirmative action in hiring and employment. Of these last two measures, the first would change the racial and ethnic composition of America and the latter establish a system of racial entitlements that would be roiling the nation half a century later.

After Bloody Sunday at the Edmund Pettus Bridge in Selma in March 1965 came the Voting Rights Act of August. But it was followed by the weeklong Watts riot in Los Angeles, the worst in an American city since Lincoln ordered Gettysburg veterans of the Army of the Potomac into New York to crush the Irish antidraft uprising that saw the lynching of Negroes.

But well before Watts in that year 1965, another war was suddenly looming. "We can never stand aside, prideful in isolation," LBJ had said in his inaugural address of January 20. Translation: The United States will do what it must to stop the Communists from conquering South Vietnam.

On February 6, 1965, the U.S. airbase at Pleiku in the Central

Highlands was hit by the Viet Cong with eight Americans dead, 126 wounded, ten aircraft destroyed. In March came Rolling Thunder, the bombing of North Vietnam, as 3,500 Marines came ashore at China Beach to protect the base at Danang. Polls showed support for LBJ at 70 percent—and support for the war at 80 percent. In June, Air Marshal Nguyen Cao Ky took over as prime minister and General Nguyen Van Thieu as president, the tenth Saigon government since the overthrow and murder of President Ngo Dinh Diem the month JFK was assassinated. In November came the first collision of U.S. troops and North Vietnamese regulars in the Ia Drang Valley. After visiting Vietnam, Secretary of Defense Robert McNamara privately warned we could anticipate a time when we would be losing 1,000 American soldiers a month.

COMING ABOARD

A conservative since I can remember, I had been a backer of Barry Goldwater from the day Nixon conceded in 1960. Arriving at the *St. Louis Globe-Democrat* from Columbia Journalism School in June 1962, I had maneuvered myself onto the editorial page by August. The *Globe-Democrat* had backed Goldwater for the nomination, but when he went down to defeat, I wrote a 2,000-word essay: "What Is the Future for Conservatism?"

"Was the Goldwater candidacy the high-water mark of a conservative tide which will now ebb back into the footnotes of history?" I asked. After detailing the mistakes of the candidate and campaign, perhaps too harshly, I answered, "No, no matter that the scribes of the left are now publishing their meticulously prepared elegies over conservatism, the movement was not repudiated and is by no means dead. It was Mr. Goldwater who was repudiated and may well be politically dead." At the essay's end, I ventured a prediction that has stood the test of time.

[T]he new conservatism ante-dated Goldwater, made him a national figure to rival Presidents, and will post-date him.

For that conservatism depends primarily for its momentum upon one fact: The abject failure of the ideology of Western liberalism to either halt or reverse the advance of totalitarian Communism. As there is no sign today liberalism has learned how to check that advance, there is no sign the conservative movement will wither and die. It has lost a battle, not the war.

In early December 1965, I learned that Nixon would be speaking at a Republican gathering in Belleville, Illinois, across the river from St. Louis, filling in for an ailing Everett Dirksen. And *Globe-Democrat* cartoonist Don Hesse, a good friend, would be hosting the reception following. I wanted to meet Nixon to see if I might get aboard his 1968 campaign early, a campaign I saw as inevitable. I was certain he was going to run, that his only serious rival was Romney, and that an alignment of the conservative movement with the Nixon Republicans could ensure his nomination.

After three years of writing editorials, I was losing my enthusiasm. Although I was perhaps in line to be editorial editor before my thirtieth birthday, the prospect of a life in St. Louis, writing editorials, no longer held the attraction it once did. "It is required of a man that he should share the passion and action of his time at peril of being judged not to have lived," said Oliver Wendell Holmes. I believed that then, and I had a card to play with Nixon.

Ten years before, I had been sitting on the caddie log at the all-male Burning Tree Club where Eisenhower golfed, when the plaid golf bag of the vice president was brought out, and the pro stared over at me and my friend Pete Cook, the only white caddies. The veteran caddies had taken out their afternoon bags. So it was that I spent four hours with Vice President Nixon. My memories of that day sixty years ago endure. In his early forties, Nixon, of medium height and build, was not a natural athlete. His swing was stiff and jerky. His drives were grounders, pop flies, an occasional single. I spent time avoiding the poison ivy finding his ball. But something else was obvious. Nixon was happy out there with the guys at that all-male club. He was enjoying himself hugely. Seeing a familiar figure across a fairway, Nixon shouted, "Hey, Stu, what are you doing out here? There's a vote up on the Hill!" "Tell 'em to shove it up their pratt!" hollered back Senator Stu Symington of Missouri. Nixon laughed heartily and played on.

In Hesse's kitchen, I brought up with Nixon our previous encounter, mentioned the plaid bag and the names of the pro at Burning Tree, Max Elbin, and the assistant pro, Don Sailer, to convince Nixon I was not making this up. "If you're going to run in '68," I said, "I'd like to get aboard early."

Unimpressed by my title of assistant editorial editor, Nixon wanted to know what I wrote. As there were only two writers on the editorial page at the *Globe-Democrat*, other than the editor, I told him I wrote on all issues, foreign and domestic, three or four editorials a day. As for my getting aboard early, Nixon said, 1968 would hinge on how the party did in recouping its losses in 1964, and that was where his energies would be directed, on the campaign a year off, in 1966.

The next morning, on the long drive from Belleville to the St. Louis airport, Nixon had questioned Hesse intently about me. My hopes dimmed when I heard nothing for days. Then came a call from New York. Could I, said the familiar voice, fly to New York to talk further? I told the former vice president he should probably ask my publisher. Richard H. Amberg was soon in my office, stunned he had just received a call from Richard Nixon asking permission for me to come visit him. Of course you can go, he said.

That meeting with Nixon after I had waited for hours in the office of his secretary, Rose Mary Woods, made an impression. I had just turned twenty-seven. Nixon was fifty-three, younger than

Rockefeller, Romney, or Reagan, though he had been a national figure since I was ten. None of his rivals had a career that remotely matched his. He moved from subject to subject swiftly and pressed me on everything from the war to the conservative movement to civil rights. He was an exhausting interviewer. When Rose interrupted to say Delaware senator John Williams was on the line, I got up to step out of his office. Nixon waved for me to stay and went on to advise Williams on strategy for the tax legislation in Congress. After three hours, Nixon returned to the issue that seemed most on his mind—ideology:

"You're not as conservative as Bill Buckley, are you?" he pressed.

I had written a *Globe-Democrat* endorsement of Buckley for mayor of New York, but felt a noncommittal answer might be best: "I have great respect for Bill Buckley." At meeting's end Nixon said he wanted to hire me—for one year. The pay would be $13,500—a rate of $12,000 for the first six months and $15,000 the last six. This was half again the $9,000 I was making at the *Globe-Democrat*, where I had reached the top five-year Guild scale in three. My assignments would be to handle his growing volume of mail, help produce a monthly column he had agreed to write for the North American Newspaper Alliance, and assist him in the off-year elections in 1966.

I accepted, but told him he should call the publisher. Nixon did. I was aboard. By Christmas I was headed for New York. From January 1966 until that August morning in 1974 when Marine One lifted off the White House lawn for Andrews, to carry Nixon to his last trip aboard Air Force One as President, I was with him.

SETTLING IN AT NIXON, MUDGE

In the office outside Nixon's corner office were three desks. Rose Mary Woods, his secretary since 1951, occupied one. I occupied the second. The third was for "Miss Ryan," who handled calls and helped Rose with the secretarial work. Patricia Ryan was the maiden name of Pat Nixon, the future first lady from whom I used to bum cigarettes.

On my first day I brought in my portable typewriter. Nixon insisted I switch to an electric. He wanted his staff proficient with the latest equipment. A first assignment was to research the origins of the Republican Party and identify the elements that had come together to create it in the 1850s. Nixon wanted to show, in his Lincoln Day speeches, how, as the GOP had been from birth a coalition that united in common purpose to become America's majority party, so the sundered party of 1964 could be brought together for victory in 1966 and beyond.

Nixon wanted the paper the next day. I took the subway to Columbia and spent until midnight at the university library. The following day I had on his desk a 700-word "Memo to RN: GOP Circa 1860." It began:

> The party of which Lincoln was leader after his nomination was a potpourri of dissident elements. It included men who seemed to be united only in the anticipation of political power and in a mutual hostility to Jacksonian Democracy as practiced by Pierce and Buchanan.

Among the groups making up the new Republican Party, I wrote, were anti-Catholic Know-Nothings, Prohibitionists "who bore no love for the whiskey-drinking Irish and beer-drinking German immigrants," Free-Soilers and Barnburners from New York, and Old Whigs, unionists who loved Henry Clay but were anathema to the abolitionists. They united behind Lincoln because he would preserve the Union, was acceptable on slavery, and could carry Pennsylvania, Indiana, and New Jersey. During the "interregnum," as South Carolina and 6 more Southern states seceded, "the Republican Party seemed to be united only in mutual hope for political spoils." Horace

Greeley's *New York Herald* "was still speaking of the 'irrepressible conflict' within the Republican Party." It was Fort Sumter that had brought the party together. I yet have a copy of the memo, but cannot recall Nixon using any of this in Lincoln Day speeches, as there was nothing romantic or relevant about the ingredients of that first Republican stew. And though a war had united the Republican Party of 1861, a war was beginning to divide the Republican Party of 1966, as it had already the American people.

EARLY IN FEBRUARY, I asked Nixon to send me to a conference of researchers being put on in Chicago by the Republican National Committee. One of the pro-Nixon men I met was Wes Adams, director of research for the South Carolina party. When I got back to 20 Broad, I sent Nixon a brief report of how impressed I had been with one particular group:

> The conference was largely a Romney show. The Michigan delegation, if it was not the largest, was the most in evidence and it was not the state committee we viewed, but the personal research staff of the Governor. Romney's executive assistant, a rather suave fellow, is a Ph.D.; he handled two of the lectures himself, and spent more than 90 percent of his time on the platform. . . .
>
> My own impression of Romney's crowd is high. They seem quite competent and exceedingly cocky. Their interest is in their own man, not in the GOP in Michigan and certainly not in the state committee of Michigan.

Two attendees who introduced themselves as Nixon men told me that at an earlier conference in Kansas City the Romney team also dominated the proceedings. The suave fellow was Walter De Vries.

NIXON MENTIONED SEVERAL individuals I should get to know in New York and DC: Vic Lasky, columnist and author of the 1963 best-seller *J.F.K.: The Man and the Myth*; Charlie McWhorter, his legislative aide in vice presidential days, who had been the national chairman of the Young Republicans, and Bill Safire, who had a PR firm. In Washington, where I would return home most weekends, I was told to get together with Bill Stover and "Sandy" Quinn, former Nixon staffers now with Senator George Murphy; and Agnes Waldron, a tough, loyal, caustic, chain-smoking lady who worked on the Hill and wrote out in longhand questions and answers to prepare Nixon for his press conferences. All were Nixon loyalists. All would become lifelong friends. Sandy would run the Nixon Foundation. Agnes was the first woman to become a special assistant to three presidents, heading the research office in the Nixon, Ford, and Reagan White Houses. In 1991, I would deliver her eulogy at St. Joseph's Catholic Church on Capitol Hill, where she lived most of her life.

My closest friendship was with Rose Woods, a woman of extraordinary efficiency and the quintessence of loyalty. She had been with Nixon almost since the Hiss case and had been beside him in 1952 when Nixon was charged by a hostile liberal media with having had his personal expenses paid by rich Republicans. Nixon answered his attackers with his "Checkers speech," the most effective use of television by a political figure up to that time, which secured his place on the ticket. Rose had traveled the world with Vice President Nixon. She was like an aunt to Tricia and Julie. When everyone else departed after 1962, Rose had stayed. From day one she took me under her wing.

One morning, on a day Nixon planned lunch with former New York governor Tom Dewey at the Recess Club, Rose went into his office and persuaded him to take me. Thus did I meet the GOP nominee who had lost to FDR in '44—and to Truman on November 2, 1948, my tenth birthday. Sitting down the table from the cool, cerebral Dewey, I recalled Alice Roosevelt Longworth's crack about "the little man on the wedding cake," and how Senator Everett Dirksen, speaking for his leader Robert Taft at the 1952 Republican Convention, had glared down from the podium at a smirking Dewey to declaim: Twice we have followed you, and twice you led us down the road to defeat. We shall not follow you a third time. As historian Richard Norton Smith describes it, "The place went wild, booing, hissing, cheering. Dewey was imperturbable because he knew he had the votes and Eisenhower wins the nomination."

That 1952 party had turned its back on Taft again, listened to Dewey, and nominated Ike. Yet, not two years before this lunch, this paragon of the establishment missed his first convention since 1936, not wanting to see his party torn away from him and his crowd forever dispossessed of what they thought had belonged to them. The great man was yesterday. We were tomorrow. Yet I remain grateful to Rose that I got to meet this legend of my boyhood.

SHOULD NIXON COURT THE LIBERALS?

Another loyalist I met early in 1966 was John Whitaker, a veteran advance man. On one of my trips home he invited me to dinner, laid out his thoughts on how Nixon ought to proceed, and asked me to convey them.

I did. A 1,000-word memo to Nixon began, "John's thinking runs thus. <u>We ought to move to the left, and not worry excessively about the conservatives in the party</u>." We should develop programs to capture from the Democrats the image of a party that cares about "the forgotten man at the bottom of the economic pyramid." John suggests "that you give some consideration to, and perhaps put some feelers out on, a possible trip to Red China." Following which I wrote, "To me this is beyond the realm of conception." Among the first strategy memos I would send to Nixon, this one dealt directly with the deep divide in Nixon's household that would last through the campaign of 1968 and into his presidency. My memo went on:

> I hope I have been fair to John who is a splendid fellow [who] . . . shares Bill Safire's conviction that we ought to vigorously and openly court the liberals and the left—and not spend any excessive hours worrying about the conservatives as they have no place to go anyway.

In rebuttal I analyzed the state of the conservative movement and predicted the reaction should Nixon pursue the Whitaker-Safire line.

> The right wing of the party is hurting psychologically. It feels the left wing stabbed it in the back in 1964 (right) and yet at the same time it recognizes that simon-pure conservatism alone will never prevail in a national election (right).
> [*National Review*] is . . . the spokesman for the intelligentsia of the right, and it is evident to me . . . that the conservatives are willing to compromise and move left a bit and throw their full support behind you.

But we will imperil any Nixon-conservative alliance, I wrote, if we pursue the Whitaker-Safire line. "[I]f we should suddenly strike out to the left of Johnson, it would produce the greatest defection in history since Constantine committed Rome to Christianity." We ought rightly to zero in on the damage done by inflation to the "little people," but,

> to move to the left of Johnson in terms of what we can promise the people in the way of goodies seems to me to be a position which would be both inconsistent and politically suicidal. . . .

Any dramatic thrust to the left of Johnson (especially in the arena of foreign policy) would send tens of thousands of conservatives packing with no commensurate gain I can see for our efforts.

Right now you are the only individual of national stature in the party who can hold the overwhelming allegiance of the right wing. . . . To retain this allegiance we need not cater to conservatives. Half of the fight in holding them is simply reiteration of your historic strong stand in foreign policy.

Rather than the *apertura a sinistra* John and Bill were pushing, I urged the opposite course: Hold the allegiance of the party rank and file by campaigning for Republicans, left, right, and center. Hold conservatives with the Nixon tough stand on foreign policy and by "not deliberately shafting them." Maintain a high caliber of dissent to give independents an alternative to "the Riverboat Gambler's antics" (whose crassness and crudity were by now alienating many who had voted for him in 1964). Hit Johnson on issues that hurt the "little man." Last, there was this possibility: The Democratic Party's left wing could break off: "I think we might get an unexpected hand from the peace-mongers and the Far Left . . . who are blind enough in their contempt for the President to generate a splinter movement [Kennedy-Fulbright ticket] and shear off half of Lyndon's left wing."

What would happen in 1968 with Senators Eugene McCarthy and Bobby Kennedy was discernible to me in early 1966. I had seen the New Left up close at the teach-ins at which I had spoken in St. Louis. Nixon, too, could see it. At the top of my memo, he wrote, "Excellent analysis. I have always shared this view—clearly apart from the politics I don't happen to believe in this 'liberal' crap!"

Nixon's last twelve words were scratched out. Not until writing this book was I able to make them out. Why had he scratched them out? They would not have offended me. My surmise: A considerate man, Nixon had second thoughts about scribbling so dismissive a comment about the liberal views of one of his best-liked and most loyal men. Yet Whitaker, in his reminiscences four decades later, wrote that while sitting beside Nixon on a plane ride to yet another "fat-cat drill," as we called fund-raisers, the Boss "lectured me on the basics of Presidential politics." What had Nixon said?

> The trouble with the far right conservatives is that they really don't give a damn about people and the voters sense that. Yet any Republican candidate can't stray too far from the right-wingers because they can dominate a primary and are even important in a close general election.

That, too, rings authentic. Nixon had grown up in poverty, lost two of his four brothers, one to meningitis, the other to tuberculosis, and likely did not look on the New Deal as taking us "down the road to socialism" but as an effort to help folks like his family. His college teacher and lifelong friend Paul S. Smith volunteered in an oral biography in 1977 that Nixon "grew up in a liberal household." His heroes, said Smith, were William Jennings Bryan, Republican Progressive Theodore Roosevelt, and Woodrow Wilson. His mother was a devout Quaker and pacifist, his father a pro-union man who had read Ida Tarbell's muckraking attack on the alleged sins and crimes of John D. Rockefeller, *The History of the Standard Oil Company,* and would tell customers at his grocery, "I hate Standard Oil and everybody who works for them." Frank Nixon got the gas for his store pump from Richfield, not Standard Oil. Nixon's wife Pat was a "rabid supporter of Al Smith when she was in high school." Smith describes Nixon as "a liberal in a conservative sort of way." The Nixon I knew had many conservative views and values, but was no ideologue. Unlike modern conservatives, he did not view government as the enemy.

Reagan had the zeal of the convert. He *was* one of us. I recall him pulling me aside once in the White House and confiding, "Pat, sometimes I think some of our friends want me to go over the cliff with flags flying." Yes, they did. But to Ronald Reagan they were *our friends*.

NO TALKING IN THE BOYS' ROOM

Our office was on the 24th floor, the senior partners' floor. On one of my first days I sauntered down to the men's room, where one of the senior partners was standing at a urinal. I asked him how things were going. He looked startled and mumbled a reply. That afternoon Rose came back from a partners' meeting to tell me I should put on a jacket before going to the men's room, and should not address any senior partner unless I was spoken to first. Nixon, Mudge was not the newsroom at the *Globe-Democrat*.

While Nixon had laid out specific duties—I worked nights until I had cleared up all his back mail with a letter for his signature or one from me as "Aide to Mr. Nixon"—my view of the job was somewhat larger: to use my position to make Richard Nixon President of the United States. And my primary means of communication with him had been established. I would write daily missives titled "Memo to RN," ranging from a paragraph to ten pages, and put them in Nixon's in-box, and they would come back from his office or apartment with scribbled comments and instructions. Over three years I would write a thousand such memos and I still have them.

My first impression was that Nixon was bored to death with corporate law. He would bring me into his office for two-, three-, four-hour sessions to talk foreign policy, politics, personalities, and he began to confide in me. If I had to practice law the rest of my life, he told me, "I would be mentally dead in two years and physically dead in four." But if he was consumed with issues and ideas, so was I. Still, in 1966, Nixon would take weeks out to argue and reargue before the Supreme Court for the plaintiff in the landmark privacy case of *Time, Inc. v. Hill.* The challenge of pleading a case before the court and his old antagonist Chief Justice Earl Warren, on the right of privacy versus press freedom—and the intense study and time of testing before the Supreme Court—this was an aspect of his legal profession that did capture Nixon's interest. By 5–4 the court ruled for *Life* magazine, and against the Hill family and Nixon.

Another assignment that first year was to travel with him and occupy the aisle seat beside him on the plane to keep people from interrupting him while he was thinking or outlining a speech on the yellow legal pads he constantly carried. On my first trip out with Nixon, to Washington, DC, he had settled into his window seat and I was in the aisle seat, when a forearm shot across my face, hand extended, and a booming voice was saying, "Mr. Vice President. I voted for you. How are you?" The passenger proceeded to start a conversation that I had been put in that first-class seat to prevent.

REPAIRING A BREACH

When I arrived at his law office in January 1966, Nixon had been the recipient of three letters from William Rusher, publisher of *National Review*, the *Iskra* of the conservative movement. Rose showed them to me. Rusher was demanding to know if Nixon had, in an off-the-record briefing with reporters in October—the contents of which had been divulged to columnist Robert Novak— "described the Buckleyites as a threat to the Republican Party even more menacing than the Birchers."

What did Nixon mean by this? Probably this: While the Birchers backed conservatives against liberal and centrist Republicans in primaries, Buckley was running as a third-party candidate for mayor in the general election in New York City against Republican John Lindsay and Democrat Abe Beame. The certain result of Buckley's candidacy would be to siphon off conservative and Republican votes from Lindsay. Buckley was thus a peril to the GOP's chances and a de facto ally of Beame. This would explain Nixon's question to me about Bill Buckley.

The first letter had arrived in October when Buckley was running against Lindsay for mayor of New York. Scribbling on a note to Rose, Nixon had dismissed Rusher's letter—"I don't want to dignify this with a comment." On November 2, 1965, Rusher had written again, saying it was "important to know the accuracy" of the "bitterly hostile words attributed to you by Mr. Novak. Quite frankly, I cannot believe that you uttered those words."

Well, I could believe it. That Nixon neither denied it nor told me to deny it was confirmation for me that he had said it. On February 28, I memoed Nixon of my deepening concern over the damage this could do to us. Evans and Novak had just run a column citing chapter and verse of Nixon's dismissals of Rusher's letters and how this "reveals the confidence gap between Nixon and the conservatives who are essential to his 1968 hopes. . . . [T]he story of the unanswered 'Dear Mr. Nixon' letters has spread all through the influential conservative circles."

In early March, Nixon got a fourth letter from Rusher, accompanied by a *National Review* editorial demanding he explain himself. This was no longer an irritant. It was a major breach, based on what appeared to be a political slur, between Nixon and the foremost conservative writer in the country, and a magazine that conservatives, especially the young, read as gospel. If *NR* started attacking Nixon for trashing Buckley and those who admired him, "the Buckleyites," Nixon could not unite the Right behind him. And Rusher was not going away. He was going to press this until he got a reply, or Nixon was denounced for having disparaged and demeaned the intellectual icon of the movement.

I crafted a response that Nixon approved. Rather than deny Nixon had said it and start a fight with Novak, I wrote that what Nixon meant was that Buckley, "by his repudiation of the Birch

Society in his magazine and syndicated column, had thereby made himself a much stronger candidate and a greater threat to the Republican candidate, Representative Lindsay."

Nixon's warning about the menace of Buckleyism was converted into a compliment to the political sagacity of William F. Buckley. This was close to confessional material.

Buckley graciously accepted my explanation, as did Rusher, the man at *NR* most skeptical of Nixon. That week *National Review* editorialized, "So, all's well that ends well. And if Richard Nixon is willing to give personal leadership to the Republican conservatives, he will find them ready to follow him."

Not only had a potentially grave breach with the Right been sutured, and a path cleared to reconciliation and collaboration, *National Review*, the voice of the conservative movement, was signaling that Nixon was the leader conservatives should follow. Rusher would describe the Buchanan letter as "a masterpiece of broken-field running." The Jesuits at Gonzaga would have called it a violation of the Eighth Commandment.

Yet it was an excellent start to what I had in mind, which was to bring the conservative movement to which I had belonged since college days into alliance with the Nixonian center of the GOP, and deny any challenger the big divisions necessary to block a Nixon nomination.

Later in 1966, in the campaign, I crafted remarks that were inserted into a Nixon speech in Indiana proposing the indexation of Social Security—an annual cost-of-living increase to compensate retirees for inflation—and a tax deduction for losses to savings due to inflation. The indexation of Social Security would become law in the Nixon administration.

In a column, Buckley criticized the tax deduction for savings lost to inflation. I responded, invoking three economists he admired, including Henry Hazlitt, whose idea it had been. There came an invitation to lunch to debate the issue, with Rusher as "moderator."

No debate ensued, but lunches with Buckley and Rusher did. By January we were friends. Buckley and Rusher were invited to meet with Nixon at his apartment. It went well. Buckley's syndicated column would provide consistent support in Nixon's run-up to the 1968 primaries. In November 1967, Buckley endorsed Nixon— over Reagan. Rusher, too, was open to the prospect of a Nixon presidency, and both knew they had a conservative and a confidant in Nixon's office. Later Rusher would ask, "Are you Nixon's ambassador to the conservatives, or our ambassador to Nixon?" The former, always.

While Buckley was a reliable Nixon man in the run-up to 1968, Rusher ran hot and cold. After I sent Nixon one *National Review* piece that Rusher wrote in that summer of '66, where he said that "conservative Republicans probably feel, rather gloomily, that Nixon is the best they can hope for," Nixon scribbled at the top: "Pat—Rusher (from my experience) has always been erratic if not a bit on the nut side." Even Rusher's close friends would not altogether disagree with the "erratic" depiction.

WHILE NIXON WOULD often describe himself as a conservative or a "progressive conservative," he was exasperated by the carping criticism from the Right. "What do they want *now*?" he would turn to me and ask. Once, in a sour moment, he told me that it was a sound rule in politics to "give the nuts 20 percent of what they want." He did not specify whether I was one of those nuts.

Healing the breach with *National Review* was the first step in knitting ties between Nixon, who had entered politics before the modern conservative movement began to flower in the late 1950s and early 1960s, and the Right. Nixon knew the older conservatives— in Congress, the party, and press. But the new conservatives were of a different breed than the Charlie Hallecks and Les Arendses whose golf bags I carried around Burning Tree. They were less tolerant of liberal Republicans and relished ideological combat. In 1964 our movement had torn the nomination away from the establishment that had imposed Willkie, Dewey, and Eisenhower upon the party, an establishment whose acknowledged leader was Governor Nelson Rockefeller of New York.

And after his shabby treatment of our candidate in 1964—he had refused to put on a Goldwater button offered to him—Rocky was dead to us. To conservatives he was a self-absorbed rich man's son who had stiffed Nixon and deserted Goldwater. He could support the nominee only if he was the nominee. But a Rockefeller nomination could not now be imposed on the conservatives who controlled the party in the South and West and had troops everywhere. *New York Times* columnist James Reston had written in 1963 that Rockefeller had as much chance of losing the Republican nomination as he did of going broke. Yet Rocky had been rejected. And he had picked up his marbles and gone home. And few wanted him back in 1968.

In 1960, Nixon had traveled to New York to negotiate the Pact of Fifth Avenue, and ordered the convention to put Rockefeller's ideas in the platform. Those days were now history. The benediction of the Eastern Establishment was no longer essential. Conservatives now held the key to the nomination. I saw my assignment as bringing them into camp to unite with Nixon Republicans to create an invincible party coalition. The threat I saw was not Rockefeller. It was a man who had never held elective office, but whose electrifying television address on Goldwater's behalf late in the campaign of '64 had made him the movement favorite for the title held by Taft and Goldwater himself, the title of Mr. Conservative. Ronald Reagan could pull the conservatives away from Nixon. Rocky was not the problem.

BRINGING IN THE SHEAVES

That same March of 1966, when the breach with *National Review* was being repaired, *Esquire* ran a cover story by Steve Roberts that had been months in the preparation titled "Who's the Next Republican Presidential Candidate?" *Esquire*'s answer was a composite face of the future candidate on the cover. The eyes and nose belonged to Nixon. In the text Roberts reported on a survey *Esquire* had conducted to which 162 GOP notables—governors, senators, congressmen, ex-officeholders, leaders of the party and allied organizations—had responded. While 54 respondents had declined to identify themselves or indicate who they thought would or should be the 1968 nominee, 108 had replied by name. No fewer than 74 named Nixon. No other potential candidate was even close. Romney was second with 14 votes, Scranton third with 10. Mayor John Lindsay and Governor Mark Hatfield of Oregon each had 4. Tied for fifth, with one vote each, were Nelson Rockefeller and Ronald Reagan.

Nixon had twice the strength of all six rivals put together. Five of those rivals were to Nixon's left and almost all had cut Goldwater dead. He had the party center and right to himself, except for Reagan, who, though he got one vote, from the mayor of Salt Lake City, was more conservative than any of the others, and a more identified champion of Goldwater. One need not have a Ph.D. in political science to see that Reagan, who had just announced for governor of California, was a potential threat to any center-right coalition forming behind Nixon to capture the nomination.

The *Esquire* article was manna from heaven. To the key officials who had named Nixon as the Republican who would or should be the nominee, I drafted, and Nixon signed, personal notes. Among the recipients was the ex-chairman of Young Americans for Freedom, Tom Charles Huston. Roberts thought Huston's analysis so representative or compelling he quoted it:

It seems to me that the most important criterion at this time is general acceptability by all wings of the party. Only Richard Nixon meets this criterion. Philosophically he is in the "mainstream" of the party. . . . In 1964 he campaigned diligently on behalf of Senator Goldwater. This certainly increased his stature in the eyes of conservatives who were very distressed with the excessive desire to placate the unreasonable liberalism of Governor Rockefeller in 1960.

Huston was saying that whatever sin Nixon had committed with his Pact of Fifth Avenue was forgiven if not forgotten because of the service he had rendered Barry Goldwater. Nixon sent a note to Huston. He was soon in New York and we were planning a series of private meetings with crucial leaders of the conservative organizations, few of whom Nixon or I had met. No one was more wired in to the organized Right than the twenty-five-year-old who led its youth arm in 1964.

Huston and I arranged for Nixon to meet at the Shoreham Hotel in Washington with the leaders of Young Americans for Freedom, Americans for Constitutional Action, the Free Society Association, the American Conservative Union, the National Right to Work Committee, the American Security Council, and several major conservative columnists and editors. *National Review* and *Human Events* were present, as was Neil McCaffrey of the Conservative Book Club.

In early September we flew by private plane to Newport, Rhode Island, where Ike's chief of protocol, Wiley Buchanan, hosted a second meeting with another cast of conservative writers and leaders at his palatial estate on the coast. Among those who flew back with us was Phil Crane of Illinois, the future congressman whose movie-star good looks had him being touted as the JFK of the GOP. Before Nixon set off on the campaign of 1966, we had working relations with the entire organizational leadership of the Right. And many had signaled their support for '68.

Prior to these meetings I sent Nixon a series of memos outlining what I thought should be our strategy: to bring the Right aboard while avoiding the perception of having been captured by or having capitulated to the Right. Nixon agreed. "Don't appear too anxious," he wrote on one memo. If they are too demanding, "[l]et them go their way. . . . We all tend to be too defensive." To a suggestion I meet with recalcitrants, Nixon wrote, "Many of these guys are unfortunately—nuts—like Joe Shell (and with college degrees). We can't go as their puppets."

Our recruitment efforts were not without opposition from within. Nixon staffers from 1960 and 1962 had never forgiven the Right or the Joe Shell crowd for what they had done to the Boss. Many detested the Right. Among the friends and loyalists Nixon instructed me to meet in New York, almost none had been for Goldwater in 1964. Some, like McWhorter, who had spent years fighting the rising New Right in the Young Republicans, reacted viscerally to the movement. Our first lunch ended with us almost shouting.

OUTED BY NOVAK

David Broder of the *Washington Post* broke the story of Nixon's session with leaders of the Right in a September 7, 1966, column titled "Nixon's Shoreham Meeting." *National Review* said that it had been "Nixon's first meeting with most of the conservatives present." Evans and Novak reported on Huston's role, mentioned the Newport gathering, and outed me:

> The key figure in all this is Nixon's new "research assistant"—a young man totally anonymous to national politics, named

Patrick J. Buchanan. In contrast to the nonideological prag-
matists who dominated Nixon's staff in the past, Buchanan is
a thorough-going conservative with close ties to the Young
Americans for Freedom, key organization of the Conservative
Youth Movement since its founding in 1960.

Novak's column pronounced the Shoreham meeting a blunder,
as it had given "the Republican left bountiful ammunition to use
in painting Nixon as the Goldwater candidate in 1968." Novak's
facts were as dead-on as his conclusion was dead wrong. That column elicited a long letter from me to the *Washington Post* listing the
meetings Nixon had held in DC in the two days during which he
had met with the conservatives. The *Post* published it in full.

Four decades after that *Esquire* article, I was with Steve Roberts
at a party in Kalorama. He mentioned a note he had gotten from
Nixon on an article he had written for *Esquire* back in 1966. I asked
him if Nixon had mentioned in the note the provocative photograph
of Angie Dickinson in flesh-colored pantyhose, wedged between
the pages of his article. Why, yes, he had, said Roberts.

COURTING THE CONSERVATIVE PRESS

After healing the rift with *National Review*, the next step was to
bring in the conservative columnists, none of whom was really hostile to Nixon: James J. Kilpatrick, Russell Kirk, Holmes Alexander,
William White, Walter Trohan, Willard Edwards, John Chamberlain, Roscoe Drummond, Ray Moley, Henry Taylor, David Lawrence, Dick Wilson, Bob Considine, Nick Thimmesch, Vic Lasky,
and Ralph de Toledano among them. Vic and Ralph were Nixon
loyalists from the Hiss days. When any sought an interview, we
sought to accommodate them. Many of them I would count as supporters of Nixon. Some, like Ray Moley, the head of FDR's "Brain

Trust" and author of his first inaugural, I would come to consider friends and counselors.

Among the people Nixon told me I must meet was Lasky. The author of *JFK* lived on Central Park South with wife, Patti, and poodle, Charlie Brown, and took me to lunch at his favorite Chinese restaurant, where he loudly introduced me to the owner and patrons as his long-lost illegitimate son. We remained friends until Vic's death, when I was honored to deliver a eulogy in the chapel at Arlington.

"MR. CONSERVATIVE"

The indispensable man in the Nixon-conservative alliance was Barry Goldwater. Nixon had campaigned tirelessly for Goldwater, and after his loss, Goldwater had publicly committed himself to Nixon should he seek the nomination in 1968. In any such run, the support of Goldwater, still seen by the Republican Right as a betrayed and martyred hero, would be invaluable.

In his letters to Nixon, Goldwater pressed three points. First was his concern that Reagan might enter the 1968 race, split the conservatives, and open the door to Rockefeller or Romney. Second, he urged Nixon to put Reagan on the ticket. Third, he believed Romney was a placeholder for Rockefeller, that should Romney falter in the early primaries, he would quit in favor of Rockefeller. In a "personal and confidential" letter in November 1967, Goldwater wrote Nixon that it was his belief "that either before the New Hampshire primary or shortly after Wisconsin, Romney will announce his withdrawal and recommend Rockefeller filling the spot." Goldwater went on:

> As you know, I have suggested that Reagan be second on your ticket and I use as an argument, it would give us at least sixteen

years of White House control. I know that you have thought about this and I know you have discussed it but, for the love of everything we want to do for the good of our country, let us not allow Reagan to get into this unless he knows full well what he is taking on and full well what it might do to his chances and the Party's chances.

Goldwater added that he had been "amazed at the great strength of Wallace throughout the South" and feared that a Wallace third-party run in 1968 might capture Alabama and Mississippi and siphon off conservative support in Florida and the Carolinas, helping to reelect Johnson. He was prescient.

On November 28, I memoed Nixon my alarm at reports I was getting of a Goldwater-Romney reconciliation. The two had exchanged testy letters in the *Times*. But Dean Burch had contacted us to say that Goldwater, who would be running for the Senate in 1968, needed to remove any image as a spoiler. Burch, Goldwater's political adviser, I wrote, has in mind "a Romney-Barry lunch of understanding and friendship." Not a good idea, I wrote Nixon. Any such Goldwater-Romney "get-together . . . would make it look as though Barry were going begging forgiveness." Nixon sent my memo to Goldwater. His reply came swiftly:

Last night when I returned to the hotel, I read the note that Buchanan had put together, and so that his mind and yours may be put at ease . . . I have not nor will I join Governor Romney in some sort of reconciliation movement. Frankly, that gesture, if you want to call it that, must come from him and to be more to the point I think he owes it to the Party and not to me. . . .

I can't believe that the Republican Party will ever give its nomination to a man who bolted that Party's team in the prior election and I feel very strong about that. . . .

Let Mr. Buchanan see this note and if he has any further comments he can get in touch with me.

Nixon scribbled across the top of the Goldwater letter, "Pat— Drop him a nice note." I wrote Senator Goldwater that there were two views among his supporters as to how those who had abandoned him might be brought in from the cold. The "stronger view" was that "the only way the Renegade Republicans could cleanse themselves of their sins was to show up in front of the Cow Palace in 1968 with the head of George Romney on a spike."

Others took a more conciliatory line, typified by a Republican comrade who said of the governors of New York and Michigan that while he personally had no objection to a couple of whores rejoining the church, he did hate like hell to see them leading the choir the first night.

From that day until his death, Senator Goldwater and I were friends.

CHAPTER 3

Comeback Year

As a practical political realist, I do not expect to
be a nominee again.
—Richard Nixon (January 1966)
to Bill Lawrence, ABC News

Nixon's comment about the threat posed by the "Buck-leyites" was not the only problem lingering from the 1965 gubernatorial campaigns in Virginia and New Jersey. At a teach-in at Rutgers in April 1965, tenured history professor Eugene Genovese, who had belonged to the Communist Party as a teenager and been discharged from the army for past associations, declared, "I am a Marxist and a socialist. Therefore . . . I do not fear or regret the impending Viet Cong victory in Vietnam. I welcome it."

Wayne Dumont, the Republican candidate, demanded that Rutgers fire Genovese. Nixon, campaigning for Dumont in late October, backed him up: Genovese should be terminated. Editorials hammered Nixon for a failure to understand academic freedom. An invitation to Nixon to accept an honorary degree from Rochester University became a subject of ferocious controversy, with students and faculty demanding he be disinvited. Declining the degree, Nixon went to Rochester in June 1966 and spoke on academic freedom. Some students and faculty rose and turned their backs.

My views on academic freedom had come from Sidney Hook,

the ex–Communist Cold Warrior who chaired the philosophy department at NYU. Hook defined academic freedom as the freedom to investigate, explore, and speak with immunity on the subject in which the professor is an accredited scholar. It did not mean a professor could call for an enemy victory over U.S. troops at war and keep his job. As a veteran of teach-ins at Washington University in St. Louis, I volunteered to write Nixon's speech on academic freedom. But at the urging of Len Garment, concerned that Nixon's call for the firing of a professor could undo his labors assuring liberals there was a "new Nixon," the Boss called in Bill Safire to take a softer approach. While Nixon's call for the ouster of Genovese was a subject of concern at the law office and among liberals, it did not seem to me that Nixon had been at all hurt. And I detected no remorse for his having made the comment. He seemed defiant.

Within days of my arrival at 20 Broad, Nixon invited me to his apartment to a meeting with half a dozen Harvard students, graduate and undergraduate, some Ripon Society members, down from Cambridge. Among them was Don Riegle, the son of a mayor of Flint, Michigan, who was thinking of running for Congress. Nixon urged Riegle to do so, telling him he would win his district in 1966. Riegle would win four terms as a Republican, then resign from the party in 1973 to protest Nixon's policies, become a Democrat, and go on to the Senate in 1976. Nixon was also considering hiring one of the Harvard men. But when the student came to the law office and we went in together to talk with Nixon—a job offer from a potential President before him—the Harvard student informed Nixon that before he could consider coming aboard, he had to be satisfied with Nixon's views on academic freedom. I could not believe what I was hearing. Nixon began to expatiate a bit on academic freedom. After we left the office, I was called back alone by Nixon, who told me, in pungent terms, he never wanted to see that kid again.

And Genovese? The Marxist socialist of 1965 repudiated his ideology, went south to teach, wrote *Roll, Jordan, Roll: The World the Slaves Made*, a new interpretation of slavery as a paternalistic institution. It won the 1975 Bancroft Prize. Genovese then helped to form the Historical Society to battle the "totalitarian assault" of political correctness. He then rejected capitalism, embraced traditionalism, converted to Catholicism, became an opponent of abortion, was remarried in the Church, argued for teaching religion in public schools, and became a Buchanan backer in the 1990s. "I never gave a damn what people thought of me. And I still don't," he told the *Newark Star-Ledger*. Gene Genovese died in 2012. Courageous scholar, courageous man.

"A CLASSIC COMMUNIST DECEPTION"

With Nixon under attack as a philistine for calling for the firing of Genovese, another embarrassment arose. The *New York Times* broke a story March 9 titled "DuBois 'Duplicity' Decried by Nixon." It quoted a March 1 statement by Nixon, as the national chairman of the Boys Club of America, charging that the similarity of the Boys Club's name to that of the Du Bois Clubs, lately declared a Communist front by Attorney General Nick Katzenbach, was "an almost classic example of Communist deception and duplicity."

The Du Bois Clubs had been named after black militant W. E. B. Du Bois, the rival to Booker T. Washington who had converted to Communism and died in Ghana in 1961. Nixon's statement alleged that Communists had cynically adopted the name "Du Bois Clubs" to confuse patriotic Americans into thinking they were the Boys Club of America.

These Du Bois Clubs, Nixon said, "are not unaware of the confusion they are causing among our supporters and among many other good citizens." These clubs are "totalitarian organizations" that do not dare to risk "full, frank, and honest disclosure of their true aims and purposes." Nixon's statement urged the media to "continue to focus the revealing light of truth on this Communist youth organization." Within days, the *New Yorker* had a gleeful lead editorial mocking Nixon's conspiratorial mindset.

When Len Garment came to my office, it was clear from his anguished expression that he thought this gaffe had been perpetuated by the right-wing editorial writer Nixon had just brought aboard. But I was as aghast as he. I had written editorials on the Du Bois Clubs, which had an active chapter in St. Louis. Their character and cause were well known to journalists. What had happened?

The Nixon statement had been issued from the Boys Club of America headquarters. Never crossed my desk. Yet Nixon had signed off on it and it was now being used to paint him as a primitive. Our operation had to be buttoned up. I called the Boys Club folks and told them: No more statements go out under Nixon's name, unless cleared by me.

Five months later, Arthur Schlesinger would cite Nixon's statements on the Du Bois Clubs in an alarmist essay in the *Saturday Evening Post* entitled "McCarthyism Is Threatening Us Again."

GHOSTING FOR NIXON

For more than a year after I came aboard in January 1966, Nixon had no other full-time paid staffer except Rose Woods. Within days of my arrival my duties began to expand. By the time the 1966 campaign began, I was handling his political mail, overseeing the in-box of clippings and memos that went into his office and briefcase, preparing the briefing books for his press conferences and TV appearances, serving as liaison to the Right, taking press calls, traveling with him, and writing speech inserts, columns, and articles for his byline. That Nixon had no one else to do these chores, no one else to talk issues, strategy, and tactics for hours, meant an unrivaled education from a master politician in his prime in that first full year at his side.

Our first collaboration on a column was less than a triumph. The column was a critique of the War on Poverty. But rather than let me write it, then edit it, Nixon involved himself for days, directing me to use as many war metaphors and analogies as I could stuff into 850 words. The column was sprinkled with references to victory, new offensive, peaceful coexistence, wholesale rout, second front, war profiteers, natural allies, concentrated fire, tide of defeat, arsenal, sergeants, generals, escalate, commanders in the field, opening guns, even the need for a Committee on the Conduct of the War. The language wholly obscured the message. Bill Buckley mocked it: "The first contribution to a sane discussion of the problem would require junking the phony military terminology. What say, General Nixon?"

Safire dismissed Buckley's objections and defended the column. As we moved along, Nixon reposed greater confidence in me and gave me widening latitude. But with major speeches he wanted to craft the ideas and arguments in his own way and with his own words. As both candidate and President he would immerse himself in the writing of his major addresses. I told friends that writing for Nixon was like Jacob wrestling with the angel—to exhaustion.

In the April 1970 speech announcing the U.S. invasion of the Viet Cong sanctuaries in Cambodia, we went through draft after draft. By the time we finished, the speech was exactly as he wanted it, which was as it should have been. No President, vice president, senator, or Cabinet officer for whom I have written was more demanding or took greater pains with his rhetoric. Nixon knew that many of the great men of history had added to their greatness not only with what they said but with how they said it.

CAPTURING THE LAW-AND-ORDER ISSUE

In the summer of '65, several months before I met Nixon in Belleville, a minor incident involving the police in the Watts section of Los Angeles had ignited a riot that lasted six days, leaving doz-ens dead, 1,000 injured, and 4,000 arrested. Thugs ranged over a 50-square-mile area of South Central, looting stores, burning buildings, and beating whites, as snipers shot at firemen and cops. After thousands of National Guard troops had poured in, order was restored August 16. In "What Did We Expect?"—an editorial that generated a stronger response than any I had ever written—I attacked America's social, cultural, and political elites for moral complicity in the Los Angeles anarchy:

> For half a decade the way has been paved for the eruptions of lawless violence. . . . Clergy have told their congregations to go ahead and break unjust laws. Priests, rabbis and nuns have paraded the streets or joined sit-ins, to show their support for civil rights—while violating ordinances that have nothing at all to do with civil rights. They have told Negroes to do the same.
>
> Civil disobedience has not only been condoned by the American Establishment; it has been encouraged and hailed. Before Adlai Stevenson died, he had said, "In the great strug-gle to advance civil and human rights . . . even a jail sentence is no longer a dishonor but a proud achievement." And the Establishment cheered. . . .
>
> If the courts are too slow in redressing your grievances, bypass the courts and go into the streets, the Negro has been told time and again.
>
> Thursday night, a Negro community took the nation at its word and Los Angeles reaped the whirlwind.

At the same time General Eisenhower was writing to a friend, "Lack of respect for law, laxness in dress, appearance and thinking, in conduct and in manner, as well as student and other riots with civil disobedience all spring from a common source: a lack of concern for the ancient virtues of decency, respect for law and elders, and old-fashioned patriotism."

The ideological premise of the Great Society—generously funded social programs would cure the pathology of the ghetto— was being tested, and failing. For days, as the Watts riot raged on, Lyndon Johnson would not accept calls. His aide Joe Califano finally got through. LBJ revealed that the rampant criminality had gotten to him. "How is it possible?" he asked Califano. "After all we've accomplished? How can it be?" The blacks, the President said, are going to "end up pissing in the aisles of the Senate."

One month before Nixon set out on the campaign of 1966, we staked out his claim to the law-and-order issue. "If Mob Rule Takes Hold in U.S.—A Warning from Richard Nixon" was the title of the essay in *U.S. News & World Report*. We tied the doctrine of civil disobedience to the riots that were "building a wall of hate between the races." Citing the latest urban riots in Chicago, Cleveland, and New York, Nixon asserted that there had been a "deterioration of respect for the rule of law all across America . . . [that] can be traced directly to the spread of the corrosive doctrine that every citizen possesses an inherent right to decide for himself which laws to disobey and when to disobey them."

"This doctrine has become a contagious national disease" whose "symptoms are manifest in more than just racial violence." He noted the contempt for police, the burning of draft cards, the blocking of troop trains.

"For such a deterioration of respect for law to occur in so brief a time in so great a nation, we must look for more important collaborators and auxiliaries" than "sidewalk demagogues." Nixon singled out "public officials, educators, clergymen and civil rights leaders," charging Robert Kennedy and Hubert Humphrey with giving aid and comfort to the lawless.

When the junior Senator from New York publicly declares that "there is no point in telling Negroes to obey the law," because to the Negro "the law is the enemy," then he has provided a rationale and a justification for every Negro intent upon taking the law into his own hands.

When the Vice President of the United States publicly declares that if he lived in the conditions of the slums he would "lead a mighty good revolt," then he is giving aid and comfort to those who revolt violently in Chicago and New York.

A second social development that had begun to define the decade was a population explosion among the criminal class and the doubling of violent crime, partly due to the maturing of the Baby Boomers, the first class of whom, born in 1946, turned eighteen in 1964. Not only did this vast generation flood the campuses, it swamped our criminal courts. When George Wallace and Barry Goldwater ran on "law and order" in 1964, the phrase was said to be code for racism. By 1966, however, a backlash had arisen against violent crimes. Law and order were now seen, and rightly so, as the indispensable preconditions of a civilized society.

In January 1958, Charles Starkweather, taking along his 14-year-old girlfriend, Caril Fugate, had inaugurated the era of mass murder by going on a killing spree through Nebraska and Wyoming and killing eleven people. But the first of the massacres we have come to know by such place-names as Columbine, Virginia Tech, Fort Hood, Tucson, Aurora, Newtown, and the Washington Navy Yard occurred in the month before Nixon's article appeared. On July 14, 1966, Richard Speck tortured, raped, and murdered eight student nurses from South Chicago Community Hospital. Two weeks later, Eagle Scout and ex-Marine Charles Whitman, after stabbing his wife and mother to death, climbed 300 feet into the clock tower at the University of Texas in Austin, and with an arsenal of rifles and pistols, killed or wounded almost four dozen people.

Nixon did not address the law-and-order issue at length again in 1966. But our trademark was on it and we had made sure that no one would get around our right flank. "Excellent job," Nixon said on my memo relating how I had worked with Len and "smoothed over any bristles which might offend without any commensurate return." We had gotten pickup on the piece from Mike Wallace at CBS and in David Lawrence's columns, and "every report we have received to date has been favorable." We would return to the theme in 1967 at length in "What Has Happened to America?" in *Reader's Digest*, with its circulation then of 19 million.

Through 1966 Nixon was working to rebuild the party base after the carpet-bombing of 1964. Yet he did not exaggerate his importance in the coming fall campaign. His appearance for a candidate, Nixon told me, was unlikely to prove decisive, but he could do three things: bring out a crowd, raise money, attract press. Having lost in 1960 after the party base had been decimated in 1958, Nixon was convinced that a far larger army of GOP state legislators, governors, and members of Congress was essential for victory in 1968. Yet, in rebuilding that GOP base, Nixon was also putting scores of Republican leaders in his debt and building a foundation for his own possible run. He was investing sweat equity in anticipation of a comeback in 1966, and gratitude in 1968 should he run again. This investment of time and effort would prove as wise as were his travels on behalf of Barry Goldwater.

BLISS, BIRCHERS, AND LEAKS

Nixon assigned Tom Evans of the firm to talk to RNC chairman Ray Bliss—"Old Nuts and Bolts," as some of us called him, since Bliss was a backroom operative—about providing an airplane. Evans reported back: Bliss had said, "No!" To provide Nixon and his small staff with a plane to travel the country on behalf of the party would be playing favorites for 1968.

"Bliss said that!" Nixon exploded. "You tell Ray Bliss I've raised my last g———n dime for the Republican National Committee!"

The explosion was justified. No one had raised the money Nixon had for the RNC. Now he was taking six weeks off to campaign for a party comeback and the RNC would not help. No one else was doing anything like what Nixon was doing. Rockefeller, Romney, Reagan were all out campaigning for themselves. Even the gentlemanly John Whitaker, a loyalist from 1960 who had volunteered two months to do our scheduling, was angry. John told me he was sending Bliss a telegram: "F——— you! Strong letter follows." When Evans told me of Nixon's reaction, I concluded that if the Boss ever became president, Old Nuts and Bolts would go to the wall.

And so it came to pass. Immediately after his 1968 victory, Nixon directed his troubleshooter Bryce Harlow to drop the hammer on the chairman. Said Bryce of Bliss's reaction when he was told, "The news almost broke his heart."

A month before Nixon set out on the campaign, in early August, an Evans-Novak column gave a description of the order of battle—who was raising money for Nixon's travels, who would travel with him, who would help defray the expenses, like the House Republican Campaign Committee.

The columnists seemed to have been sitting in on the confidential meeting of the "Stans group." Headed by Ike's ex–budget director and Nixon fund-raiser Maurice Stans, and containing several heavy hitters, big moneymen, as well as Buchanan and Safire, this group had just begun planning for the fall campaign—and beyond.

"There is a leak somewhere along the line," I wrote Nixon, and the leaker is "quite knowledgeable." Three attendees of the Stans group pointed the finger at our contact at the HRCC. "He could not possibly have known as much as appears in this column," Nixon wrote back. "The leak is obviously from someone who was present." Safire said he had heard from Bill Casey, the future director of the CIA, that he had missed "Saturday's meeting of the Group." Nixon was right: We had a major leak inside.

We never found out who the leaker was. But his motive puzzled me. Here was someone entrusted with the confidences of a potential President, blabbing what he knew to openly hostile columnists. What did this leaker, betraying our secrets, hope to achieve? To impress Evans and Novak with his insider's status and closeness to Nixon? Was it worth this to betray the trust reposed in him? If caught and exposed, how would he have defended such disloyalty?

ON HIS FIRST trip out in September, Nixon flew to Fairbanks to speak for the state ticket, headed by Wally Hickel, who was running for governor, with one exception. Lee McKinley, the GOP nominee for U.S. Senate, was a Bircher. On arrival, Nixon held a press conference and refused to endorse McKinley. That evening, true to his pledge not to campaign for a Bircher, Nixon omitted McKinley's name from his remarks. Listening stone-faced, McKinley walked out as Nixon sat down. "Nixon Rebuff to Bircher Jolts Alaskan Alliance" was the front-page headline in the *Washington Post*.

When Nixon got back, it was on his mind. He told me McKinley seemed a decent fellow and had taken his cutting of him with good grace. Yet from his tone Nixon clearly felt bad about doing what he had to do. And to me it spoke well of Nixon that he found this act of shunning distasteful. For what he had done to Dr. McKinley, Nixon knew, had not infrequently been done to him by the Republican establishment.

When Nixon went on the road in September, he left me at 20 Broad to do the "political advance." I would call ahead to each congressional district he was about to visit, talk to the candidate or his campaign manager, or both, find out what they wanted Nixon to stress and avoid, and quiz them on local news, controversies, and feuds. Nixon wanted to know the price of such items as a quart of milk and a loaf of bread in the district. Inflation was becoming an issue. If he was to speak at a college, he wanted to know the school team's nickname and what the favorite student hangout was. I would type this up and get it to Rose at their hotel before Nixon's appearance. As Nixon was hitting three and four congressional districts a day, the political advance consumed my waking hours on the phone and writing. At the end of Nixon's first week, a call came from Rose. The Boss needed me on the road to write speech inserts tailored to each district. I flew to Milwaukee and handed the political advance off to John Sears.

Sears had graduated from Notre Dame at twenty in 1960 and gotten his law degree from Georgetown. By 1965 he was rowing down in the galleys at Nixon, Mudge. Sears was a born political analyst. He had a savvy about people, motives, and strategies most professional politicians do not acquire in a lifetime. And he was excellent on the phone. He would call the candidates and their campaign managers, be on a first-name basis within minutes, find out about everything going on in the district—including conflicts, rumors, and scandals—and phone it to me on the road. Sears had a trait, however, that would prove costly to his career.

He did not tolerate fools gladly and was constantly discovering them right in front of him. Where manners had been hammered into me from childhood—to call all men "sir" and women "ma'am" when introduced or answering a phone—Sears would use the first names of people twice his age and many times more important. When Nixon once asked Sears to call Ray Bliss, I heard Sears talking to "Ray" like he was ordering burgers from a kid who couldn't get the order straight. When I reminded Sears that this was the national chairman of the Republican Party, he reminded me that Bliss had been an insurance salesman.

At the 1968 convention, where he was a delegate hunter, Sears took to calling campaign chairman John Mitchell by his first name, while instructing him on convention politics. A smoldering Mitchell directed me to follow him into his suite, spun around, stuck a finger in my face, and went into a rant about "your goddamn friend Sears." J. P. Sears had made a bad enemy.

WITH NIXON ON THE ROAD

Our traveling staff was small: John Davies, Nixon's personal aide; Rose Woods; occasionally Charlie McWhorter, Nixon's legislative aide in the vice president's office; and Pat Hillings, who, at twenty-five, had won Nixon's House seat when Nixon won the Senate seat in 1950. Hillings loved the House and had wanted to spend his life there. But he let himself be persuaded by Nixon into filing for attorney general of California in 1958 when Senate Minority Leader Bill Knowland decided to come back and run for governor. Governor Goodwin Knight was persuaded to run for Knowland's Senate seat. The musical chairs did not sit well with Californians: '58 was a bad year for the economy, and Knowland had gotten behind a right-to-work ballot initiative that brought out the unions. Republicans were wiped out and the careers of Knowland, Knight, and Hillings came to an end. A gregarious Irishman and natural-born pol, Hillings had the gifts Nixon lacked. He could schmooze the pols who wanted face time with Nixon but could not have it if Nixon was to sustain his schedule. Among Hillings's assignments in '66: collect names for '68.

Once on the tarmac at L.A. airport, I noticed reporters had gathered around Hillings. I sauntered over to listen in. Hillings was telling the press that Reagan, running for governor and under attack for "extremism," had to do more to separate himself and the California GOP from the Birch Society. When the reporters walked away with this story, I said to Hillings, "Pat, what are you doing?" Hillings replied, "The Old Man told me to do it." Not altogether consistent with our preaching about party unity.

McWhorter was an intense Scot, a liberal on civil rights and a teetotaler, devoted to Nixon. Charlie had been the national chairman of the Young Republicans in the 1950s who led the resistance to the takeover by the Right. He had battled Rusher in the YRs and was a serious man about his opinions. As I had discovered at our first lunch, he was hot-tempered. On the plane ride back to New York, after campaign appearances in Indiana, Charlie came over and engaged me in another near shouting match. I still recall Nixon, in the front of the plane, turning around, staring back in puzzlement at his two aides yelling at each other at day's end.

WHAT WAS IT like to campaign with Nixon?

In 1966, Richard Nixon was like an athlete in training. He drove himself hard, and expected everyone to do the same. Some days, he would do three or four appearances, a breakfast in one congressional district, a luncheon speech in the next, a press conference and dinner speech or rally in a third stop, then fly at night to the state where he was to appear the next morning. Working with Agnes Waldron in DC, who clipped and transmitted, page by page, stories from early editions of the *Washington Post* and *New York Times*, I would mark the key paragraphs and Rose would type them up on bond paper and we would have them in his room when he woke up. He did not want to be caught unaware of events that folks back East would be reading about that morning, or that reporters might ask about on his first stop. He insisted that I have all the statements for release in his room the night before or the next morning so he had time to edit them before we put anything out.

Nixon placed immense importance on advance work, and his advance men were as good as Kennedy's by 1968 and would become as legendary. Bob Haldeman and John Ehrlichman, who did not come aboard full-time until mid-1968, had been advance men in 1960. There were to be no half-filled halls or empty seats. Advance men would be in the district days ahead of Nixon's arrival. They would work with the locals, but were themselves responsible for ensuring the event went off smoothly, that, as the saying went, "all the fat cats got stroked"—in other words, all important leaders got to at least shake hands with Nixon.

As I had writing to do, I often did not go to the speeches or rallies, but worked in my room on the portable electric typewriter I carried. One night Nixon spoke before a crowd of only eighty in Ontario, California, in a hall that could hold hundreds. When he got back to the hotel, Nixon called in the advance men and chewed them out. This was never to happen again. Every advance man knew that 1966 was the dress rehearsal for 1968, that if they performed they would have a part in that campaign. Under the pressure, one advance man broke down, walked off, and simply disappeared. I was told he was found shacked up in a Las Vegas hotel with a lady he did not know and whose company he could not afford. Some advance men and old friends whose ties to Nixon went back years would fail to make the cut in 1968.

Nixon was in his prime this year. He had been a figure of history in the 1950s, had lost to the now legendary JFK, had been humiliated in California, but now saw a narrow opening to one of the great comebacks in U.S. history. This was the shakedown cruise. Nixon was demanding of subordinates and intolerant of failure. Speaking of a close aide from the 1960 campaign, Nixon told me, "He's eight years older than he was in 1960—and I'm eight years younger." What I saw those months was what Theodore H. White, chronicler of presidential campaigns, would see in 1968: "What [the nation] had not yet perceived was the man of extraordinary courage, of dogged perseverance, the precise thinker and meticulous planner, the character changed by learn-ing and experience."

Nixon drank little or nothing on the road. He worked him-self hard, was up early, ate little, was on time for his motorcade and rallies, napped in the afternoon, did a speech at night, came back to sip half a glass of beer and talk over the event and read his news summary or my excerpts for the next day's speeches, and went to bed. He was in three or four towns a day, doing four or five events. Though only months short of his fifty-sixth birthday, he had remarkable stamina. "When I'm campaigning, I live like a Spartan," Nixon told a reporter. He did. Rose and I and others of the traveling staff, as soon as the day's work was done, headed to the bar. Almost every event went smoothly and the press who came out to travel with Nixon were visibly impressed. When reporters ques-tioned us as to how much time we put into these events, we invoked the McWhorter Rule: "Anything planned for less than sixty days we consider a spontaneous rally."

Nixon took more than a sip when the week's work was done and we were flying back home to New York or to Key Biscayne, and no press would be waiting on the tarmac when he landed. Then he unwound on the plane. One night, after a long flight on which he had imbibed, Nixon had me ride with him in his limo to the apartment on 62nd Street. When we got out, he said, "I'll get you a cab," and ran out into Fifth Avenue in that midnight hour with cars and cabs hurtling south above the speed limit. Nixon stepped right in front of a cab and, waving his arms, brought it over to the curb.

After I got in, the cabby kept looking at me in the rearview mir-ror. Finally, he said, "Was that who I think it was?"

"Yep," I said. Had that cabby not been paying close attention on his run down Fifth Avenue, we might have lost a future President that night.

ENDORSING ROCKEFELLER

Two weeks before election day, Nixon had his lone encounter of the campaign with the man we saw as his rival in 1968, Governor George Romney. House Minority Leader Gerald Ford had invited Nixon and Romney to a rally at Calvin College in his hometown of Grand Rapids, to campaign both for him and his former House colleague Bob Griffin, whom Romney had named to the Senate that spring on the death of the incumbent Democrat. Romney was coasting to an easy victory for a third two-year term, but Griffin was in a tight race with former governor G. Mennen "Soapy" Williams. As the *Detroit News*'s Jon Lowell reported the meeting between the early favorites for '68, "The conversation went like this here yesterday":

> "Hi George," said former Vice-President Richard Nixon.
> "Hi, Dick," said Gov. Romney.
> "Good to see you."
> "Good to see you."
> "How are things, George?"
> "I've got some tough bills to handle, Dick."

"The stiff atmosphere attending Nixon's and Romney's meeting," Lowell wrote, "reflected Romney's attitude in a morning press conference in his Lansing office."

"I didn't invite him," Romney said, "but we've always had an open door policy in Michigan . . . regardless of why they come."

Perhaps both were remembering that Cleveland governors' conference at which Nixon, according to Teddy White, had tried to persuade Romney to declare for President and throw himself in front of the Goldwater express. Yet, in those years, Nixon seemed to go out of his way to say something gracious about his rivals when in their company, while the Rockefellers and Romneys and Javitses seemed to act surly and superior toward him.

Nixon predicted a record win for Romney before a crowd, mostly students, estimated at 3,500. The *Detroit News* reported that Romney's reception seemed more enthusiastic. My recollection is that both spoke strongly and well. But I was most taken by the speech of the Republican minority leader and future President, Gerald Ford, which seemed to be a long string of sports clichés about how well the party was going to do.

It was on one of the Western trips that Hillings, one afternoon, confided that "the Old Man is going to endorse Rocky"—for reelection as governor. I had heard nothing of this, and headed down the hall to Nixon's suite, opened the door, and found the room empty. I went to the bathroom door, pulled it open, and confronted the former vice president about to climb into the shower: "You're not going to endorse that sonofabitch, are you?"

A startled Nixon exploded into laughter: "Don't worry, we'll get something for it." Later, he would bring me into the room when Safire, the go-between with Rocky's man Jack Wells, discussed how Nixon would go about endorsing Rockefeller in upstate New York where the governor needed to win over Republicans who detested him and were disgusted by his treatment of Goldwater. As Nixon talked over the terms of his endorsement, I provided a running commentary on Rockefeller.

Nixon was enjoying himself in this meeting and had every right to. Since he had moved to New York, he had been treated by the Republican establishment like a distant relative of unsavory character. He had been invited to nothing by the New York party. Now here was Rockefeller, for whom the Empire State Republican Party was a wholly owned subsidiary, inquiring through intermediaries how he might get Nixon to endorse him in his own fiefdom. The unstated message: Without Nixon's help, Rockefeller could lose the governorship.

Though I shared the conservative opinion that Rockefeller was a man who used the party, while Nixon gave back as much as he got,

Nixon was right to endorse Rockefeller. For his eyes were on the prize. If endorsing Rockefeller for governor in 1966 meant Rockefeller would endorse Nixon for president in 1968 should Nixon win the nomination, it was worth it. That Nixon would make a magnanimous gesture to a man who had treated him so shabbily also spoke well of him. *New York Post* columnist Murray Kempton flew to Syracuse to witness Nixon's endorsement of the man Kempton called Nixon's "great surviving enemy":

> Richard Nixon said last night that it was 20 years ago that he was first elected to Congress from California and then he stood up and celebrated that anniversary by etching his own imperishable profile in courage. He spoke aloud and in favorable terms the name of Nelson Aldrich Rockefeller at a Republican rally in Onondaga County.

GOING SOUTH

Having seen the inroads made by Eisenhower in the upper South and by Goldwater in the Deep South, Nixon was not deterred by media hostility from seizing an opening to break the stranglehold on Dixie the Democrats had had since Reconstruction. And among the Southern Republicans we were out to recruit was the national committeeman from Mississippi.

Fred LaRue was a wealthy man who did not look the part, and a man whose soul had been seared. Out hunting with his father Ike in Canada in 1957, Fred had accidentally shot and killed him. When he spoke my name, "Pat," it came out as a three-syllable word. The night of our Mississippi event we went out for drinks. Fred had been among the party leaders who put the South in Goldwater's column at the Cow Palace.

The next morning, riding with Nixon and others on our staff—for long trips the Boss wanted only loyalists in the car and one of our own at the wheel so he could speak freely—he asked if Fred had given an indication of where he was looking to go in 1968. I replied that while Fred had not been specific, late in the evening, after many drinks, Fred had volunteered, "Pat, I've had my last dumb-o. This time I'm gonna get me a college graduate."

Nixon howled. This was excellent news. Were he to run in 1968, and were Reagan to get into the race, LaRue and Southerners like him would be pivotal.

From Mississippi, we traveled to Fort Smith, where Nixon was to campaign for John Paul Hammerschmidt in his first run for Congress. John Paul would later achieve fame by defeating Bill Clinton in his first run for a major public office. But given the last name of our candidate, we cautioned Nixon on the danger of a mispronunciation. It did not work. Nixon got up at the press conference and announced that he was pleased to be in Arkansas endorsing "John Paul Hammer-shit" for Congress. We froze. No one on our staff or Hammerschmidt's staff cracked a smile; no one laughed. Nixon stopped, repeated the name, this time correctly, and moved on.

After the press conference we went to our motel, where Nixon, as was his custom in the afternoon, took a nap to be fresh for his dinner speech or rally that evening. He instructed me to make sure no one interrupted him. The motel was a rectangular arrangement, one story high. The doors to the rooms were all on the inside of the rectangle. After about half an hour I saw a large man striding across the grounds, headed straight for Nixon's room. I must have been 75 yards away, and started running. Too late. The guy was pounding on Nixon's door, yelling, "Hey, Dick! Hey, Dick!"

I got there as Nixon was opening the door. I was aghast that I had let this clown get to him. But Nixon was suddenly all smiles.

"Pat," he said, "meet Win Rockefeller!"

The youngest of the five sons of John D. Rockefeller, Jr., Winthrop was a far bigger man than his older brothers David and Nelson, a war hero, and a hearty, gregarious fellow. In the early 1950s,

Win had been involved in a huge scandal when, after wedding Pennsylvania coal miner's daughter and beauty-queen divorcée Barbara "Bobo" Sears, the two split in a savage and salacious battle over alimony and adultery. I had read about it as a kid. He had moved to Arkansas and was now running to become the state's first Republican governor since Reconstruction. Our whole team liked him and we left Arkansas in cowboy hats bearing the label "Win with Win."

By now I was skipping evening events and spending the time writing press releases and speech inserts for the following day. After I had finished writing all three for the next day's Indiana stops, and Nixon had gone to bed, Fred LaRue and I went out. This was apparently a dry county and someone said we had to go to Oklahoma to get a drink. But someone else steered us right. For when we arrived at the bar, John Paul Hammerschmidt's campaign staffers were in a booth across the room. And at their table was a gal of about nineteen who was smiling at me. I went over to the Hammerschmidt table and invited her to join me and Fred, which she was excited to do. After we had talked awhile, Hammerschmidt's campaign manager came over and instructed the girl to come back to their table. She's enjoying herself, I said. A discussion ensued and deteriorated, and I then invited the campaign manager outside, whereupon the girl got up and went back to their table.

Suddenly, it dawned upon me that I may just have jeopardized what we were trying to do with this campaign tour: make friends and allies in the Republican Party and especially among the new members for 1968. I looked over at Fred. He had by now assumed the posture we used to take as first-graders when the nuns would tell us to fold our arms on the desk and put our heads on our arms and take a nap.

Fred, I said, waking him, I think I may have fouled up badly here.

"You did exactly the right thing," Fred said, and went back to sleep.

Seven years later, during the Watergate investigation, I ran into Fred returning from a visit to the special prosecutor.

"Pat," Fred said, "they told me that if I lie to 'em just one more time, they're gonna put me *under* the jail." Fred had been the political aide to John Mitchell, who ran the Committee to Reelect the President, or CREEP, during Watergate, and had allegedly shredded some documents for the former attorney general of the United States.

THE PRINCE OF DARKNESS

I got two hours' sleep that night, and it was dark when we started for the airport. Hillings was MIA. After a wait at the plane, with Nixon pacing, Hillings tore up in a car. And we headed for Indiana. First of the three stops was Evansville, where we were coming in for Roger Zion, who would win his race for Congress.

It was that morning that I first saw Robert Novak. We were behind a curtain waiting for the press conference to begin, when Nixon motioned me over, held the curtain open slightly, and said, "There is the enemy!" At the end of a row of reporters, sitting apart, scowling at no one in particular, was a small, swarthy man. Observing him, I said to myself, the Boss has a point. In a postelection 1966 appearance on William F. Buckley's *Firing Line*, Novak was asked about his column partner Rowland Evans's confirmation to Buckley that he never lost "an opportunity to embarrass Mr. Nixon." Said Novak, "I think it is a good answer."

Two decades later, Novak, whom even colleagues called "The Prince of Darkness," would become a friend, reliable in crises personal or political. But in the 1960s there was not to be found a journalist who more bedeviled Richard Nixon. Novak was on his case constantly. Compounding the problem was that Novak was arguably the most persistent, best-informed political reporter of his generation. Everyone read the Evans-Novak column. It was Novak who had ferreted out what Nixon said about the "Buckleyites" in late 1965, and who had kept that pot boiling by quoting Rusher's letters demanding Nixon's clarification.

On September 9, 1965, Novak had reported on a drive by Kentucky senator Thruston Morton to purge party ranks of the Birchers. At the end of his nationally syndicated column, Novak wrote, "For Richard Nixon, the defeated 1960 candidate who is now the recognized leader of the Goldwater wing of the party, the decision [to oust the Birchers] will be particularly difficult."

Nixon was incensed. He fired off a "Dear Kay" letter to *Washington Post* publisher Katharine Graham, whose paper carried the Evans and Novak column. Nixon wrote that he had "fought the Birch Society throughout my campaign for governor in 1962, with the result that many observers believe that Birch opposition was one of the major factors causing my defeat," and told Graham he put Evans and Novak in the same box as the widely reviled columnist Drew Pearson.

That evening, at an informal gathering of Indiana Republicans, mostly men, Nixon was holding forth onstage when he volunteered to his audience that he had probably been more abused by the press than any other man in politics. A white-haired fellow in front of me bellowed, "Like hell you have!"

A startled Nixon turned—and laughed. The voice was that of his old friend Charlie Halleck. I recognized the former majority leader of the House, as I had once hauled his golf bag, along with that of Les Arends, the House whip, in 100-degree heat that long, hot summer at Burning Tree more than a decade before.

ORIGINS OF A "SOUTHERN STRATEGY"

The most memorable rally of 1966 was held at the Wade Hampton Hotel in Columbia, South Carolina, an all-male event with everyone crowded together, standing near the stage in a smoke-filled room.

The speakers were Nixon, Strom Thurmond, and Albert Watson, who had backed Goldwater, been stripped of his seniority in the House, resigned, switched parties, and won in a special election in June 1965 to become the first Republican in the twentieth century to represent South Carolina in the House of Representatives.

It was boisterous and raucous and the response to all three speakers was thunderous. Nixon outdid himself. Strom outdid Nixon. Watson outdid both. With a deep, powerful voice he was shouting at the close, "Freedom is not free!" It was unlike any rally I had witnessed. When it was over I was waiting outside in the hall. Nixon came out sweating and smiling. That it had been a tremendous show was written all over him. "This is where the energy is!" said Nixon. "This is where the future of the party is!" The story of 1966, he told a larger gathering at the hotel, will be the "resurgence of the Republican Party in the United States . . . and the headline on that story will tell of the coming of age of the GOP in the South."

Among the malevolent myths about Nixon is that he set out to build the Republican Party in Dixie on a foundation of racism. That is not the man I knew and it is the antithesis of what I saw. While Nixon approved of my writings on law and order, he expressed an emotional empathy with black Americans. It was in his DNA. His Quaker mother's family had been active in the Underground Railroad in Indiana. On coming to Congress he agreed to Adam Clayton Powell's request to be part of a five-man team that would take the floor to answer the racist rants of Mississippi's John Rankin. His record as vice president, working behind the scenes for the Civil Rights Act of 1957, for which Dr. King sent him a personal letter of gratitude, marked him as a progressive. I recall him storming out of his office in a rage one morning over a story he had read about an Alabama town that had refused to bury a black soldier killed in Vietnam in its whites-only cemetery. Have a statement ready for me when I get back from lunch, he ordered.

Let me make some calls first, I replied. The story did not ring true. Southern respect for martial valor would not abide this. I called the mayor. He told me his town had been slandered. There was no room in the white cemetery to bury anyone. The town had offered to pay the full funeral costs of their soldier son. Researching the Web half a century later, I found the story of Jimmy Williams of Wetumpka, Alabama, a black soldier and Green Beret who, it was said, was to be buried in a pauper's grave in June 1966 but would be laid to rest one hundred miles away in the military cemetery at Andersonville, Georgia, site of the Confederate prisoner-of-war camp. Where the truth of this story, now half a century old, lies, I do not know. But this I do know: Nixon's visceral recoil at what he thought was a moral outrage was genuine and unforgettable.

One of the first of the monthly columns I wrote with Nixon, which was carried nationally and in the *Washington Post* on May 8, 1966, described the Republican opportunity in the South as "a golden one; but Republicans must not go prospecting for the fool's gold of racist votes. Southern Republicans must not climb aboard the sinking ship of racial injustice. They should let Southern Democrats sink with it as they have sailed with it."

> The Democratic Party in the South has ridden to power for a century on an annual tide of racist oratory. The Democratic Party is the party that rides with the hounds in the North and the hares in the South. The Republicans, as the South's party of the future, should reject this hypocritical policy of the past.

Nixon quoted Democratic senator Lister Hill of Alabama, who said that "if it hadn't been for Republicans, we would still be talking [in the Senate]. If the Republican members had voted with the South, none of that [civil rights] legislation would have been passed."

"Senator Hill is correct," Nixon wrote. Republicans were decisive in passing the Civil Rights Act and Voting Rights Act. And

Republicans "should adhere to the principles of the party of Lincoln . . . and leave it to the George Wallaces and Lister Hills to squeeze the last ounces of political juice from the rotting fruit of racial injustice."

On a June tour of the South, columnist Charles Bartlett, a friend of JFK, wrote that Nixon's line in Jackson, Mississippi, that Southern Republicans must not "climb aboard the sinking ship of racial injustice," had "served to make the moderates bolder."

In 1966 Nixon went south for Congressman Howard "Bo" Callaway, running for governor of Georgia against Lester Maddox, and Congressman Jim Martin, running against Lurleen Wallace, wife of George, for governor of Alabama. David Broder caught up with Nixon in Bakersfield, California, October 20, where we were campaigning for congressional candidate Bob Matthias, the two-time decathlon gold medalist and star of the '48 Olympics where he first achieved national glory at age seventeen. Broder had a front-page *Washington Post* story the next morning, headlined "Administration Challenged by Nixon to Repudiate Racists Seeking Office." Broder's story began:

> Former Vice President Richard M. Nixon stumped through California today, challenging the Johnson Administration to repudiate racist Democratic candidates. . . .
>
> "I have yet to find a Republican candidate anywhere who is campaigning on the white backlash," Nixon said. "It is time for the national Democratic leadership and the Johnson administration to make it clear whether it is going into the South as the party of Maddox, Mahoney and Wallace."

At this time Nixon was being pushed to make Maddox, Mahoney, and Wallace a central issue of the campaign by issuing a statement demanding that President Johnson "purge the demagogues" from the Democratic Party. Nixon asked me to think it over and work something up. I memoed back that I had "reservations" and thought that throwing the gauntlet down to the President could backfire.

> All these guys you name are running on anti-LBJ campaigns. With the possible exception of Mahoney, they are gutting Johnson every day. They are thus unconscious allies in one respect, and if we slam them they will simply turn around and start slamming us as well. This statement would be warmly received in Manhattan, but I really wonder how the South will view it.
>
> To date they [Wallace and Maddox] haven't said anything for us or against us at all. That's fine with me. It seems that today there is really hardly anybody down [south] who dislikes RN. There will be a good number of solid Nixon-haters after this statement.

McWhorter agreed. There was a danger that any such demand upon the President would backfire. Should LBJ accede to Nixon's demand, and declare Lester Maddox and Lurleen Wallace *extra ecclesiam*, Lester and Lurleen would win in landslides. Nixon would be blamed for killing two viable GOP candidates in Georgia and Alabama. This was tricky business, and as I wrote Nixon there was another consideration—1968:

> Wallace is the symbol of Southern resistance to Washington in the South, just as we would like to be the symbol of resistance to Washington and its policies in the nation. We will want, I would think, the people who are supporting Wallace now to be in our corner perhaps later.
>
> Besides, George Wallace is one hell of a popular man in the South right now. As the Governor of Arkansas said two

weeks ago, "If George Wallace ran for President right now, we wouldn't have to count the votes, we could just weigh them."

We did not make Wallace and Maddox a central issue, but neither did we ignore them. In yet another attack on the Democratic Party, on October 30, in a column for the North American Newspaper Alliance, Nixon wrote, "Below the Mason-Dixon line, the party of Jefferson, Jackson and Wilson has become the party of Maddox, Mahoney and Wallace."

Mahoney was George P. Mahoney, no true Dixiecrat, but a blue-collar Irish Catholic and perennial candidate now running for governor of Maryland on the anti–open housing slogan "Your home is your castle!" His opponent was Baltimore County Supervisor Spiro T. (Ted) Agnew. Taking on the national Democrats for their silent complicity in race-based campaigns being run by their Dixiecrat colleagues, Nixon wrote:

Lyndon Johnson, Bobby Kennedy and Hubert Humphrey have not lifted a finger or invested an ounce of their political prestige to prevent this seizure of their party in the South by the lineal descendants of "Pitchfork Ben" Tillman and Theodore Bilbo. They have allowed it to become a party in which Bull Connor is completely at home.

Boosting Win Rockefeller for governor of Arkansas, Nixon added, "[T]he Democratic Party has dredged through the early novels of William Faulkner to come up with its Snopesian candidate, Jim Johnson, whose racial views make incumbent Governor Orval Faubus, by contrast, a flaming liberal." The new Republican Party in the South should rest, said Nixon, "on four pillars: human rights, states' rights, private enterprise and a foreign policy of peace without appeasement." To those who call "states' rights" code for "segregation," he added, "Republicans have rejected the old concept of states' rights as instruments of reaction and accepted a new concept: States' rights as instruments of progress." This means states assuming their responsibilities "in the fields of health, transportation, education and welfare."

Summarizing his views, Nixon repeated lines we had used in May: about leaving it to "Maddox and Wallace to squeeze the last ounces of political juice from the rotting fruit of racial injustice."

This column, released on October 30, was carried in dozens of newspapers across the country, from the *Philadelphia Bulletin* to the *Los Angeles Times*. McWhorter, a passionate champion of civil rights, came around to say he was impressed. Some biographers, seeking to portray Nixon as "playing the race card," have ignored both of these nationally syndicated columns.

Just days after the May column appeared, Nixon received a letter of congratulations from Al Abrahams, executive director of Republicans for Progress, which had just produced, with another liberal group, Republican Advance at Yale, a Southern Project Report. These liberal Republicans did not like the way the party was evolving in the South, and had ten hard recommendations, some of them demands, to be made on state parties by the Republican National Committee. Roscoe Drummond, a columnist Nixon admired, hailed the report. David Broder, then of the *New York Times*, led his story on the report by writing, "Two liberal Republican groups urged the Republican National Committee today to help register Southern Negroes and to discipline 'lily-white' GOP organizations in the South." The report, he went on, "produced a cautious reaction from National Committee officials and immediate condemnation from some Southern state G.O.P. chairmen, presaging a major intraparty debate."

I wrote Nixon a cover memo and stapled it to the report. There is "much good material" here, I said, but the "recommendations don't seem very practical."

It is a matter of simple fact that the vast majority of Southerners (white) believe in segregation of the races if not by law,
certainly by personal choice.

These recommendations are going to bring no one racing
to the Republican banners, but if carried out they would succeed in antagonizing and angering a lot of Southerners. For
what?

I think your position is correct. Tell the Southerners what
your principles are on human rights, fight for those principles
in party councils, but take no part in any effort to purge the
party of all who oppose integration.

I told him that, looking first at the report, then at our column,
"I think the column looks quite good." Nixon wrote back on my
memo, "I agree." File the report, he wrote. That was half a century ago. Our approach was right. Wallace would sweep the Deep
South in 1968. But we would carry Virginia, North Carolina, South
Carolina, Florida, and Tennessee. Nixon in 1972, Reagan in 1984,
George H. W. Bush in 1988, and George W. Bush in 2004 would
sweep all eleven states of the old Confederacy. Wilson and FDR
had carried the same eleven states all six times they ran—but had
done so in open collusion with some of the most rabid segregation-
ists in American history. Even Adlai, who had carried the five states
of the Deep South plus North Carolina and Arkansas in 1952, did
so by putting on his ticket Senator John Sparkman of Alabama, a
future signer of the Southern Manifesto.

What was the Southern Manifesto? This declaration was written in 1956 by Senators Strom Thurmond of South Carolina and
Richard Russell of Georgia and signed by all but three of the
twenty-two senators from the eleven states of the old Confederacy.
Nonsigners were Al Gore, Sr., and Estes Kefauver of Tennessee, and
Lyndon Johnson of Texas. The congressional delegations from Alabama, Arkansas, Georgia, Louisiana, Mississippi, South Carolina,

and Virginia all signed unanimously. Only two Republican House members were among the ninety-nine congressional signatories.

What did it say? The Southern Manifesto charged the Supreme Court with a "clear abuse of judicial power" in the *Brown* decision desegregating the public schools in 1954. The court, declared these "Dixiecrat" senators and congressmen, had substituted "naked power for established law."

> This unwarranted exercise of power by the Court, contrary to the Constitution, is creating chaos and confusion in the States principally affected. It is destroying the amicable relations between the white and Negro races that have been created through 90 years of patient effort by the good people of both races. It has planted hatred and suspicion where there has been heretofore friendship and understanding.

The manifesto pledged the use of "all lawful means to bring about a reversal of this [*Brown*] decision which is contrary to the Constitution and to prevent the use of force in its implementation." In solidarity with this stand, Senator Harry Byrd of Virginia declared a state policy of "massive resistance" to desegregation in 1956. Governor Orval Faubus would block the entry of black teenagers to Little Rock Central High in 1957. Governors Ross Barnett and George Wallace would resist the integration of their state universities in 1962 and 1963. All were Democrats. Liberal hypocrisy in decrying Nixon's "Southern Strategy," after a century of liberal collusion with Dixiecrats denying Southern Negroes their civil rights, does not cease to amaze.

What the Left never understood, or would never accept, is that Nixon brought the South into the Republican column not because he shared their views on segregation or civil rights. He did not. What we shared was the South's contempt for a liberal press and hypocritical Democratic Party that had coexisted happily with

Dixiecrats for a century but got religion when conservative Republicans began to steal the South away from them.

The Goldwater-Nixon party in which I enlisted was not a segregationist party but a conservative party. Virtually every segregationist in the eleven states of the old Confederacy, and every Klansman from 1865 to 1965, belonged to the party of Woodrow Wilson, Franklin Roosevelt, and Harry Truman.

THERE IS NOTHING like a first campaign.

During the tenure of the 89th Congress, which was enacting his Great Society legislation, LBJ once brazenly boasted that this is "my Congress." We seized on the phrase, countering that Congress was not the property of any President, but "the people's house." We daily disparaged Congress for having become a "toothless old lap dog" whose role was now not dissimilar to that of Johnson's beagles Him and Her, whom LBJ hoisted by their ears for the benefit of photographers. To support the charge that Congress had ceased to represent the people and become a rubber stamp for LBJ, GOP researchers had graded all 295 Democratic House members on how often they voted the LBJ line. Almost all had voted "yes" on Johnson's agenda between 90 and 100 percent of the time. I would give Nixon the exact figure in each district where we campaigned.

And he would exaggerate the figure. If a member of Congress voted with the president 94 percent of the time, Nixon would express amazement that he had voted with Johnson 98 percent of the time. When an Indiana newspaper rapped the researcher who fed Nixon the false data, Nixon told me not to worry. This was the reaction we wanted. It "gives us a second bite at the apple." This way, he said, we can issue a statement conceding we made an error and the congressmen had voted with LBJ only 94 percent of the time. The second hit drives the point home: The guy is a poodle. Nixon related a story he relished of how he had learned this tactic years ago from an old congressman. He would imitate the old codger's voice, describing what he did, and chuckle at the memory.

On another occasion I was walking close to the Boss as he was leaving an event, when a woman rushed up to plead with him to be their Lincoln Day speaker. I was startled to hear Nixon, who had to turn down scores of such invitations, tell the lady he would be delighted. As we moved on, he said in a low voice, "Did you hear me tell that lady I would do her Lincoln Day event?" "Yes sir," I said. "Now, get me out of it!" said Nixon.

CHAPTER 4

The Manila Questions

"THAT SON OF a bitch [Nixon], did you see in the
New York Times what he said about us this morning?"
—PRESIDENT LYNDON JOHNSON,
TO VICE PRESIDENT HUMPHREY (NOVEMBER 4, 1966)

IN THE COMEBACK of Richard Nixon, the critical year was
1966, the crucial day November 4. That morning, Nixon's
Appraisal of Manila appeared in the *New York Times*. President
Johnson saw it and in a press conference that morning launched
into a tirade unprecedented in presidential lore. "It was," wrote
Jules Witcover, "the most brutal verbal bludgeoning ever adminis-
tered from the White House by Johnson, or any other president for
that matter, to a leader of the opposition party."

The roots of Nixon's strike on Johnson's policy in Vietnam, and
LBJ's enraged response, went back weeks. In September the White
House had announced that Johnson would meet in late October
with President Nguyen Van Thieu of South Vietnam in Manila.
Noting the proximity of the meeting to the midterm elections,
Nixon asked whether this was a "quest for peace or a quest for
votes," and stayed on the offensive: "There have been many firsts
in the Johnson Administration, but this is the first time a President
may have figured the best way to help his party is to leave the country."

In mid-October in Wilmington, Delaware, Johnson blundered. A Republican victory this fall, said the President, "could cause the nation to falter and fall back and fail in Vietnam." As Republicans were providing the President with more unified support on Vietnam than his own party, this was unjust. Nixon fell on the fumble. We issued a statement the next morning calling Johnson's remarks "a vicious, unwarranted and partisan assault upon a Republican Party that has given President Johnson the support for the war that his own party has denied him. With his insensitive attack, President Johnson has gravely jeopardized the bipartisan backing he should have when he goes to Manila." Nixon demanded that the President "apologize to the Republican Party for the irresponsible charge."

Nixon was clearly benefiting from these exchanges. As the leading Republican campaigning nationally, he was able both to engage Johnson on his home turf, foreign policy, and convert the '66 campaign into a Nixon-Johnson race. By urging Johnson not to weaken, Nixon was also rallying conservatives and hawks to his side. And by pointing out that on his foreign trips he had defended U.S. policy in Vietnam, Nixon showed himself as more statesmanlike than members of the President's party who were walking away from him and the war. Nixon was in what he liked to call "the catbird seat."

ON OCTOBER 24 and 25, Johnson met in Manila with presidents and prime ministers of the Philippines, South Vietnam, South Korea, Thailand, Australia, and New Zealand. On the 25th all signed a "Declaration of Goals and Freedom," and Johnson flew on to Seoul and to Saigon, where he told the troops at Cam Ranh Bay to "bring back that coonskin on the wall."

Nixon was in Portland, Oregon, at the Benson Hotel. Late that afternoon, an excited Pat Hillings came to tell me that word was out that Bill Moyers in Manila had informed the White House press corps that, after his Asia tour, Johnson would return to barnstorm the nation, campaigning across a dozen states for Democratic candidates. I rushed to Nixon's suite and told him, as he was about to leave for a rally with our Oregon candidates, including Tom McCall, who was running for governor, and Governor Mark Hatfield, who was running for the Senate.

Nixon was jolted: "Well, we'll just have to see about that." During that evening's speech Nixon forgot the name of the GOP gubernatorial candidate, finally blurting "Bob" McCall, until the audience shouted several times, "It's Tom!" McCall was miffed and the fault was mine. If an aide has unsettling news, but it is not vital that the candidate or campaigner know it, you wait until the speech-making is over and you are back at the hotel.

When Nixon returned from his Portland event he was agitated and depressed. If Johnson campaigns all out in the last week of the election, he told me, it will cost us. Our gains could be cut, perhaps as far back as 12 seats. We would win nothing like the 40 he had been predicting. Nixon was down.

Around midnight he called me back to his room. I had presented him with a problem. He had a solution. He would take the President on directly—on Vietnam. He began rapidly dictating ideas for a major policy address on the war. I scribbled a dozen pages. Nixon then told me to peel off and travel with Rose to Boise and spend the day in the hotel writing a speech based on what he had dictated. He would join us after his trip up to Seattle, Tacoma, and Spokane. This was the origin of the Appraisal of Manila, ten days later. From Portland, Rose and I flew to Boise, where I spent the day writing a new speech.

That he had been upset by the news I brought him was reflected in the *New York Times* story by Tom Wicker on Nixon's day in Washington State. The headline: "Nixon Says a 'Johnson Blitz' Threatens 'Great Republican Tide.'"

LBJ'S FORMULA FOR DEFEAT

By the time Nixon arrived in Boise, I had a completed draft. For a week we worked that speech until we had turned it into a statement, then into what I called "The Manila Questions."

In the Manila communiqué, Johnson had declared that all U.S. and Allied forces "shall be withdrawn . . . as the other side withdraws its forces to the North, ceases its infiltration, and the level of violence thus subsides. Those forces will be withdrawn as soon as possible and not later than six months after the above conditions have been fulfilled."

Johnson was signaling Hanoi that if it pulled its troops back and the Viet Cong temporarily stood down, we would pull all U.S. forces out of Vietnam in "not later than six months," perhaps sooner. Saigon would be at the mercy of the Viet Cong and the North when they chose to ramp up the war again. This told the enemy how to bring about the removal of all U.S. forces and gain a free hand in going after Saigon. It was a formula for defeat and the loss of South Vietnam. In his presidential memoir, *The Vantage Point*, Johnson concedes that he included the time line to be "specific" on what we required before getting out. The request that he be more specific had come from Andrei Gromyko. On October 10 at the White House, the Soviet foreign minister had complained to Johnson that previous U.S. statements on what it would take to get us out of Vietnam had been "very general." Responding to Gromyko, LBJ had corrected that in Manila.

And I had caught this astonishing concession. The critical passages in Nixon's Appraisal of Manila were these. President Johnson, Nixon said,

> states clearly that if North Vietnam withdraws its forces back across its border and the violence thus subsides we shall withdraw all American forces out of Vietnam, most of them ten

thousand miles back to the United States. The effect of this mutual withdrawal would be to leave the fate of South Vietnam to the Vietcong and the South Vietnamese Army. . . . [It] simply turns back the clock two years and says, "Let the South Vietnamese fight it out with the Vietcong." The South Vietnamese Army could not prevail for any length of time over the Communist guerrillas without American advisers, air support and logistical backing. Communist victory would most certainly be the result of "mutual withdrawal" if the North Vietnamese continued their own logistical support of the Communist guerrillas.

Tying allied military action to the scope of enemy action, Nixon's statement went on,

implies that a diminishing of the Communist military effort will bring a corresponding reduction in the allied effort. If this implication is accurate, then we have offered to surrender a decisive military advantage at the Manila Conference. We have offered to leave it to Communist generals to determine the timing and intensity of the war. . . . I know of no successful military effort that ever keyed its own intensity simply to match that of the aggressor—thus deliberately surrendering to the aggressors the initiative for major offensives.

Crafting these lines, I had in mind MacArthur's Farewell Address, where he declared, "'Why,' my soldiers asked of me, 'surrender military advantages to an enemy in the field?' I could not answer."

Immediately after that passage, we quoted Ike. Then Nixon rammed the sword home: "Communist victory would most certainly be the result of 'mutual withdrawal' if the North Vietnamese continued their own logistical support of the Communist guerrillas."

As we worked on the statement, I converted the points we sought to make into a series of direct questions that carried the clear implication that Johnson's war policy, outlined in his Manila communiqué, should the terms be accepted by Hanoi and the Viet Cong, pointed to an early abandonment and almost certain loss of South Vietnam to Communism, a strategic disaster for the United States. Given the gravity of the points, I went through the text again and again to ensure there were no partisan barbs or political slap shots. Safire wanted us to frame the questions as a letter to the President. Nixon thought that too gimmicky. The tone was tough but respectful.

While Nixon took off for Johnson City in east Tennessee to give a final boost to Howard Baker, the embattled son-in-law of Everett Dirksen running for the Senate, Rose and I worked on the final draft. By late afternoon a number of reporters, including Murray Kempton of the *New York Post*, whose writing I had admired since Columbia, had assembled in the law library at the firm to read copies.

Crucial to the success of the Manila questions were Safire's ties to the *New York Times*. Safire called Harrison Salisbury and persuaded him to read the Appraisal and consider running the text. The *Times* ran the text in full, accompanied by a front-page story. It went right down the smokestack.

JOHNSON UNLOADS ON NIXON

Friday morning we were headed for Maine and New Hampshire. Taping an interview at LaGuardia with Mike Wallace, Nixon asked me to monitor the President's press conference. The White House press office had announced Thursday that, as Johnson was to have minor surgery, he would be returning to the ranch for several days of rest and there would be no barnstorming for the party. In the press conference, a reporter rose to ask Johnson, "Does the cancellation of your big campaign trip mean that you do not intend to do anything to help Democratic candidates for election, such as one little speech in Texas or maybe a TV pep talk before election?"

The question set Johnson off. "First, we don't have any plans, so you don't cancel plans," he shot back, stunning reporters who had been given the details as to where Johnson would be going. Johnson then went on a two-minute rant against the press for fabricating the notion that he had ever planned to campaign. Yet, according to Joe Califano, LBJ had himself come up with the idea for the trip around the country signing Great Society bills. Wrote Califano, "The trip was set to begin on Friday, November 4, two days after he returned to the White House. Candidates across the country adjusted schedules for the President's anticipated arrival, and in some places, like Seattle . . . workers started constructing platforms."

Johnson was blatantly dissembling to an audience of reporters who all knew the truth. His mood having darkened, he got the question he had been waiting for. Chalmers Roberts of the *Washington Post* asked him about the Nixon charge that in the Manila communiqué, "it had appeared that you have proposed, or the seven powers had proposed, getting out in a way that would leave South Vietnam to the mercy of the Viet Cong."

"Sarcasm dripping from every phrase," wrote Witcover, Johnson "unloaded on Nixon":

I do not want to get into a debate on a foreign policy meeting in Manila with a chronic campaigner like Mr. Nixon. It is his problem to find fault with his country and with his government during a period of October every two years. If you will look back over his record you will find that to be true. He never did really recognize and realize what was going on when he had an official position in the government. You remember what President Eisenhower said, that if you would give him a week or so he would figure out what he was doing.

Since then he has made a temporary stand in California, and you saw what action the people took out there. Then he crossed the country to New York. Then he went back to San Francisco hoping he would be in the wings and available if Goldwater stumbled. But Goldwater didn't stumble. Now he is out talking about a conference that obviously he is not well prepared on or informed about.

Johnson went on to defend himself and the Manila communiqué against Nixon's charge that he had pledged to begin pulling all U.S. forces out if the violence in Vietnam began to subside:

Why would we want to stay there if there was no aggression, if there was no infiltration, and the violence ceased. . . . We wouldn't want to stay there as tourists. We wouldn't want to keep four hundred thousand men there just to march up and down the runway at Cam Ranh Bay. . . . Every participant in that conference, acting on good faith, with the best of motives, wanted to say to North Vietnam and every other nation in the world that we intend to stay there only so long as our presence is necessary to protect the territorial integrity of South Vietnam, to see that the violence there ceases and the infiltration and aggression ceases.

They know that and we ought not to confuse it here and we ought not try to get mixed up in a political campaign here. Attempts to do that will cause people to lose votes instead of gaining them. We ought not have men killed because we try to fuzz up something. When the aggression, the infiltration and the violence ceases, not a nation there wants to keep occupying troops in South Vietnam, and Mr. Nixon doesn't serve his country well by trying to leave that kind of impression in the hope that he can pick up a precinct or two, or a ward or two.

I sat stunned. Not only had Nixon drawn blood, the President had lost it, confirmed by his defensiveness and unbuttoned anger. With his venomous insults pouring out one after another, he was not hurting Nixon. He was drawing attention to his own state of mind. When Nixon got to the plane, he told me to sit beside him and relate as precisely as I could what Johnson had said. As the Constellation took off, Nixon knew he had been handed his greatest opening in a decade to return to center stage. This was a confrontation with a President of the United States that he could win if he handled it right. And he handled it perfectly.

NIXON'S RIPOSTE

Mike Wallace learned about Johnson's attack after Nixon had taken off. He rented a jet and flew to Waterville to catch Nixon, and caught him coming back from the event to fly to Manchester. When Wallace asked for a response, Nixon invited the nation to understand the pressure Johnson was under. While he was "surprised" by the personal character and severity of the attack, Nixon said, he would "continue to speak out." He called Johnson "probably the hardest-working president in this century" and urged that the two debate "like gentlemen." Then Nixon drove the political point home:

> Let the record show that all over the world I have defended the administration's goal of no surrender to aggression. I have defended it in the capitals of the world and here at home against members of the president's own party.

After his remarks, Nixon turned to me: "Was I too hard on him?" No, he was not. He had done it just right. "Not since the Checkers speech had Nixon more effectively seized the moment," wrote Tom Wicker. So incendiary had Johnson's remarks been that Lady

Bird could not conceal her shock. *Washington Star* reporter Jack Horner described her reaction:

> Mrs. Johnson could not hide her astonishment when she heard her husband say that the Republican "chronic campaigner" never had realized what was going on even when he was vice president.
>
> Her legs crossed, Mrs. Johnson had been sitting on the President's right, listening calmly and intently to his answers to reporters' questions. Suddenly, both her feet hit the floor. With her lips forming an "oh" or "no" of astonishment, she appeared to be about to rise out of her chair.

When we got to Manchester I had a statement written. In it, Nixon said he would issue a more formal reply to the President on ABC's *Issues and Answers* Sunday, and on an NBC show where Ray Bliss had designated Nixon as the party's national voice on the election.

Our Manchester statement anticipated in tone and substance how Nixon would react all weekend. Declaring himself "shocked that President Johnson saw fit to respond to the serious questions which I raised about American policy in Asia with a personal attack against me," Nixon declined to respond in kind and said of Johnson, "I respect both the office of President and the man who holds it for the immense energies he exerts in fulfilling his responsibility." Nixon then repeated the "serious questions" he had raised in his Manila Appraisal:

> 1. With regard to the intensity of the war, do we simply react to Communist aggression and resign ourselves to a five-year war which the administration's current policy will produce—or should we follow the policy urged by General Eisenhower and increase our military pressure to a level necessary to achieve victory over aggression?

2. Are we going to continue the President's policy of esca-
lating the number of troops to achieve our goals in Vietnam or
shall we adopt the recommendations of the Republican Coordinating Committee to increase the use of American air and
sea power to bring the Communists to the conference table?

These were the substantive points. Nixon closed with a fiscal
question: "Are we going to pay for the war by raising taxes as is
widely reported to be the administration's plan—or shall we take
the Republican way of cutting non-essential spending?"

Johnson's attack produced eight-column banner headlines on
page one of the *Washington Post* ("Johnson Berates Nixon over
Vietnam") and the *Washington Star* ("LBJ Rips into Nixon on Viet
War"). Nixon had emerged from the encounter the clear victor—
with Ike, Ev Dirksen, Gerald Ford, and Jacob Javits backing him,
and the *New York Times* conceding, "Mr. Nixon had asked some
pertinent and critical questions—which he had every right to do."
Unanimously the press came down on Nixon's side or the side of
his right to ask such questions. Columnist Clayton Fritchey, who
had served in the Truman, Kennedy, and Johnson administrations,
chastised Johnson. In this instance, Fritchey wrote, Nixon was "on
solid ground . . . raising perfectly legitimate questions—the kind
that a loyal opposition has a right, if not a duty, to raise." Kempton was even more complimentary about the new Nixon and the
Manila statement, which he had read in the law library:

Back at the office of Nixon-Mudge, one read Mr. Nixon on
Manila and remembered more than anything else the rich
compliment the late Billie Holiday paid that other monument,
Louis Armstrong, "Maybe Pops toms every now and then, but
he toms from the heart." . . .

So those eight years of ceremonies formed Mr. Nixon into a
man who, wherever he travels, will always have a significant part

of him which travels for the State Dept. And one reflected, from the sudden affection which one discovers after years of being so vindictive, that he might serve us better today if he were really the reckless partisan we had thought him and not the honorable exponent of national unity he showed himself yesterday.

On Sunday, when Nixon appeared on *Issues and Answers*, he asked anew the questions in his Appraisal of Manila, and charged Johnson with "cheap political demagoguery." On the NBC show Ray Bliss had ceded to Nixon after our staff vetoed Bliss's RNC film, *What Goes on Here?*, as too crass and partisan in its disparagement of the President, Nixon began,

> I was subjected last week to one of the most savage personal assaults ever leveled by the President of the United States against one of his political opponents. . . . I shall answer it not for myself but because of a great principle that is at stake. It is the principle of the right to disagree, the right to dissent.

Nixon "closed with a beauty," wrote historian Stephen Ambrose. Speaking directly to President Johnson, Nixon said:

> I respect you for the great energies you devote to your office and my respect has not changed because of the personal attack you made on me. You see, I think I can understand how a man can be very very tired and how his temper can then be short. And if a vice president or a former vice president can be weary and tired, how much more tired would a president be after a journey like yours?

In absolving Johnson, Nixon was inviting public understanding of his "last press conference" of 1962. "It had been a wonderful year for Nixon," wrote Ambrose:

[I]t meant the revitalization of Richard Nixon. He had just brought himself back from the humiliation of the 1962 California governor's race. Through hard work, effrontery, loyalty to the GOP, hard work, brains, brazenness, luck, hard work, and more luck, all capped by the Manila communiqué extravaganza, he had made himself the leader of the loyal opposition and had helped set in motion political forces that could soon make the GOP into the ruling party, with Nixon as President.

Mary McGrory, who would later describe Nixon as having a "switchblade grin that stops just before it reaches the eyes," ruefully conceded there was indeed a resurrected Nixon:

The President has roughly revived him.

He is no longer a has-been. He is a man to be reckoned with at the White House and his party cannot ignore this new claim. By his own lights, as the result of the presidential cuffing, Nixon is where a week ago he said Bobby Kennedy was— "sitting in the catbird seat."

During his *Issues and Answers* appearance, Nixon made a stunning announcement: "After this election I am going to take a holiday from politics for at least six months."

Is it really wise to cede the field to Romney and lock ourselves into a six-month moratorium with no flexibility? I asked him.

"Let 'em chew on him for a little while," Nixon replied.

That is what he expected the press to do to George Romney, and that is what the press did. The new year would prove an annus horribilis for the governor of Michigan, who in November 1966 had emerged in the national polls as the front-runner for the nomination and the strongest of the Republican field in any race against President Johnson.

There was another reason Nixon decided to step back. He had

a keen appreciation of the fickleness of the public. He knew the impression he was leaving in 1966, with his fighting campaign and triumphant confrontation with Johnson, would sit well with the public, and even better with his party. But if he started out on a presidential campaign in 1967, even as an unannounced candidate, he knew the press and public would tire of him and begin looking about for the "fresh face." Thus he would back away and not appear center stage as a candidate until more than a year later, on the last filing date for the New Hampshire primary. It was a risky strategy and, judging by the results, a brilliant one.

WHY NOT VICTORY?

When Nixon's Appraisal of Manila appeared on November 4, 1966, in the *New York Times*, there were 400,000 U.S. troops in Vietnam and our war dead numbered 5,700. Six years later, when Nixon pulled all U.S. forces out, ten times that number, 58,000 Americans, had died in what was then the longest war in U.S. history. And after Congress cut off U.S. military aid to South Vietnam and imposed a ban on bombing, what Nixon had predicted in 1966 came to pass: Hanoi invaded the South with a dozen divisions, overran Saigon, and inflicted on the United States the worst defeat in its history. Cambodia would undergo a holocaust with more than a million dead in the first year of "peace" under the Khmer Rouge.

The questions Nixon had asked were never answered by the Johnson administration. Yet those questions pointed inexorably to that U.S. defeat. UN Ambassador Arthur Goldberg had said we would accept a coalition government with the Viet Cong. Johnson had told Hanoi at Manila that we will get out if you will get out, and we will begin to leave as the violence subsides. This told Hanoi that America was bleeding and weary, that Ho Chi Minh could dictate the pace of the war, that the independence of South Vietnam was not a vital U.S. interest for which America was prepared to use her full military power, and that if Hanoi was prepared to fight a long war, trading dead for dead, it would emerge victorious.

"In war there is no substitute for victory," MacArthur had told the Congress in 1951. He had warned JFK not to put his foot soldiers into Southeast Asia. He had declared that you can never allow an enemy a privileged sanctuary from which to strike you with impunity. In Vietnam, we had forgotten, or we chose to ignore, all of MacArthur's lessons.

Johnson had said at Manila that we were willing to accept something less than victory and implied we were willing to accept the loss of South Vietnam in a fair fight, after our withdrawal. But if he was not resolute for victory—bring the "coonskin home on the wall!" LBJ had bellowed—why had he committed the military power and moral prestige of the United States? By the time Nixon took office in 1969, the freedom of action Johnson had in 1966 was gone, his presidency had been broken by his failure to win or end the war, and the nation was being torn apart by Vietnam.

In 1972, Nixon would bomb Hanoi and mine Haiphong harbor to bring the war to an end. He told me, after he left office, he should have done it in 1969. Johnson should have done it in 1965 or 1966, as many had urged.

America need not have lost the Vietnam War.

TRIUMPH OF THE "BIRDWATCHERS"

Election night 1966 we rented a suite at the Drake Hotel, to which Nixon repaired with his traveling staff and several advance men. We were nervous. But early in the evening, as the returns began to come in from the East, Midwest, and South, candidate after candidate for whom we had campaigned seemed to be romping home to victory. And as it appeared a Republican sweep might be developing, it swiftly became both a working as well as a drinking evening. Soon, it seemed as though Nixon's extravagant predictions of GOP gains might not only be realized but exceeded.

Our tensions dissolved into excitement and exuberance. We would get the news from television of one triumph after another, of a new governor, a new senator, a new congressman, and cheering would go up in the main suite. We would take the news into the bedroom, from which Nixon was making his calls, to tell him which candidate and state or district it was. He was as giddy as we were. John Davies would put through the calls, and tell the candidate to hold on as Nixon was finishing another call. Nixon would then get on the line and congratulate the winner, or he would commiserate with the loser, tell him he had run a gallant campaign and must not give up, but try again in 1968. But there were few losers that night. Davies, a contemporary of Nixon's who had been an executive with a California phone company and handled his calls while acting as personal aide, or "body man," on the road, was indispensable. Until the morning hours of Wednesday, when the California returns were all in, we worked those phones, confident no other potential candidate of 1968 was doing the same. Friendships formed in six weeks of campaign stops were solidified during that long triumphal night at the Drake. As Nixon had gone in for those folks in '66, many would be there for him in '68. Again, the right thing to do— put everything on the line in a fight for the party—had been the smart thing to do.

Not since Nixon was first elected to Congress in 1946 had Republicans picked up so many seats. Forty-seven House seats! And Richard Nixon had contributed more to the national victory than any other Republican. He had been the only name Republican on the road since mid-September, traveling to 35 states and into nearly 80 congressional districts. It was the greatest Republican off-year election triumph since 1946, when he had arrived to join the "fighting 80th Congress." The long string of personal and party defeats—1958, 1960, 1962, 1964—was now dramatically snapped. Nixon had gone out on a long limb and predicted a Republican sweep of vast proportions, and then gone out and helped to deliver it. Even the press was impressed.

A night or two after that evening at the Drake, Nixon invited Davies, Sears, Rose, me, and a few others to dinner with him and Pat at El Morocco for a long celebration. Never before had I seen Nixon so ebullient or happy.

The greatest comeback had taken its greatest leap forward.

At the end of each campaign, it was Nixon's custom to give his staff and traveling press a memento. My wife, Shelley, still has in our den from 1960 a small metallic map of the USA with all the states delineated to recall the first 50-state campaign. At this Republican triumph, Nixon inducted us into "The Birdwatchers of 1966," giving us a silver coin with the image of Churchill in plastic and a letter quoting the nineteen words Churchill used after Munich that Nixon had used about Vietnam in our weeks on the road: "The belief that security can be obtained by throwing a small state to the wolves is a fatal delusion."

Another memory comes to mind from this 1966 campaign. After that long celebratory night at El Morocco, Nixon flew to Key Biscayne. From there, he called to ask how I was doing. I told him that, for some reason, I felt depressed. We had been campaigning day and night for weeks with too much coffee and too little sleep. And then came the smashing success of election night, followed by the letdown of sitting in an empty office with nothing to do but to start writing thank-you notes. Nixon became paternal. This happens in all great campaigns, he said. The letdown after the great high. Do not take off work right now, stay with it, taper off for a week, then take a vacation. Don't rush it. This is what happens. And stay in touch.

The Boss, however, showed no signs of depression. He had departed for Florida exhilarated. He was back in the hunt.

CHAPTER 5

New Recruits

AND SO WE would end the Soaring Sixties with
Lazarus laughing.
—MURRAY KEMPTON, "NIXON RETURNS,"
New York Post (MAY 18, 1967)

WHEN THE NEWSMAGAZINES came out on the Monday following November 8, *Time* and *Newsweek* had identical covers, featuring the same six GOP stars: Rockefeller, Reagan, and Romney, and senators-elect Mark Hatfield, Ed Brooke, and Charles Percy. Nixon, who had traveled tens of thousands of miles and campaigned for more candidates than all of these party leaders put together, got honorable mention inside the magazines.

The polls and pundits began swiftly to move Romney's way. By the end of November 1966, Gallup had him leading Nixon among independents 34–22 and among Republicans 39–31. The Harris poll had Romney 15 points ahead of Nixon among the independents, 43–28. Harris had Romney beating Lyndon Johnson by 8, 54–46, while Nixon, Rockefeller, and Percy were all trailing the President by 8. Reagan was losing to Johnson two-to-one. In the race for the 1968 Republican nomination, the governor of Michigan had broken clear of the pack and was running to daylight.

Yet Nixon had been the big winner of 1966. An analyst had to be obtuse not to see it. In that crucial year he had solidified his alliance with Goldwater, healed a breach with Buckley and *National Review,* and personally met with and converted a large slice of the leadership of the conservative movement. He had emerged as the party's point man on law and order, Vietnam, and foreign policy. He had gone head to head with President Johnson in the last five days of the campaign and, by everyone's scorecard, bested him. Analysts were comparing his won-lost record in 1966, where Nixon focused on rookie candidates and not incumbents who had survived 1964 and were sure to win, with the lame won-lost records of Bobby Kennedy and Hubert Humphrey, who had been on the road for the Democrats.

Nixon had predicted a 40-seat pickup in the House, then gone out and helped deliver a 47-seat victory. He predicted a gain of 3 Senate seats. The party gained 3. He predicted a pickup of 6 governorships. The party added 8. Only among state legislators, where Nixon predicted a gain of 700, did he fall short. The GOP added 540. Even the farm team had had a tremendous year.

In the South, the GOP had doubled its state senators from 25 to 47 and its statehouse seats from 73 to 161. There were now 23 Southern Republican members of the U.S. House, a gain of 7, the most since Reconstruction. And the South as a region would be sending the largest number of delegates to the 1968 convention—27 percent of the total.

In New York State, an unknown academic running on the line of the five-year-old Conservative Party had captured half a million votes and come in third in the governor's race against Rockefeller, edging out Liberal Party candidate Franklin Roosevelt, Jr. While the GOP was booming in the South, it was shriveling in Rockefeller's New York. His share and the GOP share of the statewide vote had declined every time he headed the ticket. By 1966, after the third Rockefeller victory, a Republican delegation of 26 House members as of 1956 was down to 15.

In January 1967, Kieran O'Doherty, with brother-in-law Dan Mahoney a pivot of the Conservative Party, called, said he backed Nixon, and offered to find delegates to run against a Rockefeller favorite-son slate. Tom Pauken, the head of the National College YRs, had already contacted me in December. He, too, was with Nixon. Nixon told me to stay in touch with both. The American Right was not dead. It was rising again, even in the land of Rockefeller, Javits, and John V. Lindsay.

The good news did not stop. Javits, who had been touting himself as the party's "chief ideologist" and a vice presidential nominee in 1968, had lost his bid to be elected one of fifteen at-large delegates to the New York Constitutional Convention. The tide was going out on the Eastern Liberal Establishment. In 1960 Nixon had come to New York and agreed to the Pact of Fifth Avenue demands of Rockefeller. In 1966, Rockefeller had sent a secret emissary to us. He needed Nixon's help—in New York State. How sweet it was.

That Nixon was aware of the power shift was evident in a comment he wrote on my mid-December memo warning that Bill Timmons, leader of the YRs' right-wing "syndicate," and his people were concerned that "C. K. McWhorter may be influencing you in your position with regard to the YRs, toward a stance inimical to their interests."

"Tell him absolutely not!" Nixon wrote on the memo. Yet he did not have a more loyal man than Charlie, a former national chairman of the YRs. The YRs and the College YRs had now both passed to conservative control. Politically, the day of the liberal Republican was over in the GOP.

AS OF NOVEMBER 1966, Nixon was the choice for the 1968 nomination of party regulars and the Goldwater Right. He had gone into every state and congressional district where he had been invited, including the Deep South. He had endorsed a man to whom he owed nothing—Rockefeller. Scores of new congressmen were in his debt. Even losing candidates were thanking him for coming in for them. He was the lone national Republican acceptable to all factions. Tom Evans came by my desk to say, "I don't think you're going back to St. Louis." I didn't think so either.

Those of us who had been with Nixon on the road were bitter he was so conspicuously absent from the cover of those magazines. He felt it, too. Yet they were doing us a favor. In the race we knew was coming, did we want to be lead horse coming out of the gate? Nixon didn't think so. Thus, he had declared the six-month moratorium on politics.

But at 20 Broad, the rest of us were not observing any moratorium. Right after the election I wrote a 2,000-word analysis of the extraordinary Nixon effort and the fruits it had borne titled "Nixon: GOP's Big Winner in '66." It was targeted directly at the loser image. I sent it to Richard Amberg, publisher of the *Globe-Democrat*. In a weekend edition he placed it under his own byline on page one of the Features section. In it I mentioned the *Time* and *Newsweek* covers graced by the countenances of Rockefeller, Romney, Percy, Brooke, and Hatfield: "It was ironic that, two brief years later, beaming from the covers of the nation's newsweeklies would be several of the GOP's 'New Stars' that had last been seen grinning from their lifeboats in 1964." We ordered thousands of reprints and sent them to columnists, political reporters, editorial writers, and party leaders. The pickup was tremendous. The piece was quoted extensively, the facts and figures taken out and recited without attribution, which was fine by us.

Then I drafted two letters, the first to be signed by Ike's secretary of the interior, Fred Seaton, who had gone home to Nebraska. The Seaton letter succinctly made the case that Nixon was the man America needed and announced that he, Seaton, had decided to endorse Nixon for the Republican nomination in 1968, and gave his reasons why. The letter was to be sent to all 50 Republican

state chairmen and 100 Republican National committeemen and
-women, and to all Republican members of the House and Senate.
The letter invited a reply.

We had all the letters and envelopes typed up at Nixon, Mudge.
To lend authenticity, we filled a suitcase full of the letters, and one
long snowy winter day, I flew from LaGuardia to Omaha, caught a
puddle-jumper Frontier Airlines flight to Hastings, where Seaton
was publisher of the local paper, and arrived after dark. It was a short
ride to his office. So small was the town that when I got there someone at the airport phoned Seaton to say that the guy that just came
through had left his gloves. As Seaton sat signing the letters into the
night, sipping his whiskey, he told stories of his days with Ike and
Dick. After he had signed them all, we put them into the mail to go
out in the morning. They would arrive stamped with that Middle
American postmark "Hastings, Nebraska." Mission accomplished.

Though the letters from Seaton were panned by some newsmen
and Republicans as premature, Seaton got return letters from dozens of GOP leaders who signaled that, privately, they, too, liked
Nixon in '68. All those names went to Sears, who had begun building a political file for the primaries and conventions more than a
year off. Meanwhile, Nixon was observing his six-month moratorium from politics.

The week after the Seaton letters were mailed, David Broder, in
a front-page story in the *Washington Post*, "Nixon Begins Building
Up Staff for '68," wrote:

> Meanwhile, former Secretary of the Interior Fred A. Sea-
> ton . . . said yesterday that he had received a "very encourag-
> ing" response to his letter urging support for the former Vice
> President. . . .
>
> So far, [Seaton] said, he has received about 125 letters and
> half-a-dozen phone calls in reply.

"A few were highly antagonistic," he said, "but most were very favorable."

The second letter was signed by John Davis Lodge, grandson of Senator Henry Cabot Lodge, who had sunk Wilson's Versailles treaty and League of Nations, and brother of Senator Henry Cabot Lodge, Jr., who had lost his seat to John F. Kennedy in 1952, had been Nixon's running mate in 1960, and was JFK's ambassador to South Vietnam when President Diem was assassinated.

John Lodge's disposition reflected his charmed life. He had been a Hollywood actor in the late 1930s and played opposite Shirley Temple and Marlene Dietrich, whose name he would often bring up. In World War II he had been decorated for his naval service with the Croix de Guerre by General De Gaulle. He had served in the 80th Congress alongside those two other freshmen, Richard M. Nixon and John F. Kennedy, been elected governor of Connecticut, and served as Ike's ambassador to Spain. He spoke French and Spanish, and secretaries at the firm vied to take dictation from the handsome Lodge, who strode like a field marshal down the hall of the 24th floor to take over Nixon's office, where he signed letters and told stories of Hollywood days. While we had drafted the Lodge letter, he appended personal notes to the many old friends whose names were on the mailing lists of Republicans we had acquired. Inserted in the envelope with each Lodge letter was a large reprint of the Amberg analysis.

Lodge's letter began, "Richard H. Amberg, the distinguished publisher of the St. Louis Globe-Democrat, has written a truly splendid account of the yeoman labors of Dick Nixon in rebuilding our Republican Party across America." It closed, "I would be interested in your personal thoughts as to how the GOP can maintain through 1968 the spirit of unity and victory which Dick Nixon has worked so hard to create in 1966." The Lodge letter produced another harvest of return letters from Republicans confiding that they, too, thought Nixon should be the nominee. Those who did were soon contacted.

Immediately after the election, we carefully sorted the clippings from Nixon's travels and the favorable columns and editorials of his visits to every town, city, and state. Through November, December, and January and even into February, we were sending out personal letters, signed by Nixon, thanking publishers, editorial editors, columnists, and reporters. While Nixon might not have been the favorite of the Washington press corps, many in the local press outside the big cities liked and admired him, and, indeed, even wrote him private letters of encouragement. Beneath the gaze of the national press, we were seeding the ground of what we would come to call Middle America.

A BAPTISM OF FIRE

When Nixon declared his moratorium and confided to me of his future rival Romney, "Let 'em chew on him for a little while," meaning the piranhas of the press, he knew whereof he spoke. On December 4, 1966, Thomas O'Neill of the *Baltimore Sun* wrote that while Romney was the acknowledged front-runner for the GOP nomination, some of his fellow GOP governors

> have chafed and found him hard to accept during his four years as a member of the club. The nub of the complaint is that Governor Romney subconsciously, and perhaps unconsciously, approaches all others as inferiors.
>
> As diagnosed by one governor, also a Republican, Governor Romney is possessed of a superiority complex.
>
> There is his confident conviction that where Romney sits is the head of the table. Always, he is the self-constituted

chairman of the board, quick to over-rule. He is never at a loss for words.

A day earlier, Broder revealed that in August 1964, Goldwater had gone out of his way to assure Romney he would " 'lean over backward' to avoid any tinge of racism or any appeal to backlash in his 1964 campaign." Romney seemed assuaged, but then refused to back Goldwater, charging the senator had failed to make the "strong clarifying statements" Romney had demanded.

Goldwater's bitterness was understandable, as even Ike said he had done all he had been asked to do. Then, in mid-1966, as Reagan was in the midst of his campaign against Governor Pat Brown, Romney, at a Republican governors' conference in Los Angeles, volunteered to the press, "I am not satisfied with his [Reagan's] position on civil rights. . . . As far as Michigan is concerned, he would be in trouble. . . . But apparently one has to do things differently in California."

Nixon had read his man right. When Romney arrived in New York in December to address the National Association of Manufacturers, Kempton was there. His verdict: Romney's speech "showed that he had lost none of that perfect lack of pitch he has displayed in his prior biennial concert tours as a Presidential possibility." Kempton continued,

> He is an odd case. By every indication he is a successful governor; yet book him on a national tour, and he'll blow the option in two weeks.
>
> One finally decides that he must have manufactured a splendid car at American Motors. You got to have a great product for George Romney to sell it.

Before the Ides of March 1967, the press corps had concluded that Romney did not have what it takes to be President. Some reviews of a Western trip he took, all lovingly collected and preserved in my office at the Nixon law firm, were brutal. Columnist Andrew Tully kicked 1967 off by describing Romney's third inaugural address as governor of Michigan as a

> sanctimonious harangue replete . . . with the wet mackerel banalities of the breed [of presidential aspirants] . . . a stump speech aimed at stoneheads who have never fully accepted the wheel. . . . [T]he intellectual and political poverty revealed by his elocution shows him better suited for the chair of history at some backwater college.

I sent this to Nixon with a note: "This is about the roughest job I have seen done on Romney's speech." Nixon wrote back, "You should see what he writes about mine. You might see him in D.C. one day. He's an interesting character."

Then came Godfrey Sperling of the *Christian Science Monitor*:

> [T]here are emerging doubts as to whether Mr. Romney has that "something," that necessary political charisma a presidential candidate must have to evoke enthusiastic public support. . . . [His] timing on jokes is bad. Often the audience is embarrassed. And when the Governor tries to discuss issues in a quiet thoughtful way, he doesn't project too well. And he doesn't read speeches at all smoothly.

Sperling usually cut candidates slack. Others did not.

"During a press conference in Pocatello," wrote Hearst columnist Marianne Means, "Gov. Romney behaved like a novice when reporters pressed him about Viet Nam, becoming rattled, peevish, and at times almost incoherent." *Newsweek* described a gaffe in which Romney called potential rival Senator Charles Percy an "opportunist." Percy told Romney he had been "deeply hurt." Romney explained, "All politicians are opportunists. It hasn't any bad con-notations for me. Why, I call my best friends sons of bitches."

Thomas O'Neill of the *Sun* wrote, "Romney has yet to show that he can withstand the heat, and has already created questions on that score. He gets rattled under close scrutiny. . . . [T]he prevail-ing observation on the sidelines is that the front-runner is digging his own credibility gap to match that of President Johnson." When Romney announced he would stop taking questions on Vietnam, the *New York Post* wrote, "[T]his self-imposed quarantine may help him arrest his virulent attack of foot-in-mouth disease." The *New York Times* echoed, "His most recent statements on the Vietnam war are verbal smog so dense that a few more such emissions will make him subject to the penalties of the Clean Air Act."

Asked to explain his moratorium on further discussion of the great issue of 1967, Vietnam, Romney replied, "Sometimes a man knows enough about a situation not to take a premature posi-tion. . . . I know a great deal about Viet Nam that makes it wise for me not to make specific proposals until I've had a chance to look at the situation." The *Detroit Free Press*, his hometown paper, wrote of Romney's Western tour, "He blew his cool . . . in Idaho by becom-ing too specific in his charges against President Johnson and by refusing to supply reporters with any specifics to back the charges. Under questioning he reddened and became visibly rattled."

In a devastating column in his magazine, Malcolm Forbes joined others in mocking Romney's remark "I never talk politics on Sun-days," and cited other Romney comments that all added up to "ver-bal flapdoodle." Forbes closed:

> To sum it all up, I have a sinking feeling that Mr. Romney is floundering for a way to convey convictions he doesn't have, for solutions to problems that either don't exist, or if they exist, that he doesn't understand. The more he talks the less he says. . . .

[T]his is no time for another, albeit cronyless, Harding in the White House.

A March 18 Gallup poll revealed the damage. Among Republicans Romney had fallen to number two, 9 points behind Nixon. In a choice between the two, Nixon had a 12-point lead. An April Gallup poll of GOP county chairmen found Nixon ahead of Romney four-to-one nationally. In the South, Nixon led Romney twelve-to-one.

Early in 1967, the *Columbus Dispatch* in Ohio began a series of anti-Romney articles that I memoed Nixon "were too good to be true." I fished around and found out that ex-Goldwaterites and supporters of Governor James Rhodes were feeding the *Dispatch*. After listing the participants I wrote Nixon, "[I]t is apparent . . . that Rhodes is really out to gut the Mormon."

Nixon visited Rhodes, who was entertaining vice presidential ambitions. When he returned, Nixon called me into his office and, laughing, did his best to imitate what the gruff Ohio governor had said to him: "Dick, George Romney running for president is like a duck trying to ——— a football. He couldn't sell ——— on a troopship."

In May, I talked with my journalism school pal Don Oliver, who had been assigned by NBC to cover Romney. He's a "lightweight," Don said. De Vries was unable to delegate responsibility, "ready for the funny farm." Except for Travis Cross, the Romney staff was minor-league, ignorant of press needs, cowering before the governor. Romney was so enraged by *Newsweek*'s publishing his crack about calling "my best friends sons of bitches," he was demanding an apology and threatening to sue. Don said *Newsweek*'s Detroit bureau was collecting film of Romney appearances where he had cursed or used obscenities and preparing to dump them at any legal proceeding. Romney's staff convinced the governor to drop the idea.

When Romney was undergoing this scourging in the winter and spring of 1967, son Mitt was turning twenty in France, where he had gone as a Mormon missionary. The brutal treatment of his dad would endure almost without interruption until Romney dropped out of the race a year later, two weeks before the New Hampshire primary. One can imagine what the son went through as he watched from afar what was happening to the father he revered.

STAFFING UP FOR '68

Nixon was as uninterested in the practice of law as he was consumed with politics, policy, and personalities. Many days we would spend so much time talking issues and strategies, I had to wait until he went home to get my work done. Nixon relished gossip. I recall relating to him stories about a U.S. senator whose prowling had become legendary and about whom the ribald tales were hilarious and unprintable. Days later, Mrs. Nixon and Tricia were in his office. Nixon called me in and told me to tell Pat and Tricia the stories. Startled and embarrassed, I gave an expurgated version.

Len Garment, Tom Evans, and John Sears of the firm had been part-time volunteers. John Whitaker had done our scheduling and a new crew of advance men had been trained by veterans Nick Ruwe and Roy Goodearle and tested on the road. Hillings and McWhorter had traveled with us to socialize with the pols who wanted face time with Nixon but could not have it because he needed his downtime. They were to collect the names of the major players in each congressional district, and of those who wanted to be aboard the Nixon team in 1968. Both went back to their jobs when the '66 election was over.

In January 1967, in the middle of our moratorium, Nixon held off-the-record meetings in New York, the importance of which was impressed upon me when I found a man inspecting the sofa cushions in his office. Rose introduced me to the former FBI agent sweeping for bugs. Nixon had a key meeting coming up with Fred LaRue and Peter O'Donnell, the Texas state chairman. They had been at a Republican National Committee meeting in New Orleans as Nixon's agents and told Gaylord Parkinson, the retired California chairman who had played a lead role in the Reagan landslide in California and was the father of the "11th Commandment"—"Thou shalt not speak ill of another Republican"—that Nixon would like to talk to him about 1968. With the huge California victory—Nixon's former aide and 1960 campaign manager Bob Finch had been elected lieutenant governor by 250,000 more votes than Reagan's margin—Parkinson was an early-first-round draft choice for chairman of anybody's campaign. He and his deputy, Robert Walker, flew to New York and dined with Nixon.

Thirty-six hours later, David Broder had a front-page story in the *Washington Post* that Nixon had offered Parkinson a major post in his 1968 campaign. Parkinson said he was considering it, as well as an offer to manage Romney's campaign. When Broder had called me, I was taken aback at all the information he had of what had gone on only hours before. I hung up. I asked Nixon what I could tell Broder.

I never trusted these hired guns who talked to the press to get their names in the paper. Nevertheless, Parkinson was soon aboard, and Walker was interviewing me at a hotel about what my specific duties were. These fellows seemed to believe their franchise was larger than it actually was.

By late March, Parkinson and Walker had lost the confidence of 20 Broad. "No one in the office trusts them," I wrote Nixon, "not Sears or Evans or Buchanan, or Rose or Garment." While their firing might not be justified, "[t]here is certainly sufficient evidence to indicate they should not have been hired." Parkinson, or his aides, I told Nixon, had released vital data to the media he was told to withhold, had violated direct instructions by naming Walker executive director, had sent letters to newsmen to join the Nixon committee, and "let an incredibly stupid form letter go to General Eisenhower." During the next four months, regular reports came in about leaks out of the committee, and nothing being done in the DC office. As I passed them on to Nixon his anger and frustration grew. On one of my reports he wrote, "1. This office must be a disaster. . . . 2. Better get Huston or Timmons to work."

Huston, former chairman of Young Americans for Freedom, and Timmons, the leader of the "syndicate" that dominated Young Republican politics in that era, were first-rate organization men. In a note to me about one of Huston's analyses of our DC campaign operation, Nixon described him as possibly an "organizational genius." It was Huston who brought Lyndon K. "Mort" Allin in from Wisconsin to run Youth for Nixon. In January 1969, Mort became publisher and editor of the President's Daily News Summary, which Nixon had demanded be set up and which would be on his desk before he got to the Oval Office. Soon running to dozens of pages, the Mort Allin news summary would become an indispensable tool of governance for President Nixon, who would scribble orders on it to White House staffers and Cabinet officers.

ONE DECISION NIXON made at my urging came back to bite us. Jules Witcover had traveled with Nixon in 1966, when no other reporter was there. And though Nixon had declared a moratorium on politics, Jules told me we owed him, and all he wanted was one last interview. I persuaded Nixon to let Witcover ride to the airport with him. I forgot all about it. In early January, a Witcover feature on Nixon broke in the *Saturday Evening Post*, and I got an enraged call from Broder, accusing me of lying when I told him Nixon was not giving interviews. After explaining what had happened, I then spent days explaining what Nixon had meant by his observations, in Witcover's piece, about Republican women:

> They're great workers, but they're idealists and emotional-ists. . . . They're the real haters. Any Machiavellian scheme,

they go for. They die hard. They tell me, "You didn't hit them hard enough. Why don't you give them hell like Truman?" I explain that I not only have to appeal to partisan Republicans but also have to get Democrats to cross over. But the women don't understand that. Occasionally I say a good word for Johnson or Humphrey. It's a device, of course, to show I'm fair-minded, but the women don't see that. That's why the women liked Barry so. He didn't give a damn about Democrats. But to win you have to.

Astounded by this new candor, *The Spivak Report* said veteran observers were coming to believe Nixon might mean it when he said he was not going to be a candidate again.

Though impolitic, Nixon had a point about women in politics and political wives. Decades later, Paul Harvey and I were having lunch with President George H. W. Bush, when he told us how he had encountered in the press room a reporter who had covered his first Senate run. He had gone back to the mansion and told Barbara about seeing their old friend, whereupon Barbara had gone on a tear, reciting chapter and verse how this wretch had gutted him in that campaign. What President Bush had not recalled the first lady would not forget.

SHELLEY

The first recruit, in January 1967, was a veteran of three tours of duty in Nixon's political wars: Shelley Scarney, whom I had never met. A year out of the University of Michigan, she was about to fulfill a childhood dream—a job in New York. But in July 1959, before beginning a job with *Life* magazine, Shelley was visiting Washington and learned of an opening in the vice president's office. Within two weeks, she was hired, and began work following Nixon's return from his Kitchen Debate with Khrushchev.

It was August, and she was a receptionist in the vice president's Senate office, directly across the hall from John F. Kennedy's. Shelley and Pam Turnure, JFK's receptionist, would alert each other when some of the same uninvited visitors would arrive to ask, or demand, to see Vice President Nixon or Senator Kennedy. Shelley had traveled the 1960 campaign and, after Nixon's defeat, joined other staff members in California. Toward the end of 1961, she left her job at General Dynamics in San Diego to assist Bob Haldeman in opening the Nixon for Governor headquarters in Los Angeles.

In 1964, Shelley joined Rose and the Boss in his campaign for Barry Goldwater. If Nixon was going to run again in 1968, he wanted her back, handling confidential calls and greeting VIPs. To the Nixons, Shelley, like Rose, was family.

The day she returned to 20 Broad changed both our lives forever. For forty-three years Shelley and I have been married, and she has worked and traveled with me during all those four decades, including my own three presidential runs. Our experiences and adventures could fill volumes. In our living room is a picture with President Nixon, inscribed "To Pat and Shelley with best wishes from the one who brought them together. Dick Nixon."

A BRAIN BANK FOR BOBBY

On January 24, 1967, I sent Nixon a long piece from the *Daily Telegraph* by Henry Fairlie, headlined "Kennedy Millions Set Up a 'Brain Bank.'" My cover note read, "I think you might want to look this article over. . . . Some of the names mentioned are quite interesting."

Fairlie described a "move" on Harvard by the Kennedys, who had effected a name change at the Graduate School of Administration, which was now to be known as the John F. Kennedy School of Government. Attached to the Kennedy School was a new Harvard Institute of Politics, with a $10 million endowment, to be staffed by public policy intellectuals like Richard Neustadt as director, Pat Moynihan, and Adam Yarmolinsky, who had been insiders in JFK's administration. Among the first class of fellows at the institute were some of the best and brightest of the liberal Republican and Democratic staffers from Capitol Hill and the Kennedy-Johnson administration. Among the journalists invited to the institute that year were Max Frankel of the *New York Times,* Phil Geyelin, recently named to the editorial page of the *Washington Post,* and Al Otten of the *Wall Street Journal.* Wrote Fairlie:

> [T]he Kennedy Institute of Politics provides the most convenient opportunity for attracting under the name of the Kennedys men who are at present serving in the Johnson Administration, who are hoping to be employed by, and would be useful to, another Kennedy administration, and who, as influential political journalists, have valuable services to offer in the future.

The largest contributor to the institute, at $2.5 million, was the Ford Foundation, headed by JFK's national security adviser, McGeorge Bundy. "Mr. Bundy's close association with Robert Kennedy is no secret," wrote Fairlie. "Nor is his ambition to be Secretary of State."

Fairlie had revealed a new and handsomely upholstered think tank where public policy elites could be sustained while working outside government with like-minded peers for a Kennedy restoration. Nixon was taken with the article and wrote back, "Pat: This is an outstanding group of brains—you can see why we must expand our base in this area."

AS WE BEGAN to staff up, Nixon wanted another writer, a moderate or liberal, to balance me. He asked me to check around and see who was the best available. I did not know the city and asked Neal Freeman, a protégé of Bill Buckley. He gave me several names. The pride of the litter was Ray Price, former editorial editor of the *New York Herald-Tribune*, the once-mighty voice of the Republican Establishment, lately stilled. Freeman said there was one problem: Price had framed and hanging in his apartment the editorial he had written repudiating Barry Goldwater and endorsing Lyndon Johnson, the first time the modern *Herald-Trib* had endorsed a Democrat for president.

In my February 27 memo to Nixon, I gave him eight names provided by Freeman. First in line was Price, the "ex–Trib editor about whom we talked. Freeman thinks Price would come high, but would be a decided asset, and blow to Rocky-Javits-Romney types." Nixon crossed out with his pen the names of four other liberal writers, but indicated an interest in two.

As I shopped the names around, all conceded Price was first-rate. But no one knew him to be a Nixon admirer. Not to worry, Nixon told me. "He may not be a loyalist now, but he will after the first battle." Nixon was right. Whatever Ray thought of Nixon before, he would prove loyal through every fight Nixon had until the day he left office and, indeed, to the end of his life.

About Nixon, this must be said: While his judgment on people was not infallible, when it came to talent he wanted the best. And he was not put off if the best had not wanted him. Once elected, he would bring a Kennedy Democrat, Pat Moynihan, into the White House to head the domestic policy shop, Henry Kissinger of Harvard, Rockefeller's man for years, to head the NSC, and John Connally, LBJ's protégé and the governor who delivered Texas for Humphrey in 1968, as Secretary of the Treasury. The selection of these men testifies to the truth that Nixon was no ideologue, no true believer. He had instincts one could call conservative, but reflexive reactions that were liberal. He wanted to leave his mark and become a man of history, and believed that, given the chance, he could make his mark in foreign policy. He once told me about picking a national security adviser, "I don't want someone I have to teach. I want someone who can teach me."

In August 1967, I sent him a note and article by Andrew Kopkind, rising star of the *New Republic*. I described Kopkind as a "New Lefter" and "part of a group that felt the left-wing leadership of the [National Student Association] was not radical enough." Nixon responded, "I know he's . . . New Left—but he still might be worth checking out. These guys are notoriously volatile." Nixon would not reject out of hand someone who had trashed him if that someone had talent and ideas and might experience a late vocation.

"THE DAKOTA WOLVES"

Martin Anderson, a libertarian professor at Columbia who had come aboard, brought in Alan Greenspan of the inner circle of Ayn Rand, author of *Atlas Shrugged*. Alan had played clarinet in Woody Herman's band. Garment, who had played sax, was high on Alan and asked me to have dinner with him. A free-market economist, Alan spent much of the evening discoursing on the superiority of the gold standard.

On July 17, I wrote Nixon about "a friend of Len's and a most levelheaded and bright fellow" who was warning that the budget was out of control and RN should come out for cuts in "non-essential spending in space, public works, SST, and perhaps the electron volt accelerator." Greenspan said that Nixon should declare that, rather than allow inflationary forces to be unleashed, he would back "a tax increase as the lesser of two evils." How could we square cutting the budget with our programs for the Negro? I reported Alan as stating "flatly that the Negro problem is not an economic problem and it is dangerous to think of its solution in financial terms."

On July 27, Greenspan wrote me, "I should like to outline a policy position which I believe could be very effective for Mr. Nixon."

The three pages were triggered by the Newark riot that month and the Detroit riot that ended that day. These two riots, which had resulted in 70 dead, 1,200 injured, and 8,500 arrests, Alan said,

> cannot be explained in the conventional terms of "desperate ghetto conditions." Having visited Watts before the riot, I can only indicate how shocked I was to find what is by no means a ghetto in any Eastern-urban meaning of the term. As a practical matter, the average Negro family income in the United States would be considered modest affluence in virtually every other area of the world. This clearly is not a question of degrading poverty per se, but an issue of the relationship of average Negro and average white incomes in this country.

Income inequality was the problem. Yet this was, in the near term, insoluble. Wrote Greenspan, "I would state flatly that a significant closing of the relative gap is economically infeasible short of a half-century." As for the "massive handout programs . . . under the label of the Great Society," they would have the ultimate effect of "degrading the Negroes as individuals and have led to the recent upsurge in racism and class antagonism." Greenspan urged a campaign emphasis on freedom. Nixon should push hard for an all-volunteer army. Promote a tax deduction to anyone who pays for a college education for a young person. What was crucial was that Nixon "convey an image of principle rather than eclecticism."

I sent the memo on to Nixon with a cover note: "This fellow is an economist, and budgetary expert, but more than that he is a sound thinker on a number of subjects." On August 14, Nixon wrote back, "I think I should have a talk with Alan Greenspan." He told me to pass Greenspan's memo to Ray Price for inclusion of the freedom theme in future speeches. "I think his recommendation that we have to convey an image of principle rather than pragmatism is well taken," Nixon wrote. "While pragmatism is the popular and fashionable line at present, it has very little appeal to people. We may have to do what is pragmatic but we have to talk in terms of principle."

Alan seemed a man of convictions, but his own libertarian principles would collide with our political imperatives.

"The Dakota wolves are after me!" said the low voice on the other end of the phone. It was early '68 and Alan had written a speech for Nixon on farm policy that had fallen into the hands of Senators Karl Mundt of South Dakota, who had served with Nixon on the House Un-American Activities Committee, and Milt Young of North Dakota. And all hell had broken loose on the prairies. This was no minor matter. After Oregon, South Dakota was our last primary state. I called Nixon to alert him.

He was agitated. "The Dakota wolves would not be after him," said Nixon, had he not fouled something up. Came word from Bob Ellsworth in DC: Mundt was calling Greenspan's speech "Bensonism at its worst," a reference to Ezra Taft Benson, Ike's agriculture secretary, who was not beloved in the farm belt, as he had believed that farm subsidies and price supports were socialistic. Nixon told me to fix it. I wrote a new speech calling for the preservation and extension of existing farm programs, and on a trip to DC took the text to Mundt's office. The senator ordered me into his inner sanctum, and said, "Now, read it to me!" He closed his eyes and leaned back in his chair.

The speech said exactly what Mundt had wanted to hear and closed with lines from William Jennings Bryan's "Cross of Gold" speech to the Democratic National Convention of 1896: "Burn down your cities and leave our farms, and your cities will spring up again as if by magic. But destroy our farms and the grass will grow in the streets of every city in the country."

Senator Mundt smiled, said it was beautiful, and that I was a fine young man. As Nixon had said, "We have to talk in terms of principle," but "we may have to do what is pragmatic."

A DEATH IN THE FAMILY

On September 30, 1967, Hannah Milhous Nixon died. Her son's devotion and the debt he owed her cannot be exaggerated. He would invoke her as a saint on the day that he resigned his presidency.

Before he flew out for the funeral, Nixon came first to the office. Rose went in briefly, then came out and said, "He wants to talk to you." I went in, and though we spoke at length we did not talk at all of his mother and I sensed he did not wish to because, a deeply emotional man, he knew he might break down. So I did almost all the talking, responding to his questions, talking on one subject after another—issues, news, the campaign, until word came that the car was downstairs to take him to the airport.

From Hillings, who met him at the airport in Los Angeles, I learned that through the funeral and burial Nixon was bitter at the press, who appeared and hovered about. One of them shoved a microphone into his face, perhaps to catch him in an emotional moment. His memoirs, quite moving about his mother's death, reflect this bitterness.

About this time also, Rose's mother and father, in Ohio, died. Rose was shattered. When she got back from the second funeral, Nixon called her in. They were alone a long while. When she came out, Rose was smiling through tears telling me the Boss explained to her that there were now three wonderful people with God in heaven. A side of Nixon few ever saw.

"WHAT HAS HAPPENED TO AMERICA?"

As with our 1966 essay for *U.S. News & World Report*, "If Mob Rule Takes Hold in America—A Warning from Richard Nixon," in 1967 Nixon and I collaborated on a piece for *Reader's Digest*, where Nixon had a friend and ally in editor and CEO Hobart Lewis. The *Digest*, the magazine with the largest circulation in America at 19 million, had a long lead time, and I began writing after the Newark and Detroit riots. As well as telling the truth as we saw it about the roots of anarchy, we wanted Nixon to stake his claim on the law-and-order issue in 1968. At the same time, Nixon was working with Ray Price on his "Asia After Viet Nam" piece for *Foreign Affairs*.

"What Has Happened to America?" came out in the October *Digest*. We laid the blame for the nation's descent into lawlessness at the feet of the intellectual, moral, cultural, and political elites. "Why is it that in a few short years . . . America has become among the most lawless and violent [nations] in the history of free peoples?" was the question posed. Our answer: "Men of intellectual and moral eminence who encourage public disobedience of the law are responsible for the actions of those who inevitably follow their counsel: the poor, the ignorant and the impressionable."

Our judges have gone too far in weakening the peace forces as against the criminal forces.

Our opinion-makers have gone too far in promoting the doctrine that when a law is broken, society, not the criminal, is to blame.

Our teachers, preachers, and politicians have gone too far in advocating the idea that each individual should determine what laws are good and what laws are bad, and that he then should obey the law he likes and disobey the law he dislikes.

Government was failing its first responsibility, to guarantee the "*primary* civil right, the right to be protected from domestic violence."

Inside the GOP not even Reagan would be able to outflank us on law and order, which would rank with Vietnam as the decisive issue of 1968. It would propel the campaign of George Wallace. Nixon

Vice President Nixon with President Eisenhower, who twice considered dropping him from the ticket. Nixon revered Ike and would deliver his eulogy in the Capitol Rotunda in 1969. *(Courtesy of the Nixon Presidential Library)*

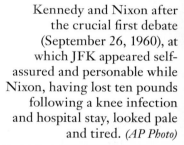

Kennedy and Nixon after the crucial first debate (September 26, 1960), at which JFK appeared self-assured and personable while Nixon, having lost ten pounds following a knee infection and hospital stay, looked pale and tired. *(AP Photo)*

Nixon, the morning after his 1962 defeat by Governor Pat Brown: "Just think how much you're going to be missing. You don't have Nixon to kick around anymore, because, gentlemen, this is my last press conference." *(Bettmann/CORBIS)*

Nixon's secretary, Rose Mary Woods, "the quintessence of loyalty," who stood by him from the "fund scandal" of 1952 through Watergate. *(Courtesy of the Nixon Presidential Library)*

Barry Goldwater at the Cow Palace in 1964. After Nixon's call for Republicans to unite behind the senator, Goldwater drove the wedge deeper, declaring, "Extremism in the defense of liberty is no vice." *(AP Photo)*

MEMO TO RN

From Buchanan

Excellent analysis. I have always shared this view — Clearly apart from [the politics I don't happen to believe in that 'liberal' crap!]

    I dined with John Whitaker and his wife over the last weekend and found them charming and friendly people. Conversation was extremely candid considering they had only met my date.

    John's thinking runs thus. <u>We ought to move to the left, and not worry excessively about the conservatives in the party.</u>

    His reasoning briefly is thus: For too many years now the Republican party has stuck fast to the image of an efficient group which is associated with the "interests" while the Democrats have established themslœves in the public mind as perhaps inefficient but a party that deeply cares about the "forgotten man at the bottom of the economic pyramid."

    There is no denying the above contention. However, I do not think it follows that we must move to the left.

    One reason is that when it comes to some new program for the people, all the room on the left has been pre-empted; <u>there is very little running room over there indeed.</u> <u>Before the Republicaж can offer a better program for some welfare idea, the program being tried must fail..</u>

    A second reason is that our position is the only one which the huge conservative wing of the GOP will currently accept, and if we should suddenly strike out to the left of Johnson, it would produce the greatest defection in history since Constantine committed Rome to Christianity.

An early 1966 memo of mine to Nixon, relaying advice of John Whitaker that Nixon should disregard the right and move left. The words partially scratched out by Nixon read, "Clearly apart from the politics I don't happen to believe in that 'liberal' crap!"

Nixon's exhaustive campaigning for Goldwater earned his gratitude and endorsement for 1968. The abandonment of Goldwater by Governors George Romney and Nelson Rockefeller would prove fatal blunders. *(AP Photo)*

June 1967. Nixon and I at the home of David Ben-Gurion, founding father of Israel, after the stunning Israeli victory in the Six-Day War.

July 1967. U.S. troops occupy Detroit following the "long hot summer" riots in Newark and the Motor City that left 70 dead, 1,200 injured, and 8,500 under arrest. *(AP Photo)*

October 1967. The siege of the Pentagon by thousands of antiwar protesters who tried to storm the building. I was caught in the clash with the troops. *(Popperfoto/Getty Images)*

October 1967. Team of Rivals: Rockefeller, Romney, and Reagan attend the Governors' Conference aboard the SS *Independence* to the Virgin Islands. If Nixon was to be stopped, one of these three had to do it. *(Stan Wayman/ Getty Images)*

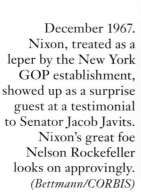

December 1967. Nixon, treated as a leper by the New York GOP establishment, showed up as a surprise guest at a testimonial to Senator Jacob Javits. Nixon's great foe Nelson Rockefeller looks on approvingly. *(Bettmann/CORBIS)*

January 1967. The core of the "new Nixon" inner circle. *Front to back:* Len Garment, Ray Price, Martin Anderson, Dwight Chapin, me, and Tom Evans.

February 4, 1968. Nixon and his family in New Hampshire at the end of the first three days of the campaign. Smiles may reflect secret polls that showed us—with the backing of the *Union Leader*'s William Loeb— leading Romney 4–1.

March 21, 1968. With Dwight Chapin. Asked by Nixon to monitor the Rockefeller announcement, we reported the startling news that Rocky was not running. *(Condé Nast Archive/CORBIS)*

March 31, 1968. After a strong showing by Senator Gene McCarthy in New Hampshire and Robert Kennedy's entry into the race four days later, Lyndon Johnson stuns the nation by announcing he will not seek reelection. *(Courtesy of the LBJ Presidential Library—Yoichi Okamoto)*

would return to this theme when the campaign of 1968 began to witness a Humphrey surge to where he almost became another Truman and nearly turned Nixon into another Dewey. Phrases and sentences from the articles and speech excerpts of 1966 and 1967— on soaring crime rates, urban riots, and campus anarchy—would reappear in Nixon speeches when he swung back to law and order to halt the mass reconversion of Wallace Democrats to the party of their fathers.

Two months before our *Reader's Digest* article hit, I sent Nixon a *U.S. News & World Report* partial reprint of a speech U.S. Appellate Court Judge Warren Burger had given at Ripon College in Wisconsin. The *U.S. News* titled its reprint "What to Do About Crime in U.S." Burger echoed what we had written for *U.S. News* in 1966. Describing the increase in murder and street crime in America, Burger had said:

[G]overnment exists chiefly to foster the rights and interests of its citizens—to protect their homes and property, their persons and their lives. If a government fails in this basic duty, it is not redeemed by providing even the most perfect system for the protection of the rights of defendants in the criminal courts. . . .

We know that a nation or a community which has no rules and no laws is not a society but an anarchy in which no rights, either individual or collective, can survive.

On May 21, 1969, President Nixon would nominate Warren Burger to replace Earl Warren as chief justice of the United States. In the White House statement announcing his appointment, I would insert the lines cited above. That *U.S. News* piece of August 7, 1967, was, I believe, critical, if not decisive, to the elevation of Burger to the highest judicial office in the land.

"LET RONNIE HAVE THE KOOKS"

Efforts to bring the conservatives into camp never sat well with many older Nixon loyalists. Some detested the Right, which did not bother me. But sometimes they seemed to be sabotaging what I was trying, with Nixon's blessing, to do. In late July 1967, Robert Novak wrote a column citing McWhorter, campaign chairman Gaylord Parkinson, and his deputy Robert Walker as disavowing a maverick Republican from Queens, Vincent Leibell. A Goldwater delegate in 1964, Leibell had filed as a Nixon delegate for 1968. McWhorter had told Novak that Nixon would not go poaching delegates in favorite-son states, and that included Nelson Rockefeller's New York.

Fine. But Novak went on to write that the disavowal and dumping of Leibell reflected a new "Parkinson-Walker strategy" where Nixon was "willing to cede Leibell-type mavericks and doctrinaire conservatives to Reagan. Or, as one Nixon insider put it to us, 'Let Ronnie have the kooks.'"

The Buchanan approach of "smoothing relations between Nixon and William F. Buckley's *National Review* set as well as the right-wing Young Americans for Freedom" has now been jettisoned, wrote Novak. "Nixon's contacts with the Right have been halted abruptly," and Nixon is now "maintaining an active though subterranean dialogue with the Rockefeller regulars through McWhorter, and several other conduits."

"Let Ronnie Have the Kooks" was the title of the column, and "desertion of these 'kooks'" was credited to this new strategy to make Nixon "more acceptable to liberal-to-moderate Republicans."

Whoever fed this to Novak committed an act of paralyzing stupidity. They had insulted Reagan, a far more serious rival than Rockefeller, shown contempt for the Goldwater Right, and left the impression that Nixon was about to go courting the liberals, the charge that had brought him such grief with the Pact of Fifth

Avenue. And the GOP was in 1967 a far more conservative party than it had been in 1960.

For days we were putting out the fires. I drafted a letter to Reagan for Nixon's signature trashing Evans and Novak and assuring the governor "no member of my personal staff" has had any contact with them for two years. Nixon promised Reagan that if Parkinson found out who had volunteered "Let Ronnie have the kooks," he would be fired. In his 2007 memoir, *The Prince of Darkness*, Novak identified his source as Robert Walker.

With his letter to Reagan, Nixon enclosed a column by conservative John Chamberlain, who poured oil on the troubled waters. Were Nixon to pursue the "new strategy" of the Novak column, Chamberlain wrote, this "would . . . provoke a migration of Republican conservatives to the Ronald Reagan camp, but it would not have any compensating virtue of luring Romney or Rockefeller supporters into the Nixon camp." Our investment of time in the conservative columnists was paying dividends.

Reagan was taking similar pains to assure Nixon that quotes attributed to him or his staff disparaging Nixon were unauthorized or untrue. Earlier in July, Nixon had received a letter from Reagan, with a copy of one Reagan had written to Hedley Donovan, the editor-in-chief of *Time*, challenging the magazine to name the governor to whom Reagan had allegedly said Nixon was a "loser." Wrote Reagan, "I have never said it or thought it." Nixon wrote back that Reagan's letter to Donovan was "right on target," adding, we have to "let them know their errors will not go unchallenged."

As for the new "Parkinson-Walker strategy," within days it was history. An amicable separation had been arranged, as Parky's wife was ill. Sears reported that Walker would be going with Parky, but might not be going quietly and could end up in some other candidate's camp. Nevertheless, we were well rid of the pair, as Governor Henry Bellmon of Oklahoma, a Silver Star winner as a Marine tank platoon leader in the Pacific, agreed to step in as interim chairman until Nixon found the man he would call his "heavyweight," his new law partner, John Mitchell.

LEVITATING THE PENTAGON

A desire to be where history was being made, part of the DNA of many a young journalist, was with me still. And I had never turned in my press card. One evening I went to the convention of the Communist Party and was steered to the press gallery, where I looked over and saw Kempton. Gus Hall was the main speaker. The gathering seemed to last as long as the conservative gathering in 1962 at Madison Square Garden to which I had escorted my Columbia classmates until, one by one, they peeled off and headed for the subway, wondering why I had remained behind in the asylum. This CPUSA gathering was much smaller but marked by the same inability to keep the speeches succinct. Ideologues are alike in that they love to talk. Yet a difference was discernible. There were far more elderly and aged in the hall than young people. And whatever one thought of the Right in 1962, our crowd was a robust and rising movement. The hostility and hatred of the protesters screaming outside the Garden that night, held back by New York's mounted police, testified to it. The time of these old comrades, the 1930s, was gone. Ours was coming.

Also in 1967 I went home to Washington to be at the first giant antiwar demonstration. Yippies and hippies had said that they were going to "levitate the Pentagon." As I told a friend, I didn't think they could do it. But if they did I wanted to be there to see it. The events of the night before the March on the Pentagon have been recounted by Norman Mailer, one of the stars of the event, in his *Armies of the Night.* I saw the climax at the Pentagon. I had gone to meet the huge crowd crossing Arlington Memorial Bridge and walked alongside until I heard the curses and shouts of "FBI! FBI!"

coming toward me. The crowd seemed to think anyone with a coat and tie at their march was a Hoover agent or informant.

It was not a pleasant crowd, and with my friend Jack Toland, who was carrying a Polaroid, I took up a position at the foot of the steps at the north front of the Pentagon, a few yards from where the demonstrators had halted to curse and chant at the building. At the top of the steps were young MPs, their officers talking to them quietly, like coaches before a game. If there was to be a collision, I was right there.

The front five or six lines of demonstrators seemed more militant than those behind—tougher, angrier, nastier in their insults, more anxious to fight. As they charged up the stairs directly in front of me, the MPs and troops, wielding clubs, came charging down. Many of the demonstrators jumped the wall in front of me and ran past, with the MPs clambering over the wall in pursuit. One enraged soldier grabbed me by the collar and raised his club over my head, when I flashed my press card in his face. He let go. From his expression this trooper was no lover of the Fourth Estate.

After the confrontation ended and the crowd began to disperse, I saw an older fellow being carried away by his arms and legs to a police van, hollering about something. I walked over. It was David Dellinger. His protests as he was hauled off seemed an appropriate end to a memorable event. What I had witnessed was in microcosm what was happening to the country. America was coming apart. These MPs looked on those leftists who were insulting and cursing them, trying to break their lines, not as friends seeking to end a war they would be fighting but as anti-American trash who ought to have the living hell beat out of them. To the soldiers, this crowd, acting like a mob and storming the Pentagon, were treating with contempt what they had been taught and believed about patriotism in a time of war and standing by their comrades in Vietnam.

The demonstrators who stormed up the steps of the Pentagon

were a different crowd from the students at the Washington University teach-ins who would ask sharp questions about France's return to Indochina after World War II, Bao Dai, and the Geneva Accords that divided Vietnam. In cursing and charging U.S. soldiers, they were repelling Middle America, splitting the nation, and leaving us with the larger half. *New York Daily News* columnist Ted Lewis, who was at the Pentagon, got it right with the four words he used to describe what we both witnessed: "venomous . . . ugly, disgusting and prejudiced." People such as these would play a significant role in creating the New Majority.

The Left seemed to have forgotten how Dr. King had succeeded in the 1950s and early 1960s. He had practiced nonviolence. His marches were provocative but peaceful. When black students sat down at lunch counters in North Carolina to have ketchup dumped on their heads, they did not turn around and sucker-punch the guys who did it. They took it, for their appeal was to a sense of justice and decency in the American majority. So doing, they won the battle for public opinion, a necessary precondition for winning the battle in Congress and the country.

The student radicals of the 1960s, from Berkeley in 1965 to Columbia in 1968, from the *Armies of the Night* antiwar militants in 1967 to Grant Park in Chicago in 1968 where Viet Cong flags were hoisted and "Ho! Ho! Ho Chi Minh! The NLF Is Going to Win!" was the chant, angered and alienated a nation and advanced their own antithesis—Nixon Republicans and the conservative and populist Right. "They won. We lost," Mark Rudd would tell Tom Brokaw four decades after the 1968 riots on the campus at Columbia. What did these fools think would happen, given their antics?

CIVIL RIGHTS—AND WRONGS

In July 1967, *U.S. News & World Report*, a fiefdom of conservative columnist David Lawrence, ran a long interview with Carl F.

Hansen, superintendent of schools in Washington, DC. Hansen had presided over their desegregation in 1954 when I was a junior and he enjoyed an excellent reputation. Yet this was his valedictory interview. He had just resigned in protest of an order by U.S. Judge J. Skelly Wright to abolish the track system in DC schools. Bright students would now be put into classrooms with slow learners, reducing the pace of the class to where the best students were bored and the slower students were deceived into thinking they were keeping up.

"What we have to deal with is people . . . having different degrees of development and capacity to improve themselves," said Hansen. "And I think we should get off the racist binge that we've gotten into in the last few years." "Government interference," said Hansen, is leading to "class warfare—class in terms of money, status, economics—the idea that I've got more money than you, therefore, I should share some of it—and race."

Wright had thrown out the "honors curriculum" Hansen had created back in 1955. Now, said the superintendent, "all of this is to be submerged in mediocrity, where a bright child doesn't dare to be too bright, and where a slow youngster is pacified into believing that he's doing well."

As for seeking "an arbitrary racial balance" in schools, Hansen scoffed:

[T]his is a ridiculous concept. And it's foolhardy, too, because you can never achieve it. You can't by edict declare that "you white folks are going to have to send your children to this school and you Negro parents are going to have to send your children to that school to get a racial balance. . . ." Schools cannot remake a family.

Backing up the superintendent was the reality. The DC public schools had already been abandoned by white parents since desegregation, with Negro enrollment now 91 percent. Hansen directed his heaviest fire at LBJ's Office of Economic Opportunity and Office of Education. These people "believe they have a kind of omniscience, that they can see and do what ought to be done for the good of the whole country." Their intentions may be good, but "the objective is tremendously dangerous to the very essence of our freedom, which is that schools be decentralized and locally operated."

I marked up the Hansen interview for Nixon, and sent him a cover memo urging that we seize upon this issue, on which I had long been in agreement with Hansen:

> I really believe we can make immense political mileage here, and still be on the side of the angels. Even the *New York Times* has argued for concentration on the upgrading of Negroes' schools as against some illusory racial balance. I think that a strong statement opposing the concept of racial balance, opposing the forced busing of whites into Negro areas or Negroes into white areas as wrong, calling for compensatory and crash efforts within the Negro community, and leaving the question of open enrollment to the local school district would be of immense value. We would be bumped by some; but if handled rightly, we can minimize the damage and maximize the mileage.

I added a postscript: "(Note: When Buchanan got together with a group of old friends in D.C., who were indifferent to every political issue five years ago, all he got after they had a few drinks was a violent anti-Negro, let's buy guns attitude.)" My memo to Nixon was written on the last day of the week of racial rioting right across the Hudson River in Newark.

At the top of my memo when he returned it, Nixon flashed a yellow light: "I think this makes sense," Nixon wrote. "Let's develop the theme."

Hansen's "honors curriculum" comported perfectly with W. E. B. Du Bois's vision of deeply educating "the Talented Tenth" in Black America. When Hansen gave that interview he noted that spending per pupil in DC schools had doubled from "something over $300" in 1957–58 to $750 in 1967. Today, it is near $20,000 per year per pupil, among the highest in the nation. Yet DC test scores remain so low that DC teachers have been caught erasing and altering answers on tests, systematically cheating, to raise the scores of their pupils. This has happened because the schools were taken from the custody of educators like Dr. Hansen and dictated to for decades by the likes of the crazed ideologue we used to call "J. Scalawag Wright."

In the 1968 decision *Green v. County School Board of New Kent County*, the Supreme Court would reject Hansen's wisdom. It would rule that desegregation and freedom of choice for parents in deciding where they send their children to school is unacceptable if it does not result in a more satisfactory level of integration. The *Green* decision and its progeny would produce court-ordered "forced busing" for racial balance in school districts across America. This would lead to racial conflict in both South and North, accelerate white flight to the suburbs, and contribute to the decline and fall of once-proud public schools in many great cities of America. Half a century on, America, with the average test scores of her schoolchildren sinking steadily in international competition, would be living with the consequences of having turned education over to social engineers and radical egalitarians like J. Skelly Wright.

THE PERCY BOOMLET

As the campaign year approached, Romney was having such difficulty that liberal and moderate Republicans were beginning to panic and to cast about for a new face. Midsummer saw a boomlet for Chuck Percy. In the Senate only six months, the "Boy Wonder," the twenty-nine-year-old chairman of Bell & Howell, had made a splash with a program for private investment in housing for the urban poor. He was also advocating an All-Asian conference on Vietnam to be called by Secretary-General U Thant, the Burmese whose removal of UN troops from Sinai virtually guaranteed the Six-Day War.

In January, I had told Nixon I thought Percy was a potential rival. Nixon agreed and said we should tone down replies to Percy's stream of letters asking for our endorsement of his ideas. "I agree on Percy," Nixon wrote. "In the future I would not be so glowing in approving his various programs. He is probably putting all the letters in a brochure. However, let this one go as is." At Nixon's direction I had already begun a file on Percy. On August 17, Evans and Novak broke some news:

> Close friends and supporters of Sen. Percy, operating with both his knowledge and concurrence, are quietly putting together what could become the nucleus of a Percy-for-President organization. . . .
>
> [Percy] is now actively and systematically trying to position himself as a backup candidate for Republican moderates should Michigan's Gov. Romney fail.

Named among the Percy supporters were Congressman Donald Rumsfeld of Illinois and Senator Thruston Morton of Kentucky, still bitter Nixon had passed him over for vice president in 1960. The first hurdle for Percy's team was to get around Minority Leader Ev Dirksen and make Percy Illinois's favorite-son candidate at the Republican Convention. The columnists concluded:

> All of this must stay in a low enough key not to sound like an anti-Romney operation. Indeed, National Committeeman George Hinman of New York, a strong Romney supporter,

has warned privately that Rockefeller forces will crush Percy if
he surfaces as a candidate.

Why would the Rockefeller forces threaten to "crush Percy"
if he moved to seek the nomination? Because a Percy candidacy
would split the liberal-moderate wing of the party, sink any lingering hopes Romney had, and put Chuck first in line to challenge
Nixon when Romney collapsed. Why should this bother Nelson
Rockefeller, who, in mid-October 1967, on the SS *Independence* sail-
ing to a Virgin Islands governors' conference, would declare again
and again, "I don't want to be president"?

Answer: It would only bother Rockefeller if, contrary to what
he was telling the press, he had in mind stepping over Romney's
corpse to challenge Nixon himself. Nixon saw this instantly. On
the Evans and Novak column he scrawled, "Note to Ellsworth et
al.—Percy's candidacy should be encouraged at all levels."

On Sept. 11, Greenspan, who had met privately with Percy,
returned astonished at how far left Chuck appeared to be. In notes of
Greenspan's meeting I sent on to Nixon, Alan said: Percy "sounded
indistinguishable from Nelson Rockefeller," refers to "Republican
mossbacks," and echoes "anti-administration liberal democrats.
Essential Point: This man is not in the Middle of the Road."

Nixon was right: A Percy candidacy would rupture the Romney-
Rockefeller coalition and hence "should be encouraged at all levels."

"THE GREATEST BRAINWASHING"

By the summer of '67, Governor Romney, who in 1965 had come
back from Vietnam to laud the war effort, was moving toward
opposition to the war. On August 30, he was invited by Lou Gordon, a friend, to tape his TV show, which was about to go national.
Gordon went straight at Romney's shift: "Isn't your position a bit

inconsistent with what it was, and what do you propose we do now?"
Romney's answer:

> Well, you know when I came back from Vietnam, I just had the
> greatest brainwashing that anybody can get when you go over
> to Vietnam. Not only by the generals, but also by the diplomatic
> corps over there, and they do a very thorough job. And since
> returning from Vietnam, I've gone into the history of Vietnam,
> all the way back to World War II and before, and, as a result, I
> have changed my mind. . . . I no longer believe that it was neces-
> sary for us to get involved in South Vietnam to stop aggression.

Not until four days later did the *New York Times* get the story,
realize the dynamite it contained, and produce the headline that
inflicted the lethal wound: "Romney Asserts He Underwent 'Brainwashing' on Vietnam Trip."

We needed to do nothing. Administration officials pounded
Romney for besmirching the reputations of Ambassador Henry
Cabot Lodge and General William Westmoreland. Editorial
pages mocked him. His hometown paper, the *Detroit News*, urged
him to get out of the race in favor of Governor Rockefeller. But
Romney dug in and, as *Newsweek* said, "brazened it out." "Yes, I
was brainwashed," he continued to insist. "We're all brainwashed.
The administration simply does not tell us the truth about Vietnam. . . . I'm glad I used that word. It woke up the country. Nobody
was paying any attention, when I only used words like 'snow job.' "

To change the subject Romney went on a walking tour of inner-
city slums, going from meetings with "poverty workers in Detroit,
to housing demonstrators in Washington . . . to black-power advo-
cates in Rochester, to moderates and ministers and teen-age delin-
quents in New York's Bedford-Stuyvesant and Harlem." He came
away concluding, "A lot of people are very frustrated and bitter,
and it's time to do something . . . because there's tinder in the cities

that will make Vietnam look like child's play, and I mean just that." *Newsweek* praised Romney's listening tour, but its headline came to a different conclusion: "The Bell Tolls for a Galloping Ghost."

The first polls after the "brainwashing" episode were devastating, deepening a decline that had already begun. Since 1966, among Republicans, Romney had been running the strongest against Johnson. Now, in the new Harris survey, he had fallen to fourth, behind Rockefeller, Nixon, and Reagan. Romney had fallen from 4 points behind the President to a 16-point deficit. In a Gallup poll of September 23, only 14 percent of Republicans wanted Romney as their nominee, a 10-point drop in three weeks. Meanwhile, Rockefeller was assuring press and public alike that he had given up on earthly ambition: "Something happens in life and you lose ambition because you have a sense of fulfillment. . . . I have no ambition, no inner drive, to get into this thing again."

The cruelty of the commentary on Romney continued unabated. Gene McCarthy was quoted as saying that in Romney's case a full brainwashing had been unnecessary, as "a light rinse would have sufficed."

THE EAGLETON MEMORANDUM

In the week the "brainwashing" incident arose, Richard Amberg, the publisher of the *Globe-Democrat* who had agreed to my leave of absence to work with Nixon, died of a heart attack. He had been both a friend and a benefactor to me and to Nixon, and I went out to St. Louis for his funeral. Nixon had lost an ally. When I got back I wrote him and Mitchell a lengthy "confidential" memo on the new lay of the land in the Show Me State. Describing the coming primary between Senator Ed Long and Lieutenant Governor Tom Eagleton for the Democratic nomination for Senate in 1968, I brought up an Eagleton matter that would ignite into headlines five years later.

Eagleton is young, bright, Kennedy-type, good looking; but there is no guarantee he can beat Ed Long, even with the current problems Long has encountered. . . .

Tom is a Catholic and rural Missouri has little enthusiasm for same. . . . Tom has had some mental problems which have put him in the hospital on several occasions, and Ed Long is saying privately that he will pour coals on . . . this. . . . It could be an exceedingly dirty campaign.

Tom Eagleton captured Long's seat in 1968. But those "mental problems" became an issue in the late summer of '72, when they exploded with fatal consequences for the McGovern-Eagleton ticket.

INTIMATIONS OF DETENTE

In mid-1967, I had gone to a party in the city where I met a member of Russia's UN delegation. As the fellow had been drinking heavily, I gave him a ride to his apartment in the cab I took to mine on East 50th. I told him I was with Nixon, and quickly got a follow-up call, asking if I could get him an autographed copy of *Six Crises*. With Nixon's approval, I got him the inscribed copy, and sent it over.

Soon, I was contacted by a fellow who called himself Edward and said he was press secretary to the legation. He wanted to meet. We did for hours one evening. Edward spoke knowledgeably about Europe and the Mideast, the geopolitical fallout of the Six-Day War, the U.S. situation in Vietnam, and American politics. He quizzed me on the private lives of the Kennedys and Johnson and seemed up-to-date on the latest rumors. I sent Nixon a three-page memo on October 17, 1967, detailing Edward's interest in whether Nixon intended to go to China: "He wanted to know was RN really going to Red China. This must have had them disturbed. That rumor that was out several months back. Anyhow, he must have a good backlog on you to be aware of it." I suggested to Nixon that we alert the authorities that the Soviets were making contact, as "I would hate to see this guy expelled some day for getting secrets from some scientist and then have it pop up that he had been in touch with an RN aide, and no one had been informed."

The memo came back with Nixon's directions scribbled at the top:

> Pat—1. Inform the local FBI Chief 2. Continue to see him— emphasizing "RN is tough—but not doctrinaire anti-Soviet— believes U.S. and Soviet must find hard headed way to get along together—that RN likes Russians etc.—& is no simplis- tic B.G. or R.R.—'bomb throwers.'"

"B.G." and "R.R." were Goldwater and Reagan.

Edward and I would stay in touch during the campaign and beyond. He would continue to ask about contacts with the Chinese, wondering if we were back-channeling through the Canadians. I last saw him at the reception in the Kremlin that Leonid Brezhnev hosted at Nixon's final summit in the summer of '74 before his res- ignation. Edward looked as though he had fallen upon hard times. But then, he probably thought the same about us.

NIXON ON CHINA

Nixon had an opening to China in mind before he entered the White House. In October 1967, *Fortune* was doing a major article on Nixon. In a memo from "DC," our code for Nixon, he instructed me to convey to writer James Reichley "a capsule of my views [on China] as I prepared them for the Bohemian Grove but did not deliver there, due to lack of time."

First laying out the menace of China as "the greatest threat to peace in the world," Nixon opposed recognition, easing of trade restrictions, or entry into the UN—so long as China is "supporting our enemies in Vietnam and exporting aggression to all parts of Asia and the world."

"On the other hand," Nixon wrote, "to permanently isolate China would . . . be a mistake. China will change as the Soviet Union has changed when necessity requires it to do so." As non-Communist Asia and Japan grow in political, economic, and military strength, this will discourage China's aggression against its neighbors. Then would come the moment for America to make her move. As Nixon dictated it to me,

> When Communist China is confronted with these conditions the dialogue between the U.S. and China can and should begin.
>
> China will change as their leaders realize that their interests will be better served by turning their energies inward rather than expanding outward—as they realize the folly of exporting revolution in the promise of internal development, which we would be willing to assist under the proper circumstances.

In 1967, the idea that Peking, then in the throes of the maniacal Red Guard purge known as the Great Proletarian Cultural Revolution, would give up the world Communist revolution, or that America would then be willing to assist the "internal development" of Mao's China, was explosive. Thus, in my letter to Reichley quoting Nixon's position, I cut out Nixon's last paragraph. My sense is that I objected that it would cause a revolt on the right and engage us in a battle over China policy we did not need. But that Nixon looked to reach out to China, and had wanted to signal this even then, is undeniable.

In a retrospective after Nixon's death, Al Haig confirmed it.

The opening to China, and it was uniquely his, was Nixon's greatest achievement. Henry thought he was crazy. I remember

[Kissinger] came into the office and said, "Nixon's gone mad. He thinks he is going to China." He thought Nixon had taken leave of his senses.

In the last week of the New Hampshire primary, when Nixon was bedeviled by the allegation that he had said he had a "secret plan" to end the war, he was asked by Ed Cox, then dating Tricia, what his plan for Vietnam was. Nixon replied directly, "I will go to Peking and Moscow."

In May 1968, Nixon had me run down a comment by Rockefeller about recognizing Red China. Marty Anderson found it. With respect to China, I wrote Nixon, Rocky "does not say recognition—just fudges around." Rockefeller's quote:

with respect to Communist China, we gain nothing and we prove nothing by aiding or encouraging the self-isolation of so great a people. Instead we should encourage contacts and communication—for the good of us both. . . . For in a subtle triangle with Communist China and the Soviet Union, we can ultimately improve our relations with each—as we test the will for peace of both.

Richard Nixon and his old antagonist were thinking the same politically incorrect thoughts about Mao's China.

A POSTGRADUATE EDUCATION

Working so closely with Nixon in those years provided me with an unrivaled postgraduate education. When Anderson and I sat down with a tiny group to discuss economics, across the table were Milton Friedman, dean of the "Chicago School" and future Nobel Prize winner, who, with Keynes, was one of the two most influential economists of the twentieth century; Paul McCracken, past member and future chairman of the President's Council of Economic Advisers; and two future chairmen of the Federal Reserve, Arthur Burns and Alan Greenspan.

Among the most impressive scholars to come regularly to Nixon's office was Robert Crane, whom Nixon personally liked and for whom he had high regard. In Harvard by age sixteen, and graduating summa cum laude, Bob Crane was a founding member of the Center for Strategic and International Studies at Georgetown who traveled regularly through Asia. He was then with Herman Kahn at the Hudson Institute. On a cover memo atop one of his articles Nixon directed me to read and mark up, I wrote, "This is vintage Crane. . . . The fellow . . . thinks like a sharp Communist, the mind unencumbered by Western emotionalism, sentimentalism, or Rousseauistic prejudices about the nature of man."

Crane called Vietnam the most complex problem America ever faced. We should look to "de-Americanization," but as of now, the United States should demand a general mobilization by South Vietnam, which might double the number of troops available. There should be a unified military command, and U.S. and South Vietnamese troops should fight in integrated units.

Crane urged a blockade of the port of Haiphong, but only after sinking barges to block the Red River down to Haiphong from Hanoi and sinking the dredge that kept the channel free of silt. We should bomb closer to China, but not send U.S. troops north. If we do, we should first take out China's nuclear capability.

Historically, our problem in Asia, Crane contended, was that we were on the wrong side. Nationalism was the winning side. When we backed the French in Indochina after World War II, we yoked ourselves to a losing cause. In August 1967 I summarized for Nixon what Crane was arguing for:

The secret of judo is that you utilize the opponent's weight and strength against him. You guide his force which is already

active. So the Communists in Southeast Asia have put themselves on the side of A) Vietnamese nationalism and B) Expulsion of Foreigners (all). While the United States tries to create
movements (i.e., the building of a Great Society for Asia) rather
than rolling with them. Crane is making the same point he has
made before: Why not get on the side of Asian nationalism?

Nixon asked me to send Crane's paper to another foreign policy
scholar for "consideration and comment." He was intrigued with
Crane's boldness. Crane urged Nixon to embrace the principle of
"independence for all peoples." Now called ethnonationalism, this
is that desire of peoples to secede from the artificial nations created
by the British and other empires, who had drawn up their borders
on maps in their foreign offices. As one sees tribalism tearing countries apart all over the world in 2014, it is obvious that Bob was a
man ahead of his time. He wanted to come aboard, but we had a
budget problem, money enough for only one foreign policy adviser.
A tough call. Crane might be "more brilliant in the abstract" but
was "a much less aggressive fellow" than Dick Allen, who is "a good
deal more politically oriented and a good deal less theoretical." My
recommendation to Nixon: "I think Allen would probably do more
for us in the way of solid production."

In staffing up for 1968, Nixon was ever conscious of what he saw
as the need to maintain ideological "balance." When I told him in
March 1968 that Dick Allen was ready to come on full-time, Nixon
wrote me, "He would be good—but with Crane—gives us two on
hard line side—which is OK if we balance with a 'career' type who
can give us reach in that area."

Nixon's purpose was not simply political, to have conservatives
and liberals alike feel they were represented in his inner circle. He
wanted to be certain he heard the ideas and opinions of a spectrum
stretching across the party and beyond the party. He was never
afraid of hearing views that contradicted his own. He sought them

out. He would often state his own position, emphatically and categorically, then turn and challenge you directly on what he had said, ending with the pointed query "Or am I wrong?"

REAGAN, NIXON, AND OPEN HOUSING

Through 1967 the specter of Reagan hovered, and on September 22 I sent Nixon a strategy memo. Right now, I wrote, Reagan is not registering well in the polls and to raise his numbers he must travel. This would call into question his noncandidacy. Also, conservative opinion leaders are now almost all favorable to Nixon, as he is positioned as both conservative and centrist. Our courtship had borne fruit. "Reagan's problem is . . . how to eject RN from the conservative territory which he is occupying."

Were I a Reagan adviser, I wrote, I would find a burning issue where Nixon had taken a more liberal stand, take the opposite view, and raise it at every press conference until conservatives saw the difference between Nixon and Reagan. The issue might be trade with the Soviet bloc. I used open housing, as it was then heating up and an issue on which the conservatives we had met with in 1966 had urged Nixon to break with Johnson. Huston had argued vehemently that Nixon meet with Dirksen and support him against "Open Occupancy." Nixon was hesitant. This would be dramatic and risky. On the last great civil rights issue of the civil rights decade, Nixon would be standing on the other side of the divide. Did he want to be there? But as of that September our staff was united against "federalizing" open housing. As I wrote Nixon:

> [O]n the issue of open housing I took it up with Greenspan, Garment, Anderson, Price and . . . to a man they feel that RN ought to oppose open housing at the Federal Level. Now, I think the thing to do is to oppose it in sophisticated terminology, using GOP principles, and talk of the right [of the]

individual to buy and sell homes. . . . (I will work this up and then run it by Ray for his approval. . . .)

The Reagan people "don't have any such issue now" where Nixon is vulnerable to attack from the Right, I wrote, "and it ought to be our policy to see that they never get one. The way you have done to date is perfect." At the top of the counter-Reagan strategy memo, Nixon scribbled "Good."

However, the issue of open housing was coming to a boil in 1967.

In 1963 California had passed the Rumford Fair Housing Act, banning any racial discrimination by homeowners or landlords in the rental or sale of their property. In 1964 the California Real Estate Association got a million signatures to put on the ballot Proposition 14 to amend the state constitution to restore "absolute discretion" to property owners to sell, lease, or rent to whomever they wished. Proposition 14 won with 65 percent of the vote. California's Supreme Court in 1966 struck it down as a violation of the Fourteenth Amendment with Governor Brown's approval. Reagan ran on a promise to repeal the Rumford Fair Housing Act, and crushed Brown by a million votes.

In January 1966, Dr. King had moved to Richard Daley's Chicago to break up the urban ghetto and integrate housing. There had been marches and demonstrations in white neighborhoods. During one march through the white ethnic enclave of Marquette Park on Chicago's Southwest Side on August 5, demonstrators were met with bottles and bricks ("Irish confetti") and King was hit with a rock. "I have seen many demonstrations in the South," said King, "but I have never seen anything so hostile and so hateful as I've seen here today."

In July, race riots had erupted on the West Side, the Guard had been called out, and Nixon was going in for a speech, for which I did the political advance. The Percy people wanted us to stay away from the riots, which was not possible, or take the line of being against violence but for addressing grievances. Joe Woods, Rose's brother, running for Cook County sheriff, and our friends at the *Trib* wanted Nixon to come down hard on the rioters.

Open housing seemed a certain issue on the congressional and national agenda in 1968, and one on which Reagan might break openly with Nixon if we did not break openly with Johnson.

IN THE FALL of '67, Joe Kraft wrote a series of columns on what his liberal colleagues were dismissing as the "white backlash." Kraft had a different take. For "ordinary whites," he wrote, LBJ's poverty programs to aid the black poor "have no appeal." Kraft went on:

> [T]he ordinary American is a forgotten man politically, and I suspect that the true representatives of the disconnected middle . . . have not yet appeared. . . .
> The point is not that Negro claims should be denied. It is that a difficult period lies ahead and that there are great strains on the low- and middle-income whites. An explosion can be averted only if there is some concern, some respectable concern for their interests and feelings.

"Respectable concern" was what Nixon could offer—and Wallace could not. I memoed Nixon on Kraft's standing request for an interview: "When and if Kraft comes in, these columns (all marked) make some damned interesting points about what is needed at this point in time in the way of political leadership." Nixon agreed to see him and told me to send back Kraft's columns on the "forgotten man" when he did.

"SCANDAL IN SACRAMENTO"

From the time Reagan was elected governor in 1966, we were reading and receiving reports of political activity and state organizations sprouting up to make him the Republican nominee in 1968. In letters to Nixon, Reagan denied he had authorized any of these efforts. But in my office, where these clippings and reports were sent, we kept a file. Trust, but verify.

In late October 1967, two months after Romney's remark that he had been brainwashed during a trip to Vietnam had wounded his candidacy, a column, "Scandal in Sacramento," appeared in the *New York Post*. The author was Drew Pearson, the most widely syndicated columnist of the day, and arguably the most detested. Westbrook Pegler had called him a "gent's room journalist."

Pearson trafficked in scandals other columnists would not touch. FDR, Truman, and MacArthur had all challenged his integrity. In an encounter at the Sulgrave Club in December 1950, Joe McCarthy either kneed Pearson or sucker-punched him. Nixon told me he had come into the coatroom, saw the fracas, and said, "Let a good Quaker stop this fight." But Joe, who had Pearson pinned against a wall, said, "Dick, this one's for you!" and kneed Pearson in the groin. Nixon's version was close to that of David Oshinsky, whose *A Conspiracy So Immense* marvelously captures the postwar town and time of *Give 'Em Hell, Harry* and *Tail Gunner Joe:*

> Joe finally cornered Pearson in the coat room. "Well, Drew," he sneered, "a pleasant evening, wasn't it?" Pearson said nothing. As he reached into his pocket for the coat check, McCarthy wheeled around and kneed him twice in the groin— an instinctive move, the senator explained later, to protect him from assassins. As Pearson doubled over, Joe floored him with an open-handed slap. At that point Richard Nixon burst onto the scene yelling, "Let a Quaker stop this fight."

Oshinsky claims Nixon exaggerated how serious the fight had been, when Nixon said he had never seen someone slapped so hard. "If I hadn't pulled McCarthy away, he might have killed Pearson,"

Nixon told a friend. When news of the incident got out, twenty senators phoned Joe to congratulate him. According to Oshinsky, when Utah's Arthur Watkins encountered McCarthy on a Capitol elevator, Watkins put an arm around him and said, "Joe, I've read conflicting accounts of where you hit Pearson. I hope both are true."

Pearson's column that October reported that the previous winter Governor Reagan, only weeks in office, had hired a Los Angeles detective to investigate a "homosexual ring" in his office and learned the allegations were true and an orgy involving staffers had been held at Lake Tahoe that included "two sons of a California state senator." Pearson said Reagan procrastinated for six months in removing the individuals, and acted only when the scandal was about to break.

Reagan held a press conference and savaged Pearson, saying three presidents had called him a "liar," adding, "Drew Pearson shouldn't be using a typewriter and paper. He's better with a pencil on [outhouse] walls."

Pearson also reported that on the ship taking the governors to their annual conference that year in the Virgin Islands, Reagan press aide Lyn Nofziger had confirmed the firing of the staffers and the reason. Rose Woods wrote Lyn a note saying I had been instructed to answer any reporter calling for comment by saying, "Mr. Nixon never dignifies a Pearson column with comment."

Much later, I heard from a Reagan staffer that the incident, wrenching as it was for the governor, did not adversely affect his sense of humor. The staffer had come into the governor's office as Truman Capote was walking out, and told me Reagan pointed to Capote and said, "Why don't you troll him up and down the hall, and see if there are any more of them out there?"

This sex scandal in the governor's office, coming just as the 1968 campaign was about to begin, told me there was no way Reagan was going to enter the primaries, that Romney was our only opponent, and that for Reagan to become the nominee, Romney or someone else was going to have to stop us first. I could not then see who that someone was. Romney had been bleeding support since spring. His "brainwashed" comment, which he stubbornly refused to recant, seemed potentially fatal. Rockefeller, or so I believed, could not be nominated by the party that, just four years earlier, had given its heart to Barry Goldwater. And Rockefeller could not even declare for President until Romney had run his course and collapsed.

A RAPPROCHEMENT WITH ROCKY AND JAVITS

In late November, Nixon, who had not appeared at a Republican event on Rockefeller's turf since arriving from California, surfaced with "a stunning Pat in tow," wrote *Newsweek*, as the surprise guest at a testimonial for Senator Jacob Javits. Since he came east, wrote Novak, "Nixon has been treated by the liberal hierarchy that runs the Republican Party here as a leper." Nixon told the press who crowded around him, "I think Javits should be elected in New York and Goldwater in Arizona." Javits responded less graciously, "I do not feel that Mr. Nixon is a candidate whom in good conscience I couldn't support as I did not support Barry Goldwater."

Grammar aside, the import was clear, and dramatic. If Nixon was acceptable to Javits, the foremost liberal senator in the party, and Nixon was Goldwater's choice, this meant his nomination could see a party united from left to right. A grinning Governor Rockefeller was photographed beside Nixon at the event. The next night, fifty conservatives gathered in New York for a testimonial to Marvin Liebman, and I memoed Nixon a summary of Huston's report from the dinner:

No one seemed either surprised or concerned that RN would be going to the Javits Dinner. Those conservatives who are for RN long ago accepted the fact that RN hob-nobs with liberal Republicans as well as Southern and Right-wing Republicans.

Even those who are not in RN's camp recognize that RN is a "Big Tent" Republican; and has been consistently so.

However, another attendee at the Liebman affair, a *National Review* conservative, wrote me a note saying some at the dinner were disgusted with what they had read in the *Times* about the Javits event:

The dinner was bad enough . . . but the announcement that he [Nixon] would vote for Javits (even against Buckley, implicitly) was beyond the call of the amenities. I would warn you very strongly against left-zags at this point—just when the right is reevaluating its commitment. One of my friends seem[ed] to put it for a lot of us: "We'd like to be for him, but Jesus he makes it hard. His first date of the political season and he rushes into Javits' arms."

I just hope you're getting something in return, something more substantial than Charlie's [McWhorter's] wide-eyed hopes of carrying New York with the Javits-pull.

My sentiments about Rockefeller and Javits were those of the brethren at the Liebman dinner. Yet Nixon was pursuing the wisdom to be found in the lyrics of the civil rights anthem "Keep Your Eyes on the Prize." Nixon was the favorite for the nomination. If endorsing Javits for Senate in 1967 and Rockefeller for governor in 1966, as he had done in Syracuse, meant this pair of deserters in 1964 would have to endorse him in 1968 should he win the nomination, Nixon was willing to pay the price—and right to do so.

And Nixon was irritated by the constant carping from the Right. At the bottom of a conservative's note to me saying "The damage done by the Javits dinner is severe" among YRs and Reaganites, Nixon shot back: "Pat—what do they say about Reagan's endorsement of Kuchel?"

Good point. Tom Kuchel was the liberal Republican senator from California who had refused to endorse Nixon for governor in 1962. And one thing Nixon deeply resented, throughout his career, was that he was held to more exacting standards than his rivals and adversaries.

ENDING THE DRAFT

By 1966 I had come around to the view that Nixon should call for an end to the draft. I was convinced America had changed irretrievably, that with the campuses on fire against the war we had ceased to be one people. The '50s were ancient history. Was it still wise to conscript into the service hundreds of thousands of young men who believed we were fighting a "dirty, immoral war," wanted no part of it, and would subvert the morale of the troops in the barracks?

This was the pragmatic argument. Philosophically, Eugene McCarthy once told me a male citizen had three duties: Vote, pay taxes, and bear arms in the defense of his country. The idea of obligation appeals to traditionalists. Libertarians argued that conscription was involuntary servitude. Politically, the idea of an all-volunteer army would appeal to the young, especially those who wanted no part of Vietnam—and to their parents.

I recommended that Nixon come out for ending the draft, but only as the Vietnam War came to an end, which, if elected, he would bring about. On October 23, 1967, I wrote him a memo of my concern about how we might be perceived when we issued his formal statement.

In the timing and writing of the volunteer army thing, we should consider carefully what the reaction will be in light of the fact that this was one of the anti-war peaceniks' major gripes at that demonstration [at the Pentagon]. Will it be said that RN is giving these guys the means to avoid service—and will then our genuine position be lost in the ensuing discussion?

Nixon wrote back, "Ike thinks so." He had taken up our idea with the General, who did not like it. Yet Nixon would keep his word and end the draft, with Marty Anderson as point man in the campaign and White House.

TRADING WITH THE ENEMY

On November 21, Nixon had spoken to a breakfast meeting of the House Republican Conference. It was a *tour d'horizon*. He spoke without text or notes for a half hour. On the volatile issue of U.S. trade with Soviet-bloc nations and Moscow, however, Nixon had said:

> Economically, we should have a policy which encourages more trade with the Soviet and East European countries. We should recognize, however, that to them trade is a political weapon. I believe in building bridges but we should only build our end of the bridge. For example, there should be no extension of long term credits or trade in strategic items with any nation, including the Soviet Union, which aids the enemy in North Vietnam.

Nixon had left the door open to trade with the Soviets and the East bloc in nonstrategic items on short-term U.S. credits, while a hundred caskets and body bags were coming home from Vietnam every week from a war that could not continue without Soviet arms and equipment. On December 5, we got a rocket from Congressman Del Clawson, the hawk on East-West trade, a cutting issue with conservatives. Was Nixon really favoring "increased trade with nations of the communist bloc"? Clawson wanted to know. I sent his letter on to Nixon with an alarmed cover note:

> East-West trade [is] a super-sensitive issue with Congress types and conservative types. . . . perhaps the number two Gut Issue with Conservatives. . . . Without a clear-cut position on this, we are going to get some terrific heat—and no benefits at all.

Not only did I agree with Clawson, this was the kind of issue that the Reaganites could seize upon if they wanted to justify challenging Nixon in the primaries. Senator Mundt, Bill Buckley, and other columnists had already begun to question Nixon's position on trade with the Communist bloc.

"Don't send me a problem without sending me the solution," Nixon once admonished me. I crafted a revised position for Nixon and sent it on to him. In it Nixon affirmed that he was "not opposed to peaceful trade with the Soviets or the Communist States," but made trade strictly conditional. "I am opposed to trading a horse for a rabbit." If the Soviets, who hold the keys to peace in Asia and the Middle East, are willing to "help us build peace, then we ought to sell them the goods they want."

> But I am not in favor of frittering away economic concessions to the Soviets, or making trade concessions to the Soviets—while Soviet and Eastern European supplies and arms and equipment are killing American boys. I am for building bridges. I am not for having Uncle Sam build both ends of the Bridge.

"Good," Nixon wrote, "send this to Clawson as a statement of RN's position." But while wary of Reagan storming into the primaries, I was also aware that suddenly, and surprisingly, the Rockefeller some of us thought dead was showing unmistakable signs of life.

THE RESURRECTION OF ROCKEFELLER

"In the last 6 months Nelson Rockefeller has gained something like 30 points on Lyndon Johnson—from about fifteen points behind to about fifteen points ahead." So began my strategy memo to Nixon, "On the Uses of Television," which dealt with the political resurrection of his old antagonist. I underlined the second paragraph:

In that period of time, the average television viewer has probably seen President Johnson an estimated, say, 60 times. He has probably never seen Nelson Rockefeller on the tube in those six months (outside the New York viewing area), unless it was a smiling still photograph of him put on the backdrop.

I argued that the "absence of TV" was responsible for Rocky's rise to where he had become the most popular politician in America. With no presence on national television, Rockefeller's media consisted of what was written about him. And most of this was friendly, favorable, or laudatory, the product of journalists who agreed with the governor of New York and would have liked to see him as President.

"Now, no man is as good as the kind of publicity Rocky gets, from the highest (Lippmann, Hughes) type of sources. So, if that is the case, keep your mug off the tube." Let them carry the ball for you. Another reason that Rockefeller might stay out of the camera's eye is that his presence in the living rooms of America would stir up his old enemies on the Right. If he is not in the public eye declaring himself on Vietnam, on the riots, on civil rights, there is no reason for anyone to attack him. Rockefeller's team had stolen our playbook. He had declared his own moratorium on politics, indicated he had no further interest in the presidency, and was concerned only with being a good governor. And the press was buying it. As I wrote Nixon,

In short the old hateful Nelson Rockefeller is dying while a new Rockefeller is in the process of being gestated by the publicists. And if I were Rocky's adviser I would tell him to keep out of sight while the metamorphosis was going on, and to emerge only far down the road as the new Nelson Rockefeller. . . .

The conservatives hate the old Rocky. But the old Rocky must have died because no one sees him in the flesh anymore. We do read about a different person now, whom the press tells us about, a fellow without ambition, a happy family man, the most popular Republican in the country.

Our objective, I told Nixon, should be to force Rockefeller to take a stand on Vietnam, expose his links to the Romney campaign, and "[f]lush him out so that the old wolves of the right can get the scent again." As it was certain Rockefeller would make a move against us, better that it come sooner than later. For Rocky was not a long-distance runner. As soon as he turned up as a candidate, munching blintzes, millions would say, "Hey, it's him again!" The new Rockefeller might be a star in the polls. The old Rockefeller could not beat Barry Goldwater in a California primary.

Sears and Ellsworth were sent my memo and recoiled. Nixon thought Sears had written their response and asked me to rebut it. The Ellsworth-Sears memo had said,

> If we draw Rockefeller out on the issues, he will receive a favorable press. . . . The worse thing that could happen to us would be for Rockefeller and Reagan to get in the race. Rockefeller could not get the nomination but he could freeze up the left. Reagan might not be able to get the nomination, either; but he would cut into us from the right.

But, I wrote Nixon, if Rockefeller were assured of a favorable press by coming out on the issues, he would have come out on the issues. He had not done so. And no one could take a stand on Vietnam or the riots that satisfied both sides. Rockefeller had conservative columnist William White and liberal Clayton Fritchey praising him. Once he takes a stand on Vietnam and the riots, he loses one or the other. Second, if we smoked Rockefeller out and he got into the race, it would be curtains for Romney. And we could beat Rocky in New Hampshire, Wisconsin, Indiana, and Nebraska before he made it to his presumed base in Oregon. Nixon agreed, scribbling, "Right"—and "Absolutely nuts!" and "naive" on the points of the Ellsworth-Sears memo.

Yet Rockefeller's rise, by being absent from television, carried a message—for us. As Nixon was already seen as the most knowledgeable and experienced candidate, we did not need to be seen on television talking about Vietnam. We already held that card. We should use television not primarily to discuss politics or issues but to show the country that Richard Nixon was personable and friendly, and not without a sense of humor. We should use television to contradict the caricature of him drawn by antagonists and enemies for more than twenty years.

A TILT TOWARD ISRAEL?

Before we traveled to Israel in June 1967, Nixon asked me to rewrite an article on John Foster Dulles for *Reader's Digest*, "since your views on Dulles are probably pretty close to mine." He wanted one major alteration:

> The draft proposed by the *Digest* from my notes should be substantially revised in one respect—the handling of the Suez crisis. Suez can be referred to, but not at such length, in view of the fact that I now have some doubts as to the wisdom of the course we followed at that time.

Nixon was referring to Ike's decision at the time of the British-French-Israeli invasion of October-November 1956 to order the allies out of Suez and tell Israel's David Ben-Gurion to get out of Sinai. Ike threatened to sink the British pound if Anthony Eden did not withdraw British troops from the canal. This brought down Eden's government and had been a subject of blazing controversy. For London had intended to overthrow Nasser, who had nationalized the Suez Canal and reoriented Cairo policy toward the Soviet Union, after the U.S. and Britain refused to finance his Aswan Dam.

Eisenhower's order to the Israelis to get out of Sinai did not sit well with many in the Jewish community, though no Republican has matched the 40 percent of the Jewish vote that Ike got that November.

During that fall of '67, I wrote Nixon my views on the Middle East, with an emphasis on the "adventurous and dangerous policy being pursued by the Soviets" and the absence of any effective U.S. counter. We ought "to assume a role of friendship with the moderate Arabs and with the Israelis," I said. Though this may be a "difficult task," it is better "than doing nothing, which appears to be American policy today." I saw the relationship with Israel and the Arab world in a Cold War context. Soviet warships were entering the Mediterranean in unprecedented numbers and Moscow was negotiating for port privileges in Egypt, Algeria, and Syria.

On November 27, de Gaulle held an explosive press conference at which he described Jews as "an elite people, sure of themselves and domineering." Referring to the 1956 crisis, de Gaulle went on, "The Franco-British Suez expedition had seen the emergence of a warrior State of Israel determined to increase its land area and boundaries." Thus France was disengaging from its close contacts with Israel and refusing "to give our official backing to its settling in a conquered district of Jerusalem." Israel, said de Gaulle, today "organizes itself on conquered territories, the occupation of which cannot go without oppression, repression, expulsions, while at the same time a resistance grows, which it regards as terrorism. Jerusalem should receive international status."

France would no longer supply Israel with the Super Mystere fighter-bombers that had enabled it to achieve victory in the Six-Day War. Ellsworth was urging Nixon to take on de Gaulle for rendering moral support to regimes seeking revenge against Israel. Bob sent a proposed statement declaring that the U.S. lifting of the arms embargo to Israel was not enough: "The U.S. should assume a much greater responsibility for Israel's military capability and provide her with the necessary arms. The U.S. should support Israel now."

I did not disagree and added that Nixon should mention de Gaulle's expulsion of NATO from Paris. But a statement, I said, was not the way to go. This would seem suited "to a press conference type answer." Nixon shot back, "I agree. But absolutely no playing for Jewish vote!" In the campaign of '68 Nixon would make a play for the Jewish vote and shift Republican policy for the next half century. Issue: Should the U.S. stand equidistant between our Arab and Israeli friends with an "evenhanded" policy? Or should we "tilt" U.S. policy to Israel?

BECAUSE OF CRUDE comments on the Nixon tapes revealed years later, many have asked, Was Nixon anti-Semitic? Not in any action I saw in these years before he took office. Two of the three men he instructed me to meet in New York were Lasky and Safire. His troubleshooter with liberals, Len Garment, was Jewish. He would name Henry Kissinger national security adviser, Herb Stein chairman of his Council of Economic Advisers, Arthur Burns chairman of the Federal Reserve. I would be with him in Key Biscayne when the 1973 Yom Kippur War erupted and Nixon ordered all-out aid to the Israelis being driven back all along the Canal. Golda Meir would call Nixon the best friend Israel ever had. Among the foreign leaders he most liked and admired was Yitzhak Rabin, whom we met right after the Six-Day War. But there was undeniably a sense on Nixon's part that many in the American Jewish community were unfriendly, even viscerally hostile. As Vic Navasky said, New York intellectuals loathed Nixon. And many were Jews.

In the early spring of 1968, Bill Timmons sent me a memo indicating that some folks he was working with were getting peeved at Nixon:

> I have received some flak from friends and businessmen I am working with in Miami Beach on the Republican National Convention regarding RN's public statements about the "convention in Miami." They point out that it should be "Miami Beach" and are quite sensitive about the distinction. Since I have to work with them it would be helpful if, in the future, RN could refer to the "convention in Miami Beach."

I sent Timmons's complaint to Nixon. He put an exclamation point on it, expressing astonishment, and instructing me to pass along a message to Bill: "B.T. We have no friends in Miami Beach! We have a few in Miami." Miami Beach was as famous as the Catskills for its Jewish population; Miami not so much.

Was Nixon prejudiced? While he enjoyed mocking Ivy League professors—he loved to quote Frederick the Great that the cruelest way to punish a province is to have it governed by a professor—as President he would put Harvard Ph.D.s in charge of domestic and foreign policy. While he denounced the press as "the enemy," his three major writers in 1968—Price, Buchanan, and Whalen—came off editorial pages. Half a dozen journalists would join his White House staff. He reviled Hollywood, but a friend whose company he enjoyed and humor he relished was Paul Keyes, one of the comedy writers for *Rowan & Martin's Laugh-In*. While he might entertain his staff by imitating the mannerisms of "queens," he had trusted

156 PATRICK J. BUCHANAN

loyalists he knew were gay. He liked Asians, supported the aspirations of blacks, and was strongly pro-Catholic, especially Irish Catholics. He admired their faith, their fierce loyalty, and that they were like him—strivers against an establishment that had its own prejudices and froze them out. Nixon carried within many of the prejudgments of the times and places where he grew to manhood and power. He contained contradictions. But then, as that most American of poets Walt Whitman wrote, "Do I contradict myself? Very well, then I contradict myself."

IKE AND DICK

I never met Eisenhower, but from the caddie log at Burning Tree, I had seen him tee off and had gotten the famous Eisenhower wave as his presidential limo rolled by when I was hitchhiking home. I had been standing on the sidewalk in Lafayette Square in front of the White House when Ike rode by with Khrushchev to Blair House. Most of us remained silent as the Butcher of Budapest passed by. When Ike walked back across Pennsylvania Avenue alone, we sent up a rousing cheer.

On Christmas Day 1967, we got both good news and puzzling news from the General. In a *New York Times* front-page story that went into Ike's thinking on 1968, he had written off Romney. Said Ike, "[H]e has been on so many sides of so many questions that one begins to wonder just where he does stand. He sounds like a man in a panic. And a man who panics is not the best candidate for President." This quotation was on page 18. On page one, however, Ike was quoted directly by a "golfing crony."

Even if I had the power to name the next Republican Presidential nominee, I would not necessarily select the man I thought most qualified to be President.

My reason for that is that no matter how well qualified I think a man might be, he still has to get elected. And I would like to see the convention pick a man who can win over Johnson in November.

Ike was implying his vice president might be a loser. Earlier, on his birthday, October 14, Ike had been asked directly who he thought might be the nominee. As the Associated Press reported,

> The General began reeling off names . . . New York Governor Rockefeller . . . Michigan Gov. Romney . . . California Gov. Reagan . . . Pennsylvania Gov. Shafer. Then his wife, Mamie, leaned over and whispered something in her husband's ear. The name of his former Vice President, Richard M. Nixon, was promptly added to his list.

The *Daily News* headline: "Psst, Ike: How About Er . . . Nixon."

In truth, Dwight Eisenhower did think Nixon was a loser. After leaving office he became close to Earl Mazo, Nixon's biographer, and as Mazo tells it, Ike "was irked at Nixon for not letting him campaign. . . . He asked me many times, 'What the hell was it, Earl? Did the son of a bitch think I was going to steal the limelight from him?'"

Mazo told Ike he had heard, as a White House correspondent, that Ike did not want to campaign for Nixon. At that, Ike exploded, "Bullshit, I wanted to get in there, get my gloves off." Ike went on, said Mazo, and he would say again and again of Nixon,

> [H]ere is a guy who is obviously the best qualified you've got in the whole damn country for President and he'll never make it, the guy can't win. Why do people dislike him? What the hell is it? . . . Why can't they recognize quality?

There is another explanation why Nixon asked Ike not to campaign for him. Mamie, "fearful of the strain on Ike's frail heart," wrote Clayton Fritchey, went to Pat Nixon to ask her to persuade her husband to ask Ike not to campaign. Major General Howard Snyder, Ike's physician, went to Nixon directly to tell him Ike "had not been sleeping well." Mamie and Snyder feared another heart attack that Ike might not survive. Nixon immediately complied, and in a campaign planning meeting with Ike, asked him not to go on the road. Fritchey got the information from Mazo's biography of Nixon, which Steve Hess updated in 1967. I drafted the letter of thanks from Nixon to Fritchey that Nixon approved. In late summer 1966, Ike had confirmed the events in an interview with Richard Tobin of the *Saturday Review*, which columnist Ted Lewis of the *New York Daily News* related on September 9.

Ike believed Nixon as man and leader was head and shoulders above JFK, whom he called "Little Boy Blue." As 1964 approached, Ike said to Mazo of Nixon, "My God, there's the man. We wouldn't have any God damned Bay of Pigs with Dick in that damn place. We wouldn't have any of this with Dick running the show." Why did so many dislike Nixon? Ike's quizzical answer: "Cause he ain't 'pretty'—because on television he don't know how to make up his face or some damn thing?"

Why Ike slighted him and how Nixon felt about it I did not know and did not ask. Murray Kempton wrote of the relationship, "I like Mr. Nixon, he is part of my youth." And the General? "Dwight David Eisenhower has a dubious character but superb political judgment; and Richard Nixon has a splendid character and atrocious judgment."

In May 1967, when he made an appearance at the "I Like Ike" exhibit of Eisenhower's amateur paintings at the Huntington Hartford Gallery, Nixon volunteered of Ike's work, "I am a traditionalist. I like the paintings because I understand them." Murray Kempton was disbelieving:

He could hardly have meant that. The painting of the great master of capitalist realism is opaque, giving away nothing of itself, another one of the masks of the most subtle and cunning politician who ever presented himself as country boy. "Complex and devious" Nixon broke once in the direction of candor, "in the best sense of those words, of course."

Never did a commander send trooper like a pig through so many mine fields. And never did trooper go more faithfully or carry away more shrapnel. Mr. Nixon is duty's child; yea, though he slay me, yet must I depend on him.

In the mid-'50s, columnist-author Ralph de Toledano, a friend of Nixon who had been with him during the wounding attempt to dump him from the ticket, had said savagely of Ike, "The son of a bitch was a no-good sadist." While Nixon was deferential and respectful of Ike, he let slip more than once that the General, who was prepared to dump him in 1952 over the fabricated "fund scandal," and to drop him from the ticket in 1956, could be devious. As Witcover writes, after the Cleveland governors' conference debacle from which Nixon fled to London, Bill Scranton made a transatlantic call to inform Nixon he had decided to challenge Goldwater, and had gotten Ike's blessing. "Watch out for the old man," Nixon cautioned. "You mean 'Ike'?" Scranton asked incredulously. "Yes," said Nixon.

Whatever Nixon felt about the slights from the man he served so loyally and so long, he still thought Eisenhower's endorsement and support could be decisive. When Humphrey, in a text released from North Dakota, attacked Ike's presidency as "the peace of just doing nothing . . . We had enough of that," leaving himself wide open, I wrote a 500-word reply for Nixon, attacking Humphrey for his "disparaging remarks."

This is an inexcusable act of petty partisanship against a former President who has time and again defended the Johnson-

Humphrey administration against attacks by the peace-at-any-price members of their own party.

President Eisenhower presided over eight years of unprecedented peace and prosperity at home; he ended one war in Korea and kept the nation out of other wars for eight years.

For Mr. Humphrey to cast aspersions on that record is truly astonishing when one considers that Hubert Humphrey is second man and chief publicist of an Administration that has presided over the near collapse of peace at home and has failed to bring an end to the longest war in American history.

"Everyone likes flattery," Disraeli said, "and when you come to Royalty you should lay it on with a trowel."

The statement contrasted the administration's troubled record with Humphrey's rhetoric and closed by characterizing Hubert as a nominee of the bosses. The people had spoken in the primaries, the statement concluded, while "the stand-ins for Hubert Humphrey in New York and California and Oregon and Nebraska and Indiana ran third or last every time." Nixon loved it. My statement came back with his writing at the top: "Buchanan 1. Send Copy to Ike. 2. Send to all RN speakers (Congressmen, governors et al.) 3. This is the basic issue of campaign." I sent the statement to Ike.

Nixon sought the General's approbation as a son might that of a father he revered. Yet I often thought that Ike denied Nixon what he sought most: an acknowledgment of his achievements and his comeback in the face of an opposition Ike never knew. Two months after Nixon's inauguration, Ike died at Walter Reed. I can still hear the motorcycle sirens as the limousine left the White House grounds.

"The President emerged from the hospital red-eyed and silent," wrote Felix Belair of the *New York Times*. Nixon gave the eulogy. Colonel Vernon Coffey, his military aide, was with him: "[A]fter delivering the eulogy in the Capitol Rotunda after Eisenhower's death, I saw a deeply shaken Nixon break down in the holding room at the Capitol, crying heavily, child like, for several minutes."

CHRISTMAS, 1967

After we moved out of the Nixon, Mudge law offices in December 1967 to a temporary headquarters on the fourth floor of 421 Fifth Avenue, I received a visit from a law student at Columbia, anxious to join the campaign. I heard him out and sent him on to the other staffers to interview, with a cautionary warning: "This guy looks like a Rockefeller plant."

The "Rockefeller plant" was Ken Khachigian, my friend of forty-six years who would remain loyal to Nixon through his presidency and depart with him for San Clemente to help write his memoirs and prepare Nixon for the David Frost interviews. Ken's loyalty became the stuff of legend in the final days of 1974 with his insistence that we fight impeachment to the finish and not even consider resignation. For those last months, Ken was known among White House senior staff as "Lieutenant Onoda," or simply "Onoda," after the Japanese soldier Hiroo Onoda who had, twenty-eight years after Japan's surrender, just emerged from the Philippine jungle in full uniform, because his emperor had not told him to surrender.

At year's end, 1967, I was invited to the Nixon Christmas party at the apartment. Seeking to be unobtrusive, I was off by myself, sampling the hors d'oeuvres, when I saw across the table a woman staring intently at me. Her eyes suddenly brightened and a look of recognition lit her face. Alerting all the guests in the apartment to her discovery, she pointed at me and started yelling excitedly, "Mr. Conservative! Mr. Conservative!"

And that was how I first met Martha Mitchell.

CHAPTER 6

The Six-Day War—and After

THAT, BUCHANAN, WAS a fascist.
—RICHARD NIXON, ATHENS (JUNE 1967)

A S GOVERNOR ROMNEY was having a hellish time getting his footing, Nixon scheduled four trips abroad, with no traveling press and one aide. The first took him to seven countries in Eastern and Western Europe, the second to Japan, Vietnam, Thailand, India, Iran, and around the world. The third was to Latin America. The fourth, on which I was his traveling aide, began June 4 with a flight to Paris. We were to continue on to Morocco, Algeria, Tunisia, the United Arab Republic (Egypt), Lebanon, Saudi Arabia, half a dozen African nations, Greece, then Israel, and home.

As May unfolded, tensions were rising across the Middle East. UN Secretary-General U Thant, foolishly responding to a demand by Egypt's Gamal Abdel Nasser, pulled out the UN peacekeeping force that had been in Sinai since the withdrawal of the British-French-Israeli invasion force of 1956. With UN troops departing, Nasser threatened to send Egyptian troops across the Sinai to Israel's border, and down to Sharm el-Sheik at the southern tip of Sinai, overlooking the Strait of Tiran, entrance to the Gulf of Aqaba. Through that strait and up that gulf passed all of Israel's oil from the Shah's Iran to the port of Eilat. The Arab world was on fire. The decisive battle with the "Zionist entity" was at hand.

Recalling the reaction of Japan when FDR cut off access to U.S. oil in the summer of '41, which led straight to Pearl Harbor, I told Nixon that the Israelis could not tolerate an Egyptian army controlling access to the oil on which their nation depended for survival. War is certain, I said, and soon. The Israel that had colluded with Britain and France in 1956 to oust Nasser was not going to have Nasser standing on its windpipe.

Nixon disagreed. Heading to Philadelphia to speak to the World Affairs Council, he told me, "When they look down that gun barrel," both sides will back away. In Philadelphia Nixon reiterated the message. There will be no war, he said, for "those parties who seem to want war in the Mid-East lack the power to wage it. And those parties who have the power to wage war in the Mid-East do not want it." Nixon's penchant for predictions puzzled me. When he was right he rarely got credit. When he was wrong, his prediction would be thrown back up at him constantly. Meanwhile, in Washington, there was discussion of a U.S.-led international task force of warships, a "Red Sea Regatta," to guarantee Israel's oil lifeline.

With the crisis unresolved we were off to Paris on June 4, and on the morning of June 5 flew on Royal Moroccan Airways via Barcelona to Rabat. When we landed, Ambassador Henry Tasca rushed aboard to tell us war had broken out. Nixon came off the plane to tell the press it would be a long war. "I do not believe that either side has the capability, without massive assistance from a foreign power, of winning a quick victory." His prediction updated, we were off to the embassy.

OUR TIME IN Morocco was tense. The Egyptians were charging that U.S. planes from the Sixth Fleet had led the dawn attack on their airfields. Arab nations had begun severing relations. We learned that our embassy people in Algiers were holed up in an "icebox," that our trip there had been canceled. Soon, our entire trip across the Arab world had been canceled.

After an embassy briefing, we met with Morocco's foreign minister. From this and other meetings it was clear the Moroccans saw themselves as friends of the United States, but were doing what they had to do for Arab solidarity in a war with Israel. That evening we could hear the sirens in the distance and were told, "The King is coming up from Marrakech." He was to address the Moroccan troops heading off to fight alongside their Arab brothers. They would not get aboard ship before the Six-Day War was over.

At every stop on a trip, Nixon would assess the U.S. ambassador. He was taking the measure of the men he would need if ever he became First Diplomat. In Henry Tasca, who had served in Italy after the war when there was a fear that nation would fall to Communism, he saw one of the best and told me so. Tasca was among those U.S. diplomats who believed the United States needed an evenhanded policy in the Arab-Israeli conflict.

A memorable moment of that Moroccan stop was when we were about to sit down to a working dinner with the foreign minister. He brought in and briefly introduced his wife, a woman of stunning beauty and regal carriage who seemed still in her twenties. After we departed that evening, I remarked on this, and Nixon went into a disquisition on the most beautiful of the queens, princesses, and royalty he had met in decades of travel abroad as congressman, senator, and vice president. The foreign minister's wife, he said, ranks right up there with Queen Soraya, the Shah's wife, who I was given to understand was the gold standard.

DE GAULLE TURNS ANTI-ISRAEL

With our trips to Algeria, Tunisia, Egypt, Lebanon, and Saudi Arabia canceled, Nixon and I—our schedule being rearranged for us back in New York—flew back to Paris, where we were put up at the

Crillon. Swiftly an invitation came from the Elysée Palace. President de Gaulle, who had lately created an alliance crisis by giving NATO notice it must get out of Paris and get out of France, wished to meet with the former vice president. Nixon was surprised and pleased. This was a gracious gesture by de Gaulle, and Nixon, who saw him as one of the giants of the World War II generation, never forgot such courtesies. The NATO issue came up in the conversation. For, the next morning, I spotted a U.S. military officer crossing the Crillon lobby to the elevator to go up to Nixon's suite—the Supreme Allied Commander in Europe, General Lyman Lemnitzer.

Unlike his countrymen, who were wild with enthusiasm over Israel's triumph, in which the Israeli air force had used French-built planes to achieve its victory, de Gaulle was angry they had started the war against his advice and would soon condemn the Israelis and their attack. From those hours we were in Paris until he left office, de Gaulle would tilt France's foreign policy toward the Arab side. He was growing increasingly nationalistic. In July in Montreal, de Gaulle would declaim *"Vive le Québec libre!"*—Long live a free Quebec!—embracing the cause of independence for the French-speaking province lost to Britain on the Plains of Abraham in the French and Indian War. In November 1967, de Gaulle would lash out at the Jews as "an elite people, domineering and sure of themselves," and call Israel an expansionist state. June 1967 was the point at which France's role as foremost Western patron of Israel was ceded to the United States. Nixon felt that high among de Gaulle's motives was a wish to reorient French foreign policy away from France's ties to NATO and the West, and adopt a more equidistant stance between East and West in the Cold War, befitting the great power de Gaulle believed France still to be.

AFTER NIXON MET with de Gaulle, we both met with Ambassador Charles "Chip" Bohlen, one of the acclaimed "Wise Men" of the Cold War. Bohlen had succeeded the fabled George Kennan as ambassador in Moscow when Kennan was declared persona non grata by Stalin in 1952. He was also a confirmed detentist who believed the Soviets should be ceded a sphere of influence in Eastern Europe. I was taken aback by what I thought were his excessively rosy views on the Middle East and the Cold War.

The Six-Day War was not yet over. Yet Bohlen was saying that Nasser and King Hussein of Jordan might be given the "heave-ho" after the "bloody noses" from the Israelis. "One gets the impression," I wrote in notes for Nixon, "that the Ambassador does not see Arab desire for revenge or Arab humiliation as being any obstacle," as Bohlen was contending that "the time is now ripe for settlement."

Bohlen also argued that after this rout of their Arab allies and the humiliation of Russian arms used by the Arabs, by French arms used by the Israelis, Moscow might be prepared for better relations with the United States. My notes went on:

> Bohlen says he is convinced that [Premier Alexei] Kosygin's real interests are economics and agriculture, that Kosygin and the Soviets having been badly burnt in the whole process will likely turn inward and give up these costly and non-productive "adventures" (Foreign). . . . While he did not say this specifically, he seems to be implying that the Middle East was something of a "last fling" and the Russians had come up with such a hangover that now they would take the pledge and do what was in their interests anyhow—namely, concentrate on domestic economy.

The ambassador was comparing the Soviet Union to an alcoholic who had fallen off the wagon, gone on a binge, regretted it, and, now chastened, would go cold turkey and could be a reliable partner. I knew Bohlen's reputation as a lion of the U.S. diplomatic corps, but was stunned by what I thought was his naïveté about the men in the Kremlin.

Bohlen said that France was concerned about another Yalta—where FDR and Churchill had divided the world with Stalin, who was ceded Eastern and much of Central Europe. Here my notes read: "(Bohlen interjected that Yalta was not so bad.)" Bohlen said the French believed the Americans and British were too closely tied to Israel and were going to lose their influence in the Arab world, leaving the region to France. My notes concluded:

> Buchanan's impression of Bohlen. He has mannerisms of speech and attitude (the affected boredom with it all) that suggest something of a pro-consul dealing with warring and unenlightened tribes. ("You know these religious things make people very emotional, etc., etc.") He seems to see the Russians as . . . just reaching the same plateau of sophistication and recognition [as us so that] between the two [we] must work out some arrangements in which the world might avoid the wars such as Arab-Israeli.

Harlan Cleveland, the U.S. ambassador to NATO, was less sanguine, arguing that Russian conduct in starting the war fit a pattern that clashed with detente. He agreed with Bohlen that the Soviets had egged the Egyptians on by telling them an Israeli strike was imminent, and if they struck first, Moscow would be at their side. He disagreed with Bohlen's thesis that Russian conduct in the run-up to war was an aberration. Too much evidence pointed the other way. In my notes, I wrote "Cleveland very impressive."

AS WE PREPARED to leave for London, Nixon told me he had made reservations at Maxim's. The legendary Parisian restaurant was empty in mid-afternoon when we arrived. Nixon ordered wines and dishes for both of us that I had never heard of before, patiently described each as it arrived in an almost paternal manner, as waiters hovered over us endlessly asking if "Monsieur le Prèsident!" might want something else. The meal must have cost a fortune. We were there hours, until embassy staff arrived and took us to the airport to make the flight to London. They would be there at every arrival and departure, a privilege accorded former vice presidents.

As soon as he was seated on the plane, Nixon set the alarm on his watch and was swiftly asleep. When it went off, a half hour later, he took a yellow pad out of his briefcase and began to write notes of his recollections of what he had heard and learned in Paris. He did this constantly on the trip. For Nixon this was no junket. These were learning experiences for a serious scholar of foreign policy, and after every meeting he wrote notes like some student after a crucial lecture on which he would be tested. On the entire trip the Nixon work ethic was on display.

"ONE OF THE WISEST WORLD LEADERS"

In London we were put up at Claridge's and the next day Nixon and I strolled across St. James's Park to the American embassy. I was taken with the beauty and cleanliness of the park, the magnificent buildings, the English schoolboys with their bowl haircuts walking with their teachers. I became an instant Anglophile. The most memorable moment in this side trip was the visit to Nixon's suite of Sir Alec Douglas-Home, foreign minister to Harold Macmillan, who had succeeded him as prime minister in October 1963. Douglas-Home served as prime minister for one year, but would return as foreign minister in the Tory government of Sir Edward Heath.

Though highly intelligent, Douglas-Home was difficult to understand, so heavily British was his accent. He was dressed in formal attire, headed later that morning for the Epsom Derby, the ancestral English horse race upon which our own Kentucky Derby is modeled. His focus was on Russia's role in the recent war. The Soviets are in this thing "up to their necks," he said. They have twin goals: make Nasser dominant in the region, and, through him, gain a Soviet foothold in Africa. Asked how this affected "detente," Sir Alec said the Soviets move when they see an opportunity. They always have. Like a knife, they push ahead when they hit butter, and back away when they hit steel. Where they run into unity and strength, relations tend to improve. Soviet policy seeks "a maximum of confusion for a minimum of commitment." The Soviets did not intervene militarily in the Arab-Israeli war because they do not commit their military power far from their homeland. On the margin of my notes recording the observations of the former prime minister and foreign secretary, Nixon wrote, "One of [the] wisest world leaders."

Sir Alec spoke of a Middle East peace conference but said it would fail unless Israelis and Arabs were looking across a table. Though this idea may be far-fetched, he added, it is the only way to true peace. Douglas-Home said that had the Israelis "taken a licking," U.S. and British troops would have had to intervene, with the British drawing forces out of Germany. At that point, my notes read:

> When RN said that he had read that some interpreters were using US-Soviet hotline conversations during the crisis as proof Soviets were in the spirit of detente working together in pursuit of settlement in Middle East, Home replied, "My God, it's incredible how silly some people can be."

After which Nixon scribbled in the margin, "RN's strong view also."

The conversation shifted to Southeast Asia, particularly the expansion of SEATO to include Malaysia, Singapore, and Indonesia. Nixon indicated that he had picked up some "foggy thinking" in India during his recent trip, to which Sir Alec replied he once asked India's president Radhakrishnan why "no Indian can think right." The latter replied in the spirit of the question with a story about how God was responsible for making Indians this way. After an hour, Nixon asked me to escort Sir Alec to the elevator. The ex–prime minister was half a head taller and rail-thin. His top hat made him seem even taller, and as he walked he seemed wildly uncoordinated. Arms and legs seemed to move as if disconnected from his body. When I returned to the suite, I told Nixon the British statesman was brilliant, but one strange-looking creature.

Nixon nodded. "It's the inbreeding," he said.

Years later, I would learn that Sir Alec, as Lord Dunglass, had been the parliamentary aide to Neville Chamberlain and was with him at the third and final meeting with Hitler in Munich. Lord Dunglass had supported the Munich agreement Chamberlain brought home as having bought Britain time to rearm, but had urged the prime minister not to make the extravagant claims about "peace for our time" that he did on his return to London. I regretted I had been unaware of this history when I had an opportunity to ask him, as he left the hotel, about that 1938 meeting that sealed the fate of Czechoslovakia and led to the greatest war in history. Something else I learned half a century later: In 1940, Lord Dunglass had come down with spinal tuberculosis and been immobilized for two years, which perhaps explains more accurately why the statesman walked as he did.

In 2013, going through filing cabinet drawers from 1966–68, I came across two notebooks on this trip. In one, a diplomat—I believe it was Sir Alec—made observations about the Israeli triumph that have stood the test of time. The Russians "must know [the] charge about the Sixth Fleet" attacking Egypt "is a phony," as they have been "tracking the damn thing," he said, and before

West and East go about "congratulating one another on ending the crisis," we should remember Moscow had acted like an "arsonist belatedly plunging in to fight the fire when his own assets began to burn."

"Last Sunday night it looked as though Nasser had brought off the coup of a decade," he said. "He was halfway to doing what Bismarck had done." Moscow seemed about to emerge as "diplomatic protector of the Arabs" and "could have put the screws to Israel." But Nasser "refused to put limits on what he had intended to do about Israel." So Israel "had to act."

This recalled the *Economist*'s depiction of Nasser's handling of the crisis as not unlike that of Bismarck in the run-up to the Franco-Prussian War, with one exception. Nasser handled the preliminaries brilliantly, said the *Economist*, the Ems Telegram, the marshaling of the armies, "only to be taken for six at Sedan." My notes on Sir Alec went on:

> Israel had won on the battlefield a generation of security. . . .
> The job of Israel's friends is to tell them they will get no support if they insist on terms that contradict their claim to have been fighting a defensive war— Arabs might agree to recognize Israel after this war—[but] not to an expanded Israel.

The "goals for Israel" should be these: Arab signatures on a treaty that recognizes Israel, which "should not be impossible." Safety from Syrian guerrillas. Safe passage at Aqaba to Eilat. Stationing an international force at Sharm el-Sheik—a force whose removal would require the consent of the United States and the Soviet Union. A similar force to allow Israeli ships to pass through the Suez Canal. A peace settlement that defines Arab borders and does justice to the refugees.

"Adversity seldom brings out the best in people—either individually or collectively," he said of the Arabs. Of Israel? "History teaches us that the winning side is storing up trouble for itself if it insists on grinding the loser's face in the dust." Sir Alec, unfortunately, was not in power as he gave us his sage counsel. The Labor Party's Harold Wilson was prime minister.

LION OF JUDAH

From London, we flew to Frankfurt, where Bob Abplanalp, a close Nixon friend who invented the aerosol spray, arranged a dinner at a castle on the Rhine while we awaited a night flight to Addis Ababa. Nixon could sleep on a plane. I could not, and was up talking all night with the stewardesses as we crossed the Mediterranean, Libya, and Chad, arriving the next morning in the Ethiopian capital, to be greeted by Ambassador Ed Korry. Nixon seemed as impressed with Korry's intelligence as he had been with Tasca's toughness and savvy. Korry noted that even with Israeli troops occupying Sinai and standing on the Canal, Nasser was unlikely to do a deal. For just as the sole conviction that united the black states of the sub-Sahara was mutual hatred of South Africa, the only conviction that united Arabs behind Nasser is that he was the foremost foe of Israel in the Arab world. "This," I wrote Nixon in my notes, "would be a reasonable explanation why we will never see Nasser's signature on a peace treaty with the Jews." His anti-Israel stand was a sine qua non of Nasser's claim to leadership of the Arab world.

After Nixon went to bed, Korry and I talked late into the night about philosophy and natural law.

By the time we got to Central Africa the Six-Day War was over. And even among Africa's leaders who sided with the Arabs, there was awe at the military feat the Israelis had accomplished, seizing Sinai to the Canal, East Jerusalem, the West Bank, and the Golan Heights in six days.

The highlight of the visit to Ethiopia was our meeting in the Jubilee Palace. Emperor Haile Selassie's beard was gray, but I could recall from my high school history book the photograph of the tiny black-bearded emperor addressing the League of Nations in 1936, warning the Western powers that if they did not stop Mussolini's invasion of his country, their turn as victims of fascist aggression would be coming. As the emperor spoke, a tiny dog leapt on his lap, stood there staring at us, then jumped down. The emperor neither moved nor interrupted the flow of the conversation.

The emperor seemed concerned about a breakup of Somalia. He regarded tribalism as the curse of Africa, saying his own country might be the only homogeneous nation on the continent. Yet, in the twenty-first century, it would be tribalism, and Eritrea's secession, that would tear his ancient nation asunder. The emperor used Israel as an example of a small state that had saved itself from Soviet-armed neighbors because she was strong. Ethiopia, too, was a state with hostile neighbors, he said. Sudan had been promised arms, and weapons were going into Somalia. But Ethiopia's request for U.S. arms had been denied: "While God helps those who help themselves," said the Lion of Judah, "we must help those who are helping themselves."

From Ethiopia we flew to Kenya, where we spoke at length with the most impressive leader we would meet in the sub-Sahara. Tom Mboya was intelligent and articulate and saw beyond the politics of tribe and nation. He was a Luo like Barack Obama's father, and unlike Jomo Kenyatta, the Kikuyu Mau Mau chief who had become the father of his country. Mboya spoke of a resource-rich Africa uniting economically and politically like the United States. His handicap was that he was regarded as pro-American. Indeed, Nixon and I encountered almost no anti-Americanism among the dozens of leaders we met. But I got from embassy briefings by the ambassador and his staff the sense that Mboya would never reach the apex of power in Kenya. His egocentricity, the ambassador told us, made him unpopular even with his own tribe. And Tom Mboya never did.

While in Nairobi we had a cocktail party with members of Kenya's cabinet. What was surprising was a phenomenon we encountered across Africa: the youth of the second echelon of leaders. Many seemed no older than I, and while a few were impressive, most seemed men of little substance, accomplishment, or capacity. You need not have been a devotee of Kipling to have wondered if these fellows could run the countries they had inherited as well as had the departed British.

"TWENTY HARLEY-DAVIDSONS!"

From Nairobi we flew south past Kilimanjaro and east to what had been Northern Rhodesia and was now the copper-rich nation of Zambia. President Kenneth Kaunda, a rising figure in Africa, was out of the country. And coming in from Lusaka airport we crossed an avenue that carried the name of Cecil Rhodes, the British imperialist and founding father of white-ruled Rhodesia. I wondered how long that road name would last.

From Lusaka we flew north to the Democratic Republic of the Congo, the former Belgian Congo. Our first stop was Lubumbashi, formerly Elisabethville, capital of Katanga province. In the early 1960s an attempt by Moise Tshombe to pull his mineral-rich province out of the Congo, establish a new nation, and align with the West had been backed by conservatives. On my first evening at the International House, where I had taken up residence to attend Columbia Journalism School in September of 1961, an African I was sharing a beer with stormed off in a rage when I told him I was for Tshombe and Katanga's secession.

Patrice Lumumba, the charismatic radical and deposed premier, had lately been murdered and a university named for him in Moscow, where future leaders of Africa and the Third World were welcomed. When we put down in Lubumbashi, we were greeted by the U.S. consul at the airport, drank Simba beer, and waited for the plane to be refueled, as we were told guerrillas were roaming the province.

From Lubumbashi we flew to Leopoldville, the capital, which had been renamed Kinshasa. The acting ambassador was Bob Blake, who seemed to me Kennedyesque and impressed Nixon. Congo does not have the religious problem that Nigeria does, said Blake, who volunteered an observation that has proven true for the last half century. From east to west, Africa, said Blake, is divided along the lines of religion, with Muslims in the north and Christians in the south, and this divide may be as historically critical as the divide between Arab Africa and Black Africa. Across the river in Congo (Brazzaville) were 300 Cuban soldiers. But as long as they did not attempt subversion, said Blake, let them have it. He was tough on the Belgians, who, when they had had imperial control of the Congo (Leopoldville), were, said Blake, interested solely in profit. Only a tiny few in that huge black country had a college education.

In Kinshasa we met with Foreign Minister Justin Marie Bomboko, a former head of government, and, in his ceremonial hut, with the new ruler, Joseph Mobutu, ex–army chief and now president, who would rule the Congo—later renamed Zaire—until his overthrow three decades later. Mobutu kept a caged leopard outside, and during our meeting, a horse antelope stuck its head into the window of the tiny hut.

At the embassy we had been told Mobutu wished to loosen ties to the former colonial power Belgium and replace them with ties to the United States. In the Cold War the general was betting on America. Like many of the Africans we met he was pro-Israel, proud that he and his elite soldiers had trained as paratroopers in Israel. What does Marxism, which was written for a nineteenth-century industrializing Europe, have to do with Africa? he said with scorn. An expressive man, Mobutu spoke as much with his hands and gestures as with his voice. Toward the end of the conversation, Mobutu leaned in close to Nixon to make a special request. Thinking I was about to be in on the origins of a major arms deal, I leaned in to listen. Mobutu told Nixon what he needed now and needed most—as Zaire was about to host the next African summit—were "twenty Chrysler Imperials and twenty Harley-Davidsons." I almost lost it. Mobutu, whom I would meet in his future visits to the White House, looked to me like one tough street dude right out of Harlem.

The meeting with Mobutu called to mind Murray Kempton's comment that wherever Nixon traveled, a part of the State Department traveled with him. After we were briefed by the ambassador and embassy staff on our arrival in a country, Nixon would ask if there was some issue, some point, they wanted him to raise or to stress in his meetings. Without being asked, Nixon would explain and defend U.S. policy in the Middle East, in Vietnam, or toward the Soviet Union, though in those years it was Lyndon Johnson's policy he was explaining and defending. Dean Rusk could not have been more supportive of the President and U.S. policy than Nixon in those meetings. He seemed to relish the role, acting at hours-long lunches with these African leaders like a patient professor, tutoring them, answering their questions, and speaking for minutes in response to each. Nixon was a relentless advocate for America. When he said on campaign stops in 1966 that he had defended Johnson's policies abroad better than many in Johnson's party on Capitol Hill were defending them at home, Nixon spoke the truth.

From Kinshasa we flew to the sole Francophone country on our tour of sub-Saharan Africa, the Ivory Coast. Before reaching Abidjan, our plane put in at Lagos, Nigeria, at night. The airport was bustling with activity. Soldiers were everywhere, and journalists and travelers were talking of the civil war that had just broken out. Colonel Ojukwu, an Ibo, had declared independence and was pulling his "Republic of Biafra" out of Africa's most populous country. And, as with the earlier effort of Tshombe to lead Katanga into secession, Ojukwu and his Ibo, in their drive for independence, had the support of American conservatives.

In 1967 the Ivory Coast was a jewel of Africa. Unlike many emerging nations that had sent the colonials packing, Ivorians were proud to tell us they had asked the 500,000 French living and working there to stay and help build their new nation. Abidjan, the capital, seemed a bustling success. The Ivorians seemed to have found the formula: Assume power, but to run the economy and to advise the nation, keep those French who had made the Ivory Coast a successful colony, and be open to more. The U.S. deputy chief of mission said there were twice as many Frenchmen in the Ivory Coast now as there were at independence. While the government was 90 percent Ivorian, the folks running the economy were 90 percent French.

With President Houphouët-Boigny out of the country, acting president Auguste Denise hosted us. His central concern: Communist China, which he said had designs on Africa. That explained why the Ivory Coast backed the U.S. position to keep China out of the UN. He pressed Nixon on why America was giving aid to Guinea's Ahmed Sékou Touré, a Marxist, who was China's agent in Africa. Denise said the Russians told him in Paris that they had given up on Africa, as the spiritualism of its peoples made them resistant to a Communist appeal. The Russians seem to have realized that subversion in Africa is unworkable and unrealistic, he said, but this could be a cover, a part of a strategy to return to the old ways as Africa dropped its guard. In the margin of my notes on Denise, Nixon wrote: "(RN: Note: Angola)." In Angola, a guerrilla war was under way to overthrow Portuguese colonial rule.

At the lunch hosted by the foreign minister, a huge man still in his mid-thirties, Nixon got the best test of the trip. For the Ivorian would not simply nod at his answers on the Middle East, but come back with rebuttals tacked on to his next question. Mboya alone excepted, Arsène Usher Assouan was the most impressive figure we met in sub-Saharan Africa. He turned the lunch into a debate, with his young subordinates laughing at his responses and cheering him on as he challenged the former vice president of the United States. Everyone, Nixon included, enjoyed the session. Lubricated by a variety of French wines, this was the most lively lunch of the trip.

WHAT BECAME OF THEM ALL?

We arrived late at night in Liberia, and the drive into the capital was a long one. Monrovia was named for President James Monroe, one of the luminaries of the American Colonization Society whose policy was to repatriate American slaves to the land of their ancestors. There were almost no lights on the road, but after some time I saw in the distance what seemed an enormous and brilliantly lit oil refinery. I was told by the droll embassy staffer that this would be the presidential palace.

President William Tubman was out of the country and we were hosted at an official lunch by long-serving vice president William R. Tolbert, with his wife, members of the Cabinet, and their wives. All were Americo-Liberians. Their friendliness, mannerisms, jocularity, and speech all said: These folks are from the USA. It was as if we had come across a colony of black Americans in the heart of Africa, which was partly true. These descendants of American slaves ran the country—the main port was Buchanan, named after our 15th president—and I was told at the embassy that they ran the place as a wholly owned subsidiary of the Firestone Tire and Rubber Company. Iron ore and rubber were its exports, and the prices of both were down. Firestone was the nation's number-one employer and the crucial factor in Liberia's economic life. At our meeting with the U.S. "country team," we learned that Firestone had hired only one native Liberian as a legal adviser. I got the impression that this situation could not long endure.

If I had to summarize in a few words the attitude of the Africans

Nixon and I met on our journey, it would be friendly, respectful, curious, and anxious for greater contact with America. We encountered almost no hostility, and significant sympathy for Israel, and even awe at how the Israelis had routed three Arab armies in six days. These Africans seemed to see us as the world's first power and the probable winner of the Cold War. What became of them all in the years that followed?

Haile Selassie, King of Kings, Lion of Judah, was overthrown in 1974 and is believed to have been murdered in bed in 1975 by agents of the Derg, the Communist military junta that had seized power. The new regime would switch Ethiopia's allegiance in the Cold War, bring in Cuban troops, fend off U.S.-backed invasions from Somalia. Its leader, Colonel Mengistu, would flee to sanctuary in 1991 to the Zimbabwe of Robert Mugabe.

Kenya's Tom Mboya was assassinated in Nairobi two years after we spoke with him. Suspicion fell upon associates of President Jomo Kenyatta, as Mboya was a rising rival for the presidency. Among those who would testify at the trial of Mboya's killer was Barack Obama, Sr., who had been with Mboya just before his death. Obama would later say he had been the target of a hit-and-run incident because of his testimony.

In the year after our visit, President Kenneth Kaunda of Zambia would ban all political parties but his own and begin to drive his mineral-rich nation into unpayable debt. After our visit to the Congo, President Mobutu sentenced Tshombe to death in absentia for treason, and a plane on which Tshombe was traveling was hijacked and diverted to Algeria. In August 1967, Nixon sent Mobutu a tough letter warning that should Tshombe be sent back to the Congo and should he, Mobutu, execute him, it would cause a serious breach with the United States:

I recognize that your government considers the case of Mr. Tshombe to be an internal matter. But I think I can say with certitude that Mr. Tshombe's transfer to The Congo and execution, in accordance with the penalty imposed upon him in absentia, would drain off much of the good will that currently exists in America toward your government and country.

Tshombe never left Algeria. In June 1969, he died of "heart failure." Mobutu, his name augmented to Mobutu Sese Seko, would rule until 1997 and become the richest man in Africa. I assume he got his Harleys.

The Biafra secession, whose birth we witnessed, would last three years and consume a million lives. The Ibo would be dragged bleeding and broken back to the embrace of the mother country in 1970. The Ivory Coast would prosper, then be torn asunder by civil wars in the twenty-first century. Many French would give up and flee.

Vice President Tolbert became president on Tubman's death in 1971 and would be murdered in that same Monrovia palace where we dined by Master Sergeant Samuel Doe, who led a coup in 1980. Tolbert's body, with those of other murdered officials, was dragged out and stoned by a mob. Some of the Cabinet members and wives with whom we had lunched would end up in ditches or tied to stakes on the beach after kangaroo-court trials. Here they were bayoneted to amuse the cheering crowds of Liberians who had grown to detest the privileged rule of these descendants of American slaves.

"THAT, BUCHANAN, WAS A FASCIST!"

With our tour of Africa ending, we flew to London, then to Greece, which had just undergone a "colonels' coup" in April, which many Greeks cheered. A junta was ruling the country. We first met with Prime Minister Kollias, who defended the coup as a necessity, which was aimed against the radicals. He promised an early return to parliamentary rule and said that if the United States was apprehensive, its worries would soon be put to rest: "We will be true to our heritage as Greeks. . . . democratic principles are in our bloodstream. . . . we will not desert that heritage." Kollias urged the U.S. to resume aid. At the bottom of my notes is typed, "This gentleman is not the stuff of which autocrats are made."

Our embassy arranged a meeting with Brigadier General Stylianos Pattakos, the armor commander who had helped execute the April coup. Nixon asked the ambassador if there were any questions he wanted asked. Ask him what the junta will do if students and workers go into the streets, said the ambassador.

Pattakos was a stolid bald-headed man who sat across from Nixon, the fingers of his hands touching at the tips to form a steeple in front of his face. He wore something between a smile and a smirk. His answers were clipped. The translation took no time. And the general was not lacking in self-confidence. He looked straight in Nixon's face and never looked at me, though I sat right beside Nixon. When Nixon asked Pattakos if they were prepared for demonstrations or disorders by students and workers, and how they planned to handle that, Pattakos said this was no problem. "We have excellent surveillance and we will arrest them." He smiled and awaited the next question. I glanced over at Nixon. His face did not change expression. As we left the building, Nixon said to me, "That, Buchanan, was a fascist."

Melina Mercouri would say the same of the interior minister who had stripped her of her citizenship: "I was born a Greek and I will die a Greek. Mr. Pattakos was born a fascist and he will die a fascist!" At the top of my notes of the meeting I had two words about Pattakos: "Inarticulate, hard-nosed." When the junta was overthrown, Pattakos was tried for treason and sentenced to death, later commuted to life imprisonment. Kollias was ousted as prime minister that December after the king sought to execute a counter-coup, and Colonel Georgios Papadopoulos, the coup leader, took the portfolio for himself. As the Greek-American Taki Theodoracopulos has written, "President Nixon was among the few who saw the colonels as they were: pro-West, very Christian, patriotic, honest, and not at all sophisticated."

A MEETING WITH BEN-GURION

On arrival in Israel, Nixon and I were taken into custody by a colonel in the Israeli army, a graduate of Columbia, proud he had taken the course of historian Henry Steele Commager. The colonel had lost an arm in the Sinai in the '56 war. An Israeli diplomat was a second chaperone. Early in the morning after our arrival, they drove us to an airfield, where we got on a small spotter plane to fly north to the Golan. There we got into a jeep and drove into the hills captured only days before. Off the narrow road we could see the burnt-out shells of Syrian tanks. When we asked to take a closer look we were told there were mines all around. The colonel cheerfully said that if the vice president got out of the car and lost a leg, he would lose his head.

When we came down from the Golan we had lunch at a kibbutz and saw the marked contrast between Israel's side of the frontier, green and cultivated, and the Syrian side, brown and desolate. And we were told the story of the storming of the heights by an Israeli brigade commander who had also fought in '48 and '56. Among the first to reach the top, he had telephoned the kibbutz below that had gone through repeated shellings over the years, and said, "From this great height I see how big you are."

Fifteen years later, leading a tour group for my *Buchanan and* [Tom] *Braden* WRC radio show, we would be taken to that same kibbutz. A woman there would remember me.

We got back on the plane and headed south. I saw in the distance a lake, and as we began to pass over, the colonel turned in his seat and said over the noise of the propeller, "This is Genesareth, what you call the Sea of Galilee." It was a thing of stunning clarity and beauty. I was silent as the plane flew straight down the middle of the lake and the Jordan River valley to Jericho, then turned west. "This is the first time we will enter Jerusalem from this direction," The colonel laughed. Up until two weeks before, the land below had belonged to Jordan.

As the plane turned west through the hills, the colonel motioned to me to look down. Below, on the bare, winding, hilly road Christ had traveled up from Jericho to Jerusalem, were the carcasses of trucks and tanks of the Arab Legion. This Jordanian column had been sent to recapture the city. With Israel having air supremacy from the dawn attacks that destroyed the air forces of Syria, Jordan, and Egypt on the ground in the first minutes of the Six-Day War, the killing of this column had been a turkey shoot. Defenseless against air strikes, these brave Arab soldiers had been sent by their king on a suicide mission. The grisly results lay directly beneath us.

On landing in Jerusalem we got into a jeep and were driven through the captured eastern sector along a teeming street on one side of which was the Wailing Wall of the Second Temple. We were told the gutter along the wall had been used as a common urinal.

While in Israel, we could not have had greater access to her leaders. We met with Prime Minister Levi Eshkol and founding father David Ben-Gurion. A tiny ball of a man, Ben-Gurion pressed upon Nixon the need for America to engage China, which he saw as the power of the future. He was alarmed by reports that Nasser's crushing defeat and loss of Sinai might cause him to resign. Nasser is the only leader with the stature to make peace with Israel and make it stick, said Ben-Gurion. Nasser must survive. And Ben-Gurion believed Nasser could make peace with Israel. He told us he had made two or three attempts since 1956 to get together.

With the exception of Jerusalem, which Israel would keep, Ben-Gurion said he was ready to give back the Sinai to Egypt and the Golan to Syria and set up an autonomous state on the West Bank economically tied to Israel. He spoke of a united Europe as a magnet for America and Russia so all could confront China together, and predicted that in any Russia-China war, Asians inside the USSR would side with China. He related the story of Masada in A.D. 73, where 750 to 1,000 Jews had committed collective suicide rather than let themselves be taken by the Romans. Now our armored troops take their oath at Masada, he said.

Eshkol said the Americans had told Israel to wait two days, then two weeks, for us to manage Nasser's threat to close the Gulf of Aqaba. We had failed. They had acted. Eshkol said America was "waffling" in the crisis. If the Russians began sending fighter aircraft to Egypt and Syria to replace the planes destroyed by Israel, Eshkol wanted a speed-up on promised deliveries of U.S. planes. As for Jerusalem's sovereignty, it is "Israeli," Eshkol said, a fait accompli, nonnegotiable. All other matters were negotiable.

THE GENERALS: RABIN AND DAYAN

In Tel Aviv we toured an Israeli military hospital where wounded Egyptian POWs were being treated. One of our escorting officers told us he had captured an Egyptian officer whom he had known as a POW in 1956. "Why do you keep fighting us?" the Israeli officer said he asked the Egyptian. "Three times we have fought you and three times we have won."

To which the Egyptian replied, "Yes, and we will fight you eleven times, and eleven times you will win. But the twelfth time, we win!"

"We only have to lose once," said the Israeli, implying a lost war to the surrounding Arab nations meant the annihilation of Israel.

We were taken into the command post of the Israeli armed forces, deep below ground, where we met for an hour with each of the victorious generals: Moshe Dayan and Yitzhak Rabin. Dayan was world-famous as the architect of the most stunning victory in modern warfare. With a black eye patch to cover an empty socket caused by a Vichy sniper in 1941, who put a bullet through his binoculars, Dayan's face had graced the covers of the world's weeklies. The *Economist* featured a picture of the Sphinx with a black eye patch. Dayan's voice was high and British and he spoke with what seemed a lilt. He had achieved much, and seemed cocksure, and pressed Nixon on what America would do if Russian troops fought on Egypt's side. He raised the issue of nuclear weapons, saying he feared China might provide them to the Arabs. "If they dropped three (Haifa, Jerusalem, Tel Aviv), then you don't need brave soldiers."

Dayan put us on the defensive throughout. He said casualties among the young frontline officers had been high, with 20 percent losses, and that soldiers raised on the kibbutz, where they developed a spirit of camaraderie and competition, with many joining the same units, fought best.

The Russians, he said, had to respond to this humiliation. They had lost prestige because they had failed to aid their allies who were being routed. Also, it had been Russian weaponry defeated and destroyed. And Russia had backed the Arabs by sending their top military leaders and the president of the USSR to Egypt after the defeat, to shore up their comrades. Now the Russians had to do something. He wanted Nixon to press the U.S. administration to send planes right away, not later. "What will the U.S. do if Soviet pilots man the Egyptian jets?" Dayan asked Nixon. "We have only five airfields."

Six years later, as defense minister, Dayan would be caught off guard when the Egyptian army crossed the Canal and the Syrians attacked on the Golan, inflicting costly defeats in the Yom Kippur War. President Nixon would order a massive airlift of tanks and heavy guns to save Israel, even as Dayan was said to be loading F-4s with nuclear weapons, reportedly warning, "This is the end of the Third Temple."

Rabin spoke English with a guttural East European accent and was a man of few words. What will the United States do, he asked Nixon directly, if Soviet pilots fly the new MiGs being flown into Cairo? The reason we did not go all the way to Damascus, he said, was fear of what the Russians might do. Unlike Dayan, Rabin seemed almost shy. Yet I came away feeling he was the more impressive general—indeed, the most impressive figure I had met. His appearance in a simple soldier's uniform, weariness and anxiety etched in his face, in his command bunker far below ground, the fate of his country having been in his hands while he had waited out reports from the front, contributed to that impression.

Rabin would go on to become ambassador to the United States, prime minister, and, with Yasser Arafat and Shimon Peres, win the Nobel Prize for Peace for the Oslo Accords. For coming to believe in the necessity to trade the Arab land his army had captured in 1967, and to give up West Bank settlements for peace with the Palestinians, he would be assassinated by a Zionist fanatic in 1995. He was buried on Mount Herzl, and with him may have died the best chance of a permanent peace in the Middle East.

On our last evening in Israel, we met with the head of the Mossad and his senior staff. As they joked and questioned Nixon on what was going on in the States, they made sure his glass was never empty. At the end of this trip it was clear to me the Israelis had read our political scene closely and read it right. Regardless of what was being written about Nixon back home, these Israelis saw him as a potential President and ensured he had privileged access, that he saw what they wanted him to see, and that he heard what they wanted him to hear.

While in Israel we heard nothing of the devastating Israeli air and sea attack on USS *Liberty* during the Six-Day War. Though aware we were in the care and keeping of people who knew how to make their case, I came away an admirer and supporter of Israel and would remain so for decades. In those years I saw the world through a Cold War prism, and saw Israel as an ally in that war that would decide the fate of my country and civilization. Late one night in Tel Aviv, after Nixon was asleep, I went out into the square in front of the hotel. Young Israeli soldiers and their girls were laughing and celebrating. I thought to myself: This is how it must have been in Boston when news came that Cornwallis had surrendered at Yorktown.

When Nixon and I deplaned in New York at JFK, our staff was there as we came through customs. They were exhilarated by Israel's triumph and the press reports of our visit. None were enthusiastic about the war on the other side of the world in Vietnam, where 400,000 Americans were fighting. Yet that trip to Galilee, Jerusalem, and Israel had made an indelible impression upon me as well.

TRAVELING WITH NIXON

After I got back to the office, Rose Woods pulled me aside. "How did it go?" In her voice one caught the sense that the Boss could be a difficult traveling companion, given to exasperation or anger at staff when things went awry. She had a point, though the only tense moment came early. We had taken off from New York in the morning and, given the time difference, arrived in Paris at bedtime. But with the jet lag I had never experienced before, I did not fall asleep until sunrise. Hence, I was feeling miserable on the morning flight to Rabat. As we were about to land in Barcelona, the first stop, I looked over. Nixon had the cap of his fountain pen in his mouth, and was about to close the pen after making notes. When the plane hit the runway and bounced, the cap fell out and disappeared.

"Find it!" Nixon commanded. "We're not getting off this plane until you find it." Waiting until the plane emptied, I got down on the floor, felt under the seats, then concluded the cap must be wedged in the seat. I tried to pull the cushion out. Grunting and sweating, I attracted the attention of a Moroccan steward looking on in horror at this berserk American who by now seemed to be tearing his first-class cabin apart. French-speaking, he could not understand what I was yelling about the pen top. After we got someone to translate, the steward joined me in the search, which proved successful. But by now I was seething, and, as we deplaned, remained stone silent. But Nixon's mood brightened instantly. He began to discourse on the beauty of the Barcelona morning and the scenery, like a friendly tour guide.

The incident, however, was a rarity during the nine years I worked for Richard Nixon. And on the trip we became closer. With the war, and the leaders we met who were riveted by it, we were aware a historic event with consequences far-reaching for the Middle East and the East-West struggle was happening. And we had been witnesses to it.

Moreover, Nixon made every effort to include me in meetings with national and world leaders and U.S. diplomats in every capital we visited. The closer one got to Nixon, the more he revealed himself. Here was the statesman on tour, studying, listening, learning, the diplomat who made the case for his country and cause abroad, and the companion with whom one drank and talked at day's end. When Nixon trusted you he would let down his guard, and I got to know him better than any other boss I ever knew.

A WILSONIAN IDEALIST

Nixon was captivated by foreign policy, as was I. While I had spent three years writing about city, county, and state issues in St. Louis, and the domestic policies of the Kennedy and Johnson administrations, my main interest remained the Cold War. For upon its outcome would rest the fate of Western civilization. This was why I had gone into journalism.

I had been raised in Washington, DC, where there were no elections and no one voted for anything. The three commissioners who managed city affairs were appointed by the President and reported to Congress. Except for one neighbor who was appointed, we didn't even know their names. The DC government was a fraction of the size it is today. We paid no attention to it. No one talked about congressional legislation, though the Capitol was not a mile from my high school. The issues my father discoursed on in nightly seminars at the dinner table were big issues: Was the *Lusitania* carrying contraband when it was torpedoed? British treachery in dragging America into the war. Franco and the Spanish Civil War. FDR's role in Pearl Harbor. Yalta and the abandonment of Eastern Europe to Stalin. How Truman and Marshall lost China. The firing of MacArthur, "the greatest general since Julius Caesar." George Sokolsky and Westbrook Pegler were the columnists my father admired, and the *Times-Herald* was his newspaper until bought and merged with its liberal rival the *Washington Post* in 1954.

Herman Kahn once told me that for most people their life's beliefs are formed between three and seven years of age, or in college. If you wish to convert someone, those are the periods in which to do it. For me that meant World War II. December 7, 1941, came one month after my third birthday, and Hiroshima, Nagasaki, and Japan's surrender on the *Missouri* two months before my seventh birthday.

Kahn's insight helps to explain Nixon's thinking. Born in January 1913, Nixon had a deep admiration for Woodrow Wilson, who, in the years three to seven for him, was a titan. Wilson had won reelection in 1916, led America into the "war to end all wars" and "make the world safe for democracy," emerged triumphant, received a hero's welcome in Paris, and come home with the Treaty of Versailles and League of Nations—only to see them rejected by the Senate. Traveling across country by train, fighting for his League, Wilson suffered a stroke and ended his presidency a cripple in the month that Nixon turned eight. In the years Nixon grew up, Wilson would be portrayed as a tragic figure, an idealist whose fight for his League had been sabotaged by vindictive and reactionary Republicans, and who had died a martyr's death—for peace—defeated and broken in a great and noble cause.

As one of Nixon's teachers at Whittier, and a lifelong friend,

Paul Smith, relates in a 1977 interview on *The Life and Times of Richard Nixon*:

> Dick Nixon was a great admirer of Woodrow Wilson. When Dick was growing up in the grocery store in 1916, his mother Hannah, who was from a family of Milhouses that were 100 percent dyed-in-the-wool Republicans, voted for Woodrow Wilson . . . because of Wilson's stand on peace and his platform pledge that there would be no entrance into war. . . .
>
> [T]he personality of Woodrow Wilson fascinated the mind of young Richard Nixon. Richard Nixon, through his whole political life, quoted Woodrow Wilson more than any other man. . . . [T]here was a fixation in Nixon's mind on Woodrow Wilson that stayed all the way through.

The Wilson legend had a tremendous hold on Nixon. In the decisive speech of his first term, to rally the great Silent Majority against the mass demonstrations to break his presidency, Nixon invoked Wilson, and identified with the tragic figure of history and icon of his youth:

> Fifty years ago, in this room and at this very desk, President Woodrow Wilson spoke words which caught the imagination of a war-weary world. He said: "This is the war to end war." His dream for peace after World War I was shattered on the hard realities of great power politics and Woodrow Wilson died a broken man.
>
> Tonight I do not tell you that the war in Vietnam is the war to end wars. But I do say this: I have initiated a plan which will end this war in a way that will bring us closer to that great goal to which Woodrow Wilson and every American President in our history has been dedicated—the goal of a just and lasting peace.

Though Nixon had thought it was Woodrow Wilson's desk at which he was sitting, it was not. Nixon once gave me a book of Wilson's speeches that I still have, and urged me to read it. These were the kinds of speeches he wanted to give. *Woodrow Wilson: Selections for Today* had been published in 1945. The author-editor began, "A quarter of a century ago, after the First World War was over and a tired world had turned its back on the hard task of organizing a lasting peace, a Berlin editor said in summary, 'Only one conqueror's work will endure: Wilson's thought.'"

The most moving speech in the book, the last, was delivered in St. Louis, the fifth of September, 1919, when Wilson feared Congress was about to repudiate his treaty and his League.

> If it [the Covenant of the League of Nations] should ever in any important respect be impaired, I would feel like asking the Secretary of War to get the boys who went across the water to fight, together on some field where I could go and see them, and I would stand up before them and say,
>
> "Boys, I told you before you went across the seas that this was a war against wars, and I did my best to fulfill the promises; but I am obliged to come to you in mortification and shame and say I have not been able to fulfill the promise. You are betrayed. You fought for something that you did not get."
>
> And the glory of the Armies and Navies of the United States is gone like a dream in the night, and there ensues upon it, in the suitable darkness of the night, the nightmare of dread which lay upon the nations before this war came; and there will come sometime in the vengeful Providence of God, another struggle in which, not a few hundred thousand fine men from America will have to die, but as many millions as are necessary to accomplish the final freedom of the peoples of the world.

192 PATRICK J. BUCHANAN

In this moving, powerful passage one sees the idealism of Wilson, the prophetic insight about what would happen a generation on, a second world war. Yet one also sees how far Wilson's thought departs from that of the men who created America. Why should "many millions" of Americans die for "the final freedom of the peoples of the world"? When had the freedom of the captive peoples of six continents become the moral responsibility of the soldiers and sailors of the United States who would, one day, have to lay down their lives in the millions to attain it? When had Wilson, an avowed segregationist, become concerned about the colonized black, brown, and yellow peoples of the earth? Had Wilson not himself taken us into war as an "associate power" of the British, French, Russian, Italian, and Japanese empires? Had he and those empires not carved up Europe, Africa, the Middle East, and Asia, and divided and distributed the spoils at Versailles?

The disconnect between Wilson's words and actions yet astonishes.

Why did Wilson appeal to Nixon? Because Wilson had dared greatly. Because the cause in which he believed, a lasting peace for all mankind, was a noble one that Nixon shared. Because Wilson had a vision and had sacrificed himself and suffered greatly to attain it. Because Wilson had given up his life for a cause he believed must one day triumph. Nixon identified with this and it explains his preoccupation with "a generation of peace" and the utopian and neo-Wilsonian character of his first inaugural:

> The greatest title history can bestow is the title of peacemaker. This honor now beckons America—the chance to help lead the world at last out of the valley of turmoil, and onto that high ground of peace that man has dreamed of since the dawn of civilization.
>
> If we succeed, generations will say of us now living that we

mastered our moment, that we helped make the world safe for mankind.

"No man can be fully free while his neighbor is not," said Nixon.

But is this true? For this would imply that Americans had never been "fully free," nor would they ever be fully free until all the peoples of the earth were free. Years later, after I had dropped off a speech draft in the Oval Office, the President read it and muttered, "For God's sakes, Buchanan, get some lift into it!" As I reached the door, he said loud enough to hear, "Why can't I get speechwriters like Wilson's?" Not until I was outside the Oval Office did I retort, sotto voce, "Wilson wrote his own speeches."

My views were closer to those of MacArthur in his "Duty, Honor, Country" address at West Point: "But always in our ears ring the ominous words of Plato . . . 'Only the dead have seen the end of war.'" Yet this idea—that world peace was attainable and he was uniquely qualified and skilled to attain it, perhaps a legacy of the deeply influential Quaker mother to whom Nixon was so devoted—was a motivating force in Nixon's life and career. His enemies might laugh at the idea, but beneath that surface cynicism Nixon loved to exhibit, there beat the heart of a Wilsonian idealist.

A philosophical idealist, not an operational one, for in retrospect that admirer of Wilson would conduct a foreign policy of ruthless realism. He would play the Chinese off against the Russians, go to Peking and shake hands with the greatest mass murderer of the century, Mao Tse-tung, discard old friends like Chiang Kai-shek on Taiwan, mock liberal statesmen like Pierre Trudeau and Willy Brandt, embrace tough-minded butchers like Nicolae Ceausescu to split him off from Moscow, and demand an Israeli military halt before General Ariel Sharon could annihilate Egypt's Third Army east of the Suez Canal in the Yom Kippur War. While he did not go so far as General de Gaulle—"The state is a cold monster"— Nixon could be cold toward old friends if it required cutting deals with enemies to advance American interests. Even as Hanoi felt his Christmas Bombing fury at backsliding on the peace accords, so, too, did Saigon sense he was forcing them to make concessions at the expense of their security to end the war for the United States.

CHAPTER 7

"Year of the Dropouts"

RICHARD MILHOUS NIXON has performed the most remarkable feat of self-levitation in modern political history.
—STEWART ALSOP, *Saturday Evening Post* (1967)

THE NEW NIXON is a Nixon with a sense of humor, an attitude of detachment . . . a new political style and, lo, there is a new man.
—WARD JUST, *Washington Post* (MAY 1968)

I DON'T THINK Nixon can win elections . . . and particularly against a tremendous vote-getter like Romney.
—ROBERT NOVAK, ON *Firing Line* (1967)

IN EARLY DECEMBER 1967 Safire recommended that on the day he announced, Nixon should challenge Senator Eugene McCarthy to a debate on foreign policy. But with us far ahead of Romney, and his foreign policy preeminence conceded, I wrote Nixon, "Why do we want to put these kinds of stakes on the table against the meager benefits we might get of besting Eugene

McCarthy?" Why throw this "desperation pass" when we are far ahead in the polls? Debate challenges are for losing candidates.

"I agree," Nixon wrote back. But as he was looking for "something bold and imaginative," Rose and I had a suggestion. Given the multiple crises confronting the nation—race conflict, soaring crime, inflation, the war in Vietnam, the mounting Soviet missile threat—and the difficulty of dealing with them all at once, we suggested that Nixon in a single declaration destroy the image of him as a consummate politician and tell the nation "that the next President should be a one-term President." Our memorandum urged that Nixon close his announcement of candidacy with words like these: "I think that the next President must be a new President and he must enter office on the assumption that he will be there for four years only, one term. That is the assumption I would enter the Presidency with."

This would stun the press and nation. The idea had zero appeal to Nixon. When I spoke to him about it, he agreed the next President should govern as though he would have but one term to accomplish his goals, but make no such commitment. For he would then be a lame duck from his inaugural, and the campaigns to succeed him would begin as soon as he was elected. I never heard again about the idea. In retrospect, Nixon was right. Yet when one looks at what he accomplished in his first term and what became of his second, he would today be listed, like Polk, who sought and served but a single term, among the near-great Presidents.

"WHISKEY BEFORE BREAKFAST"

Soon after I began writing editorials for the *Globe-Democrat* I learned that publications like *Human Events* were reprinting them. One such was the *Manchester Union Leader*, run by the formidable William Loeb III, a godson of Theodore Roosevelt. His father, William Loeb, Jr., had been secretary to the President.

Loeb's *Union Leader*, known across New England as "whiskey before breakfast," was the most powerful voice in the first primary state. No other newspaper, radio station, or TV channel came close.

While at the law firm, I had begun a correspondence with Mr. Loeb, who wrote Nixon often, and with ruthless candor. In January 1968, Nixon got a letter from Loeb saying he had spent several hours with former governor George Wallace and was quite impressed. "This fellow is no dope," Loeb wrote, and added, "If Wallace runs as an independent, you might just as well forget the Republican nomination—it will be worthless."

"Find out what he wants and give it to him," he told Nixon. "It would be the best political bargain you ever made." At the top of Loeb's letter Nixon scribbled, "Pat, go up and have a chat with Loeb."

So it was that I paid a midwinter visit to the publisher of the *Union Leader*. However, the afternoon I flew to Boston and took the cab ride to Prides Crossing, where Loeb and his wife, Nackey, lived, there was a blizzard. The impatient cabby drove me up and down the long road on which the Loebs lived, but we could not see the numbers on the houses. We could hardly see anything. The cabby was about to dump me, when I asked him to make one more run up the road. As the cab crawled through the dark, snowy night, I suddenly told the driver to stop. In front of us was a parked vehicle with a bumper sticker that read "Stand Up for America!"

"I'll get out here," I told the driver.

Though I had never met them, Bill and Nackey Loeb treated me like the Prodigal Son. They prepared dinner, put me up in the guest room, offered me sherry, and brought cookies and hot chocolate and a book to read before I went to sleep. When I got back to New York, I told the Old Man we had a good friend at the *Union Leader*. And Bill and Nackey Loeb would remain my friends, backers, and benefactors for the rest of their lives.

———

DAYS AFTER NIXON announced, we were staying at a hotel in Boston and Loeb wanted a confidential visit with the candidate. However, a *Boston Globe* reporter had been assigned to cover Nixon, and told not to let him out of his sight. The reporter staked out a position on our floor and would see any visitor who got off the elevator. And Bill Loeb was famous, controversial, and recognizable, especially to a reporter for the liberal *Globe*, which would want to know what was up with a Nixon-Loeb secret meeting in Boston.

What to do? As the reporter was a red-faced Irishman, I suggested, at 9:30 a.m., half an hour before Loeb arrived, that we repair to the lobby bar. He readily assented. From where I positioned myself in the bar I watched Loeb enter the hotel and stride to the elevator. An hour later, Loeb exited the elevator and departed the hotel. The reporter never saw him. Mission accomplished. I told my new reporter friend I had to get back to work. A couple of beers before breakfast was not my idea of how to start a day.

THE HALDEMAN MEMO

One of the operative assumptions of the 1968 team was that the 1960 campaign had been mismanaged and the candidate mishandled. Nixon had pledged in 1960 to campaign in all 50 states and spent time in states he had no prayer of winning, such as Massachusetts, and no chance of losing, like Nebraska. Before the first debate he had been hospitalized for two weeks for a staph infection beneath the kneecap. When he left the hospital on September 9, Nixon added campaign stops to states he had missed. The Sunday before the first debate, he arrived in Chicago at 10:30 p.m., addressed a rally of 5,000, then motorcaded through five wards doing rally speeches in each, arriving at his hotel after 1 a.m.

Shelley said she was sleeping sitting up on the staff bus on the way to the hotel.

The morning of the debate, Nixon addressed the Carpenters Union convention, mostly Kennedy supporters. Nixon was campaigning till noon on the day he would be seen alongside Kennedy by 70 million Americans.

Nixon arrived at the studio first, Kennedy ten minutes later. Nixon commented on Kennedy's deep tan, which JFK said he got campaigning in convertibles in southern California. An aide urged Nixon to put on makeup. He rejected the idea, but accepted some "beard stick" powder to cover up his perpetual five o'clock shadow.

I heard the debate on radio with a Kennedy man. He agreed Nixon might have had the edge. On television it was a disaster. Nixon was ten pounds under his normal weight, and his face showed it and appeared abnormally pasty. When he got back to the hotel, Rose Woods told him her parents had called and asked if he was well. Nixon's mother called Rose to ask if her son was "feeling all right."

The impression Kennedy left in that first debate, his assertiveness, his youthful good looks, his relaxed demeanor, may have been decisive. The dramatic contrast, not so much in arguments as in appearances, cost Nixon the presidency. In a campaign, as critical as what a man says is how he looks—on television. While unfortunate, it is true. And that Nixon forgot this in the crucial first debate before the largest audience that had ever witnessed a political event remains astonishing.

NOT ONLY WAS Nixon's writing and media staff entirely new in 1968, we were all versed in the mistakes of 1960. We were not going to let that happen again. In 1968, we threw out the 1960 playbook and followed "the Haldeman memo," named for its author, who had run Nixon's 1962 campaign for governor. Bob Haldeman argued that in a presidential campaign, from Labor Day to election day, a candidate might be seen in person by 1,440,000 people—if he did six speeches a day, six days a week, for eight weeks, and had a spectacular advance team that produced an average of 5,000 people for every speech. Three of every four of these folks would already be loyalists, said Haldeman, asking, "What happens to the candidate in this process?" He answered his own question:

> He becomes punchy, mauled by his admirers, jeered and deflated by his opponent's supporters (and paid trouble-makers), misled by the super-stimulation of one frenzied rally after another. He has no time to think, to study his opponent's strategy and statements, to develop his own strategy and statements. No wonder the almost inevitable campaign dialogue borders so near the idiot level.

However, tens of millions would see the candidate on the evening news on any given night or on Sunday interview shows. With only one TV story about the candidate each night, and only two headlines a day—morning and evening newspapers—why should a candidate produce more than two fresh stories or pictures each day? All the candidate needed to provide the print and television media was a good story for the morning papers and a fresh story for the evening papers and evening TV.

All else was redundant or superfluous. Indeed, it might be worse than redundant or superfluous. Six or seven appearances a day must necessarily result in an exhausted, irritable Nixon and an uncontrolled message. Fewer appearances, better appearances—this was the formula, especially with Nixon, whose natural disposition was to drive himself to exhaustion.

We would road-test the theory against Romney, who was driving himself as hard in early 1968 as Nixon and Kennedy had in

1960. And it would work. Nixon's 1968 campaign was the first of the modern campaigns. Four years later, President Nixon would conduct a "Rose Garden" campaign and almost never mention the name of his opponent.

In late December 1967, Nick Thimmesch, who had been with *Time* and was now a columnist, came to see me at the Park Avenue headquarters to which Nixon's staff had moved from the law firm. Romney is a demon campaigner, said Thimmesch, he is tireless. He is hitting six and seven coffee klatches a day and speaking at night. You had better get up there before he wraps up the state. Nick, who liked Nixon, was a friend. I went to see Nixon. Should we step up the schedule? No, Nixon said. We have our plan. We stick to it. Not until the last day before the filing deadline did we fly secretly to Boston, drive up into New Hampshire, and announce the next morning, six weeks before the primary. We could not have cut it closer.

My concern about the intensive grassroots campaign Romney was running was that while he might not win, he could do well enough to claim a moral victory and lend credence to press claims that Nixon had fallen short of expectations, reinforcing the "He can't win in November!" theme.

THE *PUEBLO* AND THE TET OFFENSIVE

On January 22, 1968, a North Korean commando unit almost succeeded in an assassination attempt on President Park Chung-hee at the Blue House in Seoul. Two days later, the USS *Pueblo*, an intelligence and surveillance vessel, which had not been notified about the assassination attempt, was intercepted by North Korean gunboats, boarded, and seized in international waters, 16 miles off the coast, outside the 12-mile territorial limit. One U.S. crew member was killed and several wounded. This daylight hijacking of a U.S. naval vessel and North Korea's taking hostage 82 U.S. sailors was a national affront and humiliation. But Lyndon Johnson, fearing for the lives of Captain Lloyd "Pete" Bucher and his crew, did nothing to retaliate or retrieve the ship. Not until Nixon had been elected would North Korea, a month before his inauguration, let the American crew go. The next Democratic President, Jimmy Carter, would face a similar hostage crisis for 444 days, which would not end until his successor, Ronald Reagan, was also about to raise his hand and take the oath of office.

On the evening of January 31, a limo took Nixon, Price, Chapin, and me to the private terminal at LaGuardia. It was a horrible night. We flew through a snowstorm to the private terminal at Boston's Logan Airport, where we were met by Nick Ruwe, our advance man in charge of New Hampshire. We drove to Nashua and registered Nixon in a motel under the name "Benjamin Chapman," bringing him in through a side door. An inebriated fellow stumbling our way walked by in the hall, not recognizing one of the most recognizable faces in the world.

Before leaving LaGuardia, we had heard reports of heavy fighting in Vietnam with attacks on provincial capitals and Saigon. This was the Tet Offensive, launched on the lunar new year holiday during which the North Vietnamese had declared a truce. In the first days of Tet, 50,000 Viet Cong and North Vietnamese would strike across South Vietnam and lose tens of thousands in a drive to bring down the government and break the Americans who were facing rising opposition to the war at home. With their Tet Offensive and siege of the Marine base at Khe Sanh that had begun January 21 and would last into April, Hanoi thought it could break America as the Viet Minh had broken the French in 1954 at Dien Bien Phu.

Of concern to me was that my brother Jim, who had just graduated from dental school, had asked to be sent to Vietnam to fulfill his military obligation and had volunteered for the 101st Airborne. He had broken his foot on his first jump, missed the December deployment, but arrived in January and been assigned to a village between Saigon and Cambodia. The enemy who stormed Saigon and breached the U.S. embassy grounds passed him by coming and going.

On February 2, the *New York Times* carried a one-column story on page one—"Nixon Announces for Presidency"—beside a four-column lead story headlined: "Street Clashes Go On in Vietnam; Foe Still Holds Parts of Cities; Johnson Pledges Never to Yield." Beneath that headline was a four-column photograph of General Nguyen Ngoc Loan, the national police chief, putting a pistol inches from the head of a "Vietcong terrorist," and executing him. Eddie Adams's photo would win the Pulitzer. The Viet Cong prisoner had been caught murdering civilians. The "Saigon execution" photo would be one of the iconic images of the war, along with that of the naked little girl running down a road screaming after being burned by napalm.

Through February we followed the Tet Offensive. At its climax, 3,000 South Vietnamese civilians were found to have been executed, their names on lists handed to enemy soldiers in Hue, and U.S. Marines would spend the month eliminating resistance in the old imperial capital. While I did not hear the news until later, the prefect of discipline at Gonzaga my last year there, Father Aloysius P. McGonigal, SJ, had died in Hue, where he had gone to be with his beloved Marines when they charged the Citadel.

The photograph that went around the world from Tet, however, was not any picture of the 3,000 murdered South Vietnamese in Hue, but the Adams photo of the summary execution of that Viet Cong prisoner being shot in the head by Saigon's chief of police.

A "GOLDWATER PROBLEM"

Before departing for New Hampshire, Nixon received a warning from Robert Ellsworth, the Kansas congressman who had lost a primary challenge to Senator James Pearson in 1966. Ellsworth had belonged to the Wednesday Group, a small contingent of liberal House members led by John Lindsay of New York. Bob had met Nixon on a plane in 1966, impressed him, and been hired to run our Pennsylvania Avenue campaign office.

Ellsworth told Nixon he had a Goldwater problem that was "largely responsible for the 'Nixon Can't Win' syndrome." While Goldwater's "abstract conservative ideology" had broad support, wrote Ellsworth, the perception that Goldwater was an "operational conservative," who would reduce or repeal aid to education, Medicare, urban renewal, public housing grants, and jobs and poverty programs, had killed him. For 85 percent of the people were opposed to operational conservatism. They wanted America's problems dealt with and expected the federal government to play a major role. When talking of lawlessness, inflation, or other crises, Ellsworth wrote, "Nixon should express his . . . strong support for effective federal government action to bring it under control. The same may be said with respect to education, medical care, housing, race, jobs, pollution, etc."

Our weakness and Rockefeller's strength are tied to the perception, said Ellsworth, that Nixon, who had gone all out in 1964 for Goldwater, is like Goldwater an operational conservative, while Rockefeller comes across as a champion of government action. Nixon must dispel this impression by assuring the electorate he knows the federal government has a crucial role in dealing with "current domestic social problems." Ellsworth's arguments were drawn from *The Political Beliefs of Americans,* by Hadley Cantril and Lloyd Free, which had analyzed the operational and ideological concerns of Americans. At the top of the Ellsworth memo, Nixon wrote "good" and "Ray, Pat, read."

The Ellsworth memo of January 27 touched on the great divide of the party from the days of Goldwater, through the Nixon and Reagan eras, Bush I and Bush II, to the Tea Party. No president after Coolidge had been an operational conservative. None rolled back the Great Society. None sought to repeal the New Deal. Not even Reagan, who made the effort but failed to carry out his commitment to shut down Carter's departments of education and energy. It would be the inexorable growth of the Leviathan state under Republican and Democratic Presidents alike that would lead to the fiscal crisis that struck the U.S. in the twenty-first century. Undeniably, Ellsworth had a point. By 1968 Americans, whatever they told themselves and others, had come to accept Big Government as a permanent feature of public life. Selling TVA and making Social Security voluntary were dead ideas before Nixon headed for New Hampshire. Nixon could be a social and cultural conservative in that revolutionary decade, and a foreign policy hawk. But he risked defeat if he was perceived as a threat to Social Security or Medicare. Nobody in our camp was for that.

PRESS SECRETARY—FOR A DAY

On his third night in the Granite State, Nixon gave his maiden speech, featuring a Ray Price phrase he would use again and again in this era of acrimony and division: "We need the lift of a driving dream." After the speech in Concord we talked with Teddy White. He thought it good but not great.

On the opening trip to New Hampshire, Nixon and Haldeman, who had come east for the first days of the campaign, suggested that I act as press secretary, a role about which I was more than ambivalent. I had no desire to be the man between Nixon and those he routinely referred to as "the enemy." I told Thimmesch of this decision and he suggested I get on with it by going down with him to the bar and having drinks with the reporters.

We sat down at a table with Pat Ferguson of the *Baltimore Sun* and Robert Novak, whom I had not met. It was late afternoon and I ordered a beer, whereupon Novak began to unload on Nixon, who had slipped off that morning to Hillsborough to tape commercials without telling the press where he was going. When the press discovered Nixon had given them the slip, they were enraged. That this "new Nixon" was reverting to his old tricks was the conditioned reflex. As soon as I sat down, Novak, voice dripping with venom and sarcasm, started in. This talk of a "new Nixon" is flackery. This is the same old lying Nixon. Novak proceeded for five minutes to vomit on the candidate while treating me as some lackey sent to listen and report back to his masters.

Before I finished the beer I got up and went back to tell Haldeman to tell Nixon I was not cut out for this, that I had come close to sucker-punching a columnist on my first day, that I lacked the temperament to deal with these people, and to get someone else. Fortunately, Ron Ziegler came in from California to serve as press aide and would play that role until August 1974. In 2013, during an interview at my home about JFK and what our world would have been like had he lived, Tom Brokaw told me he had been offered the job by Haldeman. So, too, had Mike Wallace.

In 1982, when we became co-panelists on *The McLaughlin Group* and CNN's *Crossfire*, Novak became a cherished friend. I was at St. Patrick's when he was baptized. Still, Pat Moynihan had a point when he told me at Novak's party following the baptism, "Buchanan, now that we have made Novak a Catholic, do you think we can make him a Christian?"

TEN DAYS AFTER we got the Ellsworth memo, a column by Novak appeared, reporting on a "deep but hidden conflict among his advisers over the nature of the new Nixon":

A highly sophisticated group of Nixon advisers, not associated with disasters of the past and convinced that changes must be more than cosmetic, have been opposed at every turn by old-line Nixonites who resist any real change. The campaign kickoff made it clear that the new advisers have not yet won out.

Should Nixon not make these changes, the advisers were warning, he could be stopped by Rockefeller at the convention, or lose to Johnson in the fall. "[H]eaded by Robert Ellsworth, the innovative former Congressman from Kansas," the group was said to include Richard Whalen and Garment, and they "want Nixon to establish himself as an operational liberal . . . attuned to solving real problems." The columnists mentioned an "obscure new book, *The Political Beliefs of Americans*," by Cantril and Free. On Vietnam, these advisers "would like to see Nixon disassociate himself from the LBJ war policy" and attack President Johnson "for leading the U.S. into an 'unwinnable war.'" These advisers dismissed Nixon's Concord speech as a bore.

An almost identical story appeared in the *Economist*, which said that "a new group of youthful advisers to Mr. Nixon, calling themselves 'liberal' . . . believe that he must modernise himself in a post-Dulles mould to become president":

Most influential of these is Mr. Robert Ellsworth. . . .

The Ellsworth-Whalen group is privately advising Mr. Nixon that he must alter his frame of reference radically.

Primarily they believe that he should soften his line on Vietnam to the extent of saying that the war is now militarily unwinnable and that . . . the United States must now accelerate its efforts to bring an end to the fighting.

But for Nixon to declare himself now opposed to Vietnam and charge Lyndon Johnson with having led us into an "unwinnable war," then to convince primary voters he was an "operational liberal," would have been suicidal. I wondered: Could "these advisers" think that by pushing their side of our internal debate in the

Economist and a Novak column, they would persuade the candidate? What were they doing? Did they not know Nixon?

ROCKEFELLER VS. LINDSAY

After our first trip to New Hampshire we returned to a New York City whose sanitation workers, in defiance of the Taylor Law, had been on strike since February 1. Ten thousand tons of garbage had been piling up daily on city sidewalks. Mayor Lindsay had offered the workers two-thirds of the pay hike the union was demanding. It was not enough. As the *Daily News* described the city those days, "Ten thousand persons walked off their jobs. Rubbish fires flamed nightly. Storm sewers backed up. Hungry rats swarmed in by the battalion. The grim specter of deadly disease stalked the streets."

For the first time since a polio outbreak in 1931, the Board of Health declared a state of emergency. Lindsay asked Governor Rockefeller to call out the National Guard. But rather than confront the union and risk a general strike, Rockefeller stepped in and ended the strike—by giving the union all that it had demanded. Whereupon, all hell broke loose.

"Sellout," said the *Daily News*, "unforgivable betrayal of the public interest!" By fifty-to-one, New Yorkers backed Lindsay's stance over Rocky's capitulation. We issued a statement saying that neither the health of a city nor the safety of its citizens should "be made hostages on the table of collective bargaining," and in echo of Governor Cal Coolidge in the Boston police strike, that "no union has the right to strike against the public health or safety." Blackmail, Nixon said, must not succeed. Rockefeller, who prided himself on being a problem-solver, never did understand the new conservative party to which he now belonged—or the Middle America of '68.

"A LOSER" NO LONGER

Nixon's New Hampshire campaign was a masterpiece, flawless in conception and execution. Among the reasons we exhibited what Mark Twain called the calm confidence of a Christian with four aces is that before we arrived in New Hampshire we had polls showing us beating Romney 4– and 5–1. The pressure was on Romney, not us. I had sent an "Outline of Strategy" to Nixon—which would be leaked by our media people to Joe McGinniss and reprinted in *The Selling of the President*—urging that we make the minimum number of appearances in New Hampshire necessary to show we cared. We simply needed to avoid mistakes and run out the clock. From announcement day to election day was six weeks. To Romney's call for debates, Nixon should respond that our debate was with Lyndon Johnson, that all Republicans should make the case against his administration in what Nixon called "the fires of the primaries." This underscored the point that neither Reagan nor Rockefeller had dared to challenge Nixon in those primaries. While Nixon believed he had to win the primaries, probably all of them to ensure his nomination, we had a retort to Republicans feeding the press on background that Nixon was a loser. If Nixon is such a loser, we said, why don't they come out into the primaries and prove it?

I always felt we benefited from our adversaries' focus on Nixon as loser. For the loser label would disappear if we simply started winning. On November 22, I had sent Nixon a paper about this entitled "The Loser Problem." Romney and the liberals, I wrote, are making "a grave error in placing all their chips in the 'loser' basket." Should we win in New Hampshire, where we were running far ahead, they "are going to have to shift the entire emphasis of their attack. . . . They can't very well say 'Nixon is a loser but he can beat the hell out of us.'"

My concern is not too much with the loser, as long as we get a hung jury on this until we win N.H. . . . My fear is that they will revive the "ruthless," "tricky" crap. . . . This is the sort of thing that could not only damage us in the primary, but could stick to us and damage us in the General.

Nixon thought this a "good analysis." To my surprise, our opponents never really went after Nixon's character as the Kennedy crowd had in 1960. Perhaps what they had done to Goldwater and how they alienated so many for having done it inhibited these attacks. Given the rising hopes of the GOP that winter of 1968, perhaps they realized that any personal attacks would backfire inside the party. Those were the days, at least in public, when the 11th Commandment—Thou shalt not speak ill of another Republican—still seemed operative.

FOLLOWING THE HALDEMAN memo, we would schedule Nixon hard for two or three days in New Hampshire, then pull him out of the state, fly him to some other primary state, or Key Biscayne, and let our ads carry the campaign, while Romney was doggedly and desperately trooping across the state trying to get traction. As in 1966, Nixon was a Spartan campaigner. He would come back from the evening event, sip a beer, and be quickly in bed, while those of us on his small traveling staff repaired to the bar to join the traveling press. But when Nixon headed for Florida, he began to unwind—on the plane.

I recall one of our first trips out of Manchester in a four-seat Learjet, where Nixon, sitting beside Ray, behind Dwight and me, asked for a vodka and Fresca. Dwight fixed it and handed it back. Then we fixed our own drinks. We had not finished our first when we heard from behind us Nixon bellowing, "I love those little brown people!"

Dwight looked at me and it was all we could do not to start laughing. Nixon had finished one drink and was burbling his affection for Asians. But to a listener hearing him it would have seemed like he had had five. Over the years, people would ask me about his drinking. My assessment: Nixon worked so hard, was wound up so tight, was so exhausted from his work that, when he let down, all it took was one or two to make it appear he was sloshed when his blood alcohol level might have passed a police sobriety test.

When we landed at an airport in South Carolina that night to refuel, Dwight and I left Nixon on the plane when we went into the terminal for snacks. We had been there but minutes when we saw Nixon strolling toward us smiling. Doing our best to avoid any untoward encounter, we hustled him back to the plane and flew on to Miami, where Bebe Rebozo picked us up at 2 a.m. Nixon said he wanted a bowl of chili. So we all headed to a chili parlor in downtown Miami Bebe knew about. It was nearly empty. But as the five of us sat eating chili at our table, a guy sitting at the counter kept turning around, not believing who it was he was seeing there in the middle of the night at a chili parlor in Miami.

Bebe dropped Ray, Dwight, and me off at the Key Biscayne Hotel on the ocean side. He and Nixon headed to his house a mile away on Biscayne Bay. There we would stay for two or three days as the Boss charged his batteries. Meanwhile, Romney, tireless, was trudging through the snows of New Hampshire, his polls, like ours, showing us beating him five-to-one. His billboards— "ROMNEY FIGHTS MORAL DECAY!"— while ridiculed as reading like toothpaste ads, indicate that the governor or his pollsters were plugged in to the rising alarm in the heart of America over the soaring crime rate, the drug culture, and the sexual revolution. Romney's perseverance was attested to at one duckpin bowling alley, where, after knocking down several pins with three balls, he went on to roll thirty-four balls before he downed the last pin, to the anguish of his staff and amusement of bystanders.

"The episode was a metaphor for George Romney, the man who never knew when he was licked," wrote Witcover in *The Year the Dream Died*. Meanwhile, Nixon would spend two or three days in New Hampshire, fly to New York or Key Biscayne, then to Wisconsin, Indiana, Nebraska, or Oregon, the next battleground states. Our media strategy was to go over the heads of the writing press, using television, both bought and free. We wanted to bypass the print press who stood between Nixon and the voters and, as best we could, control the message that went to the country.

Our political strategy was to engage only Democrats. We had not invented the 11th Commandment about not speaking ill of another Republican, but Nixon scrupulously observed it in his public treatment of Romney, Rockefeller, and Reagan. By focusing his attacks on Johnson and his record, and on Humphrey and Robert Kennedy for rendering aid and comfort to protesters and urban rioters, Nixon unified his party. His GOP rivals, running behind Nixon and raising questions about his electability, appeared to be reopening the wounds of 1964. Nobody wanted that.

Privately, through a mail operation Nixon was aware of, we made sure the worst attacks on him were made known to Republican officeholders and party officials so they could see who was trying to unite the party and who was seeking to divide it for his own benefit.

As NIXON WAS speaking on February 28 in Milford, New Hampshire, a reporter told me that Don Oliver of NBC, my friend from Columbia J-School, was trying to reach me. When I contacted Oliver, who had been assigned to cover Romney, he told me Romney was dropping out, the announcement was imminent, and word was spreading through his press corps. I ran back to the hall and told Dwight, and we waited to intercept Nixon and cut him off from the press as he came down from the platform. Reporters were starting to crowd around, but we hustled Nixon into the men's room, where I told him the news and the name of my source. By then the news had reached our press corps, and they were waiting for us. When Nixon exited, I think it was Mike Wallace who told him Romney was dropping out and asked his reaction. Feigning astonishment, Nixon said this was the first he'd heard of it. I stood back and said nothing.

By day's end Nixon had scored "the first TKO in the history of presidential politics." Even the *New York Times* was conceding that it was "difficult to continue describing as a loser a man who is so overwhelmingly powerful that no challenger will even take him on." Yet Governor Romney had cheated us of the victory we were about to win. "Just like a businessman, no guts," said Nixon that night. Many of us shared the sentiment. What would the press have said about Nixon, had he, to rob an opponent of his moment of triumph, sat on his stool and refused to come out for the final round?

The day after Romney withdrew, I sent a memo to Bill Loeb asking for his thinking on how serious the write-in effort for Rockefeller in New Hampshire would be now, and how we should play it. Attached to my memo was an editorial I had worked up to which I gave the title "Nelse the Knife." It described how Rocky "sat on his backside" and refused to help Nixon in 1960, ran "one of the dirtiest and most divisive and most destructive political campaigns in history" against Goldwater, reneged on his deal to support Senator Jacob Javits—who had had his eye on the VP nomination in 1968, as New York's favorite son—and stabbed Mayor John Lindsay with his "backroom sellout to the garbage collectors union" whose strike Lindsay was resisting. And by telling the press—in Michigan while Romney was in New Hampshire—that he would run if drafted, Rocky had cut the legs out from under Romney. "Nelse the Knife" concluded:

The political history of Nelson Rockefeller is one of exploitation of his party for personal gain. He is a man who has used the political corpses of his fellow Republicans as stepping stones to power. The latest former friend and national figure to turn up in the Rockefeller body count is George Romney.

Loeb loved it. He put his own byline on it and ran it on page one. I had not known this when we flew back to the Granite State. But a Nixon man came aboard our plane, wild with excitement about Loeb's front-page editorial, and was showing it to Nixon. Nixon called me forward, handed me the guy's *Union Leader* with the "Nelse the Knife" front-page editorial, and said, "Buchanan, why can't you write like this?" It was Nixon who had told me to send the editorial to Loeb.

HUNTER THOMPSON

That February, Hunter Thompson, already a minor legend, arrived in New Hampshire. Hunter had achieved fame with a book about the Hells Angels, after having horsed around for a year with the motorcycle gang in San Francisco. Hunter said he was writing a piece on Nixon for *Pageant* magazine. My first date with Shelley was spent in the hotel room of *Newsweek*'s Jayne Brumley, to which Hunter had brought half a gallon of Wild Turkey. He and I consumed it while getting into a shouting match about the Soviet Union. The row continued almost to daylight. We would later become friends, but Hunter would write in *Pageant* that July that Buchanan is "a rude sort of geek with a Southern accent."

We promised Hunter face time with the candidate, who was skeptical of freelancers. From a hall in Nashua to the Manchester airport Hunter rode in the car with Nixon. They talked football. When we got to the airport, Nick Ruwe, Nixon's driver, was overseeing the fueling of the Learjet that would take us to Miami.

Hunter, cigarette dangling from his lips, started flicking his lighter while standing beside the wing of the plane as it was being refueled. Nick almost slapped it out of his hand. The possibility existed that Hunter that night could have blown himself, Nixon, and the rest of us into the next world.

NIXON'S "SECRET PLAN"

The lone Nixon gaffe of the primaries came after Romney pulled out. It was a product of the pressure Nixon was under from liberal advisers to say he would end the war in Vietnam. Egged on by ex–attorney general Herb Brownell among others, Nixon altered his position slightly at the American Legion Hall in Hampton, New Hampshire, on March 5, declaring, "I pledge to you that new leadership will end the war and win the peace in the Pacific." I was in Washington when I heard this and was alarmed. How Nixon was going to do this, he did not say. The press seized on "the pledge" and distorted it to say that Nixon had claimed he had a "secret plan" to end the war. This was patently false. They then demanded that Nixon reveal his plan—to save American lives. This forced Nixon to deny repeatedly he ever said he had a secret plan and to fall back on his formulaic response that "new leadership" could use the diplomatic, military, and economic resources of the nation "to end the war and win the peace."

When Nixon won in November, press cynics, after castigating him for months for allegedly claiming he had a secret plan when he had none, spun around, and said Nixon had won only because he lied about having a secret plan. To this day the myth lives. The truth: Nixon never said he had any "secret plan" to end the war in Vietnam.

Our Washington staff, however, was still testing the patience of New York. Hours after our New Hampshire triumph, the *Cleveland Plain Dealer* ran a story out of its Washington bureau, quoting a "top figure in the Nixon campaign" as declaring, "Absolutely not," in answer to a query as to whether Ohio governor Jim Rhodes might be a running mate for Nixon.

This was gratuitous and stupid. Rhodes, as a favorite son, would be leading one of the largest delegations at Miami Beach. Since 1966, we had been courting him. When Ohio newsmen pressed me in 1966 about Rhodes, I told them, at Nixon's instructions, that not only would he be on any short list for VP, he should have been on the cover of *Newsweek* and *Time* with Rockefeller, Reagan, and Romney, as he had won as impressive a victory and had helped bring in new GOP House members. So serious was this uninformed insult to Rhodes, Mitchell directed his top aide, Tom Evans, to call James Naughton of the *Plain Dealer* to ask who this Nixon strategist was, as he did not speak for the campaign.

When we got to the convention in Miami Beach, Rhodes would refuse to release his Ohio delegates on the first ballot. Had he done so, we would not have needed to sweat all the way down the roll call to Wisconsin to win the nomination.

WITH ROMNEY'S DEPARTURE from the race, press attention went to the Democratic side and Eugene McCarthy's challenge to Johnson, whose name was not even on the ballot in New Hampshire. The President of the United States was a write-in candidate. Why the White House allowed this escaped me. By not filing, by not having Lyndon Johnson's name on the ballot, the White House was assuring McCarthy a larger share of the vote than he would otherwise receive. Democratic voters, arriving at the polling place, must have been puzzled at the absence of the President's name from the ballot.

To show we had bipartisan strength in the state, I drafted a letter to New Hampshire Democrats, urging them to write in Richard Nixon. This operation had no connection to our campaign. Nixon read it and told me to cut it down to one page. The four issues hit in the mailer—"greatest crime wave in our history has swept across this land," "successive summers of race violence," "piecemeal escalation in Vietnam" frittering away "the greatest military advantages in history," and "Johnson Inflation." We had more than 100,000 printed up and addressed to New Hampshirites, and I made a cash contribution one night to a Conservative Party leader to have the letters trucked up to the Granite State to be mailed from there so they would carry a New Hampshire postmark. This secret project was a smashing success. Nixon won almost 5 percent of the votes cast in the Democratic primary, four times the number of Democratic write-in votes for Robert Kennedy.

So impressed was Nixon with the success of our secret direct-mail write-in campaign in New Hampshire that when Huston suggested we use this under-the-radar approach in Oregon, I sent his memo to Nixon. Nixon wrote back "good idea," adding "1. We may want a write in in California (Keep this in confidence now). 2. If no direct mail in Oregon Budget—see what it would cost. . . . 3. What other states have write in possibilities?" A clandestine write-in campaign in California would have been costly, given the size of the state, and risky. For Governor Reagan had planned to come to Miami Beach as the Golden State's favorite son.

Though Romney had dropped out twelve days before the primary, Nixon's vote total, 80,667, was the largest cast for any candidate in a New Hampshire primary, larger than the totals of Romney, Rockefeller, Johnson, McCarthy, and Kennedy combined. A record number of independents had gone for Nixon. Understandably, the press was caught up in the dramatic showing of McCarthy, 42 percent to Lyndon Johnson's 49 percent write-in vote. And though half of the McCarthy voters were said to have wanted a tougher policy in Vietnam, the President was cut and bleeding. Lyndon Johnson sat atop a majority party at war with itself—over the war.

THE TIME OF THE OPPORTUNIST

Since I first arrived at Nixon's office, Robert Kennedy's star had been rising. In a February 1966 Gallup poll of potential Democratic nominees for 1968, which listed President Johnson, Robert Kennedy, Hubert Humphrey, and Robert McNamara, Johnson led Kennedy among Democrats 52–26. But by January 1967, the situation had been reversed. Kennedy led Johnson 43–34. In the head-to-head poll it was Kennedy 48, Johnson 39.

By 1966 Kennedy had begun his trek leftward, which, if he did plan to challenge Johnson in 1968, was the way to go. After the Watts riot of 1965 Kennedy had given conditional absolution to the rioters: "There is no point in telling Negroes to obey the law [because] to many Negroes the law is the enemy."

On March 25, 1966, I memoed Nixon that "RFK is scoring heavily with these trips to Alabama and Mississippi and with the future trip to South Africa." He "loses nothing in the Deep South," as he has "nothing to lose there," but because "it is a jaunt into Indian country it captures the attention of the people and press."

"[B]y stating his opinions openly and frankly to people hostile to both him and what he stands for, he strengthens his support among his own who come to think of him as a fearless leader of their cause," I wrote, and he "appeals to young people . . . who admire any individual who will take the trouble to come to them and spell out his views—even if they disagree."

> [I]nvariably some of the hooded knights of the KKK or their fellow travelers can be counted upon to put abroad some rumor that Kennedy will be shot . . . and thus it looks to the country as though Robert Kennedy is explaining his views to the South at personal risk. And there are few things the American people admire more than individual guts.

Kennedy's opening to the Left continued. On *Face the Nation*, November 26, 1967, RFK had done a passable imitation of Jane Fonda: "We're killing children—we're killing women—we're killing innocent people because we don't want to have the war fought on American soil or because [the Communists] are 12,000 miles away and they might get to be 11,000."

Four days after the returns came in from New Hampshire, Kennedy, who had spurned appeals to run against Johnson, jumped in. His belated entry fairly reeked of opportunism, and in a *New York Post* column, "Sen. Kennedy, Farewell," Kempton lacerated the man he had admired. Noting that in January, after McCarthy had declared, Kennedy approved a resolution pledging New York Democrats to "continued loyalty and vigorous support" of the President, Kempton went on brutally, "He did that from cowardice; nothing has happened since, except that President Johnson was bloodied in New Hampshire; and Sen. Kennedy is just as much a coward when he comes down from the hills to shoot the wounded."

He has, in the naked display of his rage at Eugene McCarthy for having survived on the lonely road he dared not walk himself, done with a single great gesture something very few public men have ever been able to do: In one day, he managed to confirm the worst things his enemies have ever said about him. We can see him now working for Joe McCarthy, tapping the phones of tax dodgers, setting a spy on Adlai Stevenson at the UN, sending good loyal Arthur Schlesinger to fall upon William Manchester in the alleys of the American Historical Association.

With his late entry to shoulder aside McCarthy, who had the courage to take on the President when all thought it a futile and fatal enterprise, Bobby Kennedy had reinforced his reputation from

his days as campaign chief to JFK and years as attorney general—
that of "ruthless Robert."

After declaring, Kennedy began savaging the wounded President he had never wanted on his brother's ticket in 1960. On
March 22 in Nashville, he blamed the nation's divisions not on the
rioters or campus anarchists but on the architect of the Great Society:

> Who is it who is truly dividing the country? It is not those
> who call for change. It is those who make present policy, those
> who bear the responsibility for our present course, those who
> have removed themselves from the American tradition, from
> the enduring and generous impulses that are the soul of this
> nation.

On March 24, the *Times* quoted him: "Poverty, death and the
maiming of young men in the swamps of Vietnam is indecent." The
next day, Kennedy laid it all at the feet of Lyndon Johnson, charging
that our "national leadership is calling upon the darker impulses of
the American spirit." I pulled together and sent to Nixon a collection of such quotes. He wrote back, "Pat: Collect—Get others
to work on it. There are much better ones available." Nixon was
anticipating that Robert F. Kennedy just might be his opponent in
the fall.

Many in the Nixon camp, with memories of 1960, were fearful
of Kennedy, the name, and the magic. I never was. I preferred him
as the Democratic nominee, but doubted he would be the man. To
me Bobby was nothing like his charismatic brother, nor had he any
of JFK's conservative and centrist appeal. By 1968 he had moved
far to the left to attract the students and antiwar movement and he
was savaging his own President. I did not think he could take the
nomination from Johnson. And if he did, I did not think he could
unite his party. A Kennedy-Johnson battle would be their version of
our Goldwater-Rockefeller war. In a Kennedy-Nixon-Wallace race

in the fall, we would likely have the silent support of the President of the United States, so great was Johnson's detestation of Bobby. We might even have Governor John Connally lending us a hand in Texas if Robert Kennedy was at the top of the Democratic ticket.

While it was too late for Kennedy to enter the Wisconsin primary of April 2, he headed for Indiana, whose primary was May 7. There were now two challengers to President Johnson on the Democratic side. But with Governor Romney's withdrawal 12 days before New Hampshire, Nixon had no declared rival. And only two men could now conceivably stop him: the governor of California, Ronald Reagan, and the governor of New York, Nelson Rockefeller, the leader for a decade of the Eastern Liberal Establishment of the Republican Party.

BEHIND ROCKY'S RELUCTANCE

Immediately upon Kennedy's entry came word that Rockefeller would hold his own press conference March 21. Having repeatedly expressed his lack of interest in ever running again, would Rockefeller now plunge in to challenge us in the middle and late primaries, as he had fought Goldwater to the convention floor in 1964?

We did not fear a Rockefeller challenge. I did not believe that after his performance at the Cow Palace in 1964 and his refusal to endorse Goldwater he had a prayer of beating Nixon. But if a Rockefeller entry was followed by a Reagan entry, they could deadlock the convention. If Rockefeller and Reagan could amass sufficient votes, they, along with favorite-son candidates like Romney in Michigan and Governor Jim Rhodes in Ohio, could prevent a first-ballot nomination for Nixon and throw the convention wide open. Should that happen, there was a possibility that, given the conservative character of the post-Goldwater party of 1968, this could produce a stampede to Reagan, once delegates had been released from their obligations to vote for primary winners and favorite sons.

While it was difficult to believe Rockefeller would hold a press conference five days after Kennedy had plunged in, unless he, too, had decided to run, there were reasons to believe he might not. In late December, Drew Pearson had written—not in his column, which was carried in more papers than any other column in America, but in his private newsletter—that Rockefeller was involved with a young staffer. After his divorce from his wife of many years, Mary, known as Tod, and his marriage to divorcée "Happy" Murphy, who had given birth to his son three days before the California primary in 1964, which Rockefeller lost, another scandal would have dynamited any remote chance he had of being the nominee. No divorced man had ever been elected president. A source deep inside Rockefeller's office said it was true, and gave us the girl's name. The Albany press corps had to know this. Yet no one wrote it. Rockefeller was not a candidate and had declared he would not be a candidate. In those days, as JFK's charmed career testifies, politicians who were press favorites got a pass on their personal lives. Yet to announce for President with this rumor hanging out there seemed a huge personal and political risk.

A generation later, in a more permissive and indulgent era, an extramarital affair would destroy the candidacy of the front-runner for the Democratic nomination, Gary Hart. A similar report almost derailed Bill Clinton in New Hampshire in 1992. An extramarital affair terminated the career of the 2004 vice presidential nominee, John Edwards.

Something else might hold Rockefeller back: the primary calendar. Should he declare on March 21, Rockefeller would face Nixon in Indiana on May 7 and in the Nebraska primary on May 14. And Rocky was a mortal lock to lose both. Indiana, where Hannah Milhous had been born, was Nixon country, and Nebraska had been Nixon's strongest state against JFK.

Not until May 28 did the Oregon primary come around, which Governor Rockefeller had won in 1964. But a thrashing by Nixon in Nebraska, two weeks before Oregon, would be a humiliation that would demoralize the Rockefeller supporters in Oregon. Rocky was boxed. For him to enter before the filing deadlines passed for Indiana and Nebraska would be suicidal, drawing him into battle on turf where Nixon not only held the high ground but held unassailable ground. And we were in touch with Nebraska governor "Nobby" Tiemann and his secretary of state. We had their assurances that if Rocky delayed announcing for President until the filing deadline had passed in the Cornhusker State, they would open up the ballot and stick Rocky's name on it so Nixon could give him a thrashing on May 14.

Yet Rockefeller had called this press conference and we wondered: Would he do this if he were not running? In Annapolis, his most outspoken supporter and admirer among the governors, Ted Agnew, had invited the press to join him in watching Rockefeller declare. At the New York hotel suite where we were that day, Nixon retreated to the bedroom and told Dwight and me to watch the press conference and to report exactly what Rockefeller said. He was not going to watch himself, but he wanted our immediate reactions and impressions.

As Rockefeller began, Dwight and I sat stunned:

> I have decided today to reiterate unequivocally that I am not a candidate campaigning, directly or indirectly, for the Presidency of the United States.
>
> I have said that I stood ready to answer to any true and meaningful call from the Republican Party to serve it and the nation. I still so stand. . . .
>
> I expect no such call. And I shall do nothing in the future, by word or deed, to encourage such a call.

Rockefeller said he had written an affidavit to have his name removed from the Oregon ballot: "It is my complete conviction that this is the truest service I now can give to my party and my country."

Dwight and I rushed to the bedroom. "He's not running!"

"It's the girl," said Nixon.

During his disavowal of any intention to run, Rockefeller decried the cynicism of the times and asked America to accept the sincerity of his words: "We live in an age when the word of a political leader seems to invite instant and general suspicion. I ask to be spared any measure of such distrust. I mean—and I shall abide by—precisely what I say."

Well, we *were* suspicious of his motives, and we *did* distrust him, and we were right. Six weeks later, Rockefeller declared his availability and was fishing for an alliance with Reagan to block Nixon from being nominated on the first ballot.

Rockefeller's stunning announcement had unintended consequences. He had failed to alert his most devoted followers, among them Governor Agnew, national chairman of the three-week-old "Rockefeller for President" citizens' committee. As Jules Witcover wrote, Rockefeller had humiliated Agnew, a proud man, who had invited the press in to watch as his champion declared for the Republican nomination:

[T]he governor of Maryland was mortified. If ever there was a politician who climbed out on a limb and had it sawed off behind him, that politician was Spiro Agnew. It might not have been so bad had he not confidently invited the local press to share his moment of glory. But here he was, not only naked in his humiliation, but naked on television.

"Almost immediately," wrote Witcover, "political agents of Richard Nixon had been in touch with Agnew, eager to field him on the first short bounce." Within a week Agnew was in New York meeting with Nixon.

Just days after Rockefeller announced he would not run, an astounding column appeared. Drew Pearson, who first aired the rumors of Rocky's girlfriend, and first published reports of a "homosexual ring" in Reagan's office, announced that he—after being pressed by newspapers and magazines as to whether he planned to break a story about a Rockefeller affair—had decided to investigate. He had found, said Pearson, that Rocky's "second marriage is most harmonious and compatible," and "there is no truth to the report"—that is, to the rumor Pearson had himself first circulated.

Who could have been the source of such nasty rumors? Pearson had a prime suspect:

> It was impossible to trace the rumors to their exact origin, but it was ascertained that they had been spread in part by supporters of Richard Nixon. It was also ascertained that Nixon has compiled dossiers on men who might challenge him for the Republican nomination.
>
> At the time of the controversy over the two homosexuals on the staff of Gov. Ronald Reagan of California, it became known that Nixon's "Reagan file" was in the possession of ex-congressman Pat Hillings (R-Calif.), one of Nixon's close associates. Hillings could not leak information from the file, however, without Nixon's personal approval, which in this case was not given.

Without a shred of evidence, Pearson was trying to shift to our office and Nixon personal responsibility for two scandals I had never heard of—until reading Pearson. What a snake! Fortunately, we had friends in the press. Reporters covering Nixon said they never heard Nixon aides discuss any Rockefeller affair, but "first heard rumors about the Governor's personal life from aides of Governor George Romney." The *Richmond News Leader* nailed the bastard. "One gags" at this smear of Mr. Nixon, said the *News Leader* editorial:

The Rockefeller rumor has been circulating through every cocktail party in Washington for the past four months. The tale has been passed along and clucked over by liberals, conservatives, Democrats, and Republicans, by people who are pro-Nixon and anti-Nixon. But do you know what the one prime source of the rumor was?

Not Richard Nixon or any person close to him.

The one prime source was Drew Pearson himself in his "Personal from Pearson" newsletter of December 23, 1967. It was Drew Pearson himself who first put in writing and circulated the item "even including the name of an alleged girl friend."

The *Richmond Times-Dispatch* called the "sly imputation" that Nixon was behind the rumors Pearson had spread himself "a classic example of the Drew Pearson technique in action." Jack Anderson, Pearson's colleague, who inherited his column, confided to me one day in the White House that his former partner was not always a truthful man.

In mid-June, as Rockefeller began to savage Nixon, we were provided, courtesy of an ex–FBI agent, a clipping from 1963 about an ex-senator who had given the commencement address at Rosemary Hall girls' school in Greenwich. The senator believed the conduct of the governor of New York was symptomatic of America's sinking moral standards:

Have we come to the point where a Governor can desert his wife and children, and persuade a young woman to abandon her four children and husband?

Have we come to the point where one of the two great parties will confer its greatest honor on such a one? I venture to hope not.

Have we gotten so the American people will elect such a man? I venture to hope not. . . .

Are we ready to say goodbye to the solemn pledge "to have and to hold until death do us part"? Young ladies, I hope not, for your sake.

The senator who spoke these words to the graduates at Rosemary Hall on June 7, 1963, was Prescott Bush, the father and the grandfather of future Presidents and a moral and social conservative who believed that adulterous misconduct betrayed a lack of character in a man, and took a stand in those early days of America's culture wars. Not until rummaging through old files in writing this book did I stumble on the ex–FBI man's letter to Rose.

THE WAR DEBATE

Even before the victory in New Hampshire we had campaigned in Wisconsin, where we had a crack organization built by John MacIver, a big, burly, boisterous man who took the Nixon staff out to dinner one night at his favorite restaurant. As we entered, MacIver bellowed, "Bartender! Drinks all around and fresh horses for my men!" The whole restaurant burst into laughter.

Nixon was at the top of his game, and cruising unopposed toward the nomination. Yet, with the Tet Offensive, Kennedy entering the race, and Gene McCarthy's showing in New Hampshire, Vietnam was the blazing issue, and an intense battle was going on in Nixon's inner circle: Should Nixon deliver a national address modifying and updating his position on the war and the bombing of North Vietnam? Clearing up the problem of the Nixon "pledge" in New Hampshire to end the war was a propellant for those who wanted a speech.

The protagonist was Richard Whalen, another ex–editorial

writer and author of *The Founding Father*, the best-seller about Joe Kennedy, patriarch of the Kennedy clan. Whalen, as he relates in *Catch the Falling Flag*, wanted Nixon to break with Johnson on the war and move toward a more dovish position.

I was against any shift, or any speech. I had argued successfully against Nixon's writing a book, contending that no matter how many copies sold, our adversaries—in the White House, press, and party—would seize on some passage or shift in position to drive a wedge through our center-right coalition. No potential gain from a Nixon book outweighed the risks. If even Nixon's enemies were conceding he knew more about foreign policy than any of his rivals, we already held the knowledge and experience cards. What we had to prove was that Nixon was a winner.

My theory of the campaign of 1968 was that the Democratic Party, eight years in power, was at a natural disadvantage. They had a record—on crime, Vietnam, spending, the riots. They had to defend fixed positions. While the Democratic Party may have been twice as large as ours, we had the mobility of an Indian raiding party—to attack where and when we chose. For us to move to a new position on Vietnam would cause people to question our constancy and consistency, and Nixon's commitment to victory. Any shift on Vietnam would surrender the advantage a challenger almost always has. He attacks. The incumbent defends. I was most fearful of Nixon's adopting a dovish position that would provide an opening to attack us and a reason to plunge into the race for the conservative governor of California.

Moreover, there was no need to change. We had no opponent in the race. We had won New Hampshire with a record turnout. We were headed for a triumph in Wisconsin. If there was a necessity to revise our position on Vietnam, as events unfolded after Tet, we had months to do it. Why move now? When it is not necessary to change, it is necessary not to change.

At one point in the argument in front of Nixon, Whalen, after making the case for what was his speech, looked over at me and said, "Now, let's hear from the bomber lobby." And I did believe that we ought not rule out escalation—bombing the North, mining Haiphong harbor, destroying the dams on the upper Mekong to break Hanoi, prime mover of this war to conquer the South. For Hanoi now enjoyed the privileged sanctuary MacArthur said we must never tolerate. Long after he departed the presidency, Nixon came to the same conclusion, telling me he should have done in 1969 what he did in 1972: mine Haiphong and put the B-52s over Hanoi.

NO MORE TROOPS

As the March debate among Nixon, Whalen, Price, and Buchanan went on, and the issue of 200,000 more troops for General West-moreland was being argued in the administration, I wrote Nixon, "[W]e are at a watershed now."

> There is no question in my mind but that if the Administra-tion had closed Haiphong and torn up North Vietnam in a month or so in 1965 that we could have prevailed in the South and the war would be at a level where we could reduce our commitments. We lacked the guts to act then—preferring to let the US ground troops take the risk of fighting it out with the Vietnamese rather than take the risk of our going eyeball to eyeball with the Russians.

"[P]iecemeal escalation, gradualism . . . [have] failed dismally" as a war strategy, I wrote. We have "closed off a number of options, such as an invasion of the North, crossing the DMZ, invading Laos or Cambodia, and yet if we favor 200,000 more [troops] we almost de facto commit them to the same old strategy." Nixon underlined the last paragraph of my memo.

There are one hell of a lot of hard questions which time and circumstance are forcing us to answer and I think it would be criminal for the United States to pour more troops into South Vietnam—if we know beforehand that these troops and this strategy are going to be no more successful than what we have followed in the past.

"War's very object is victory, not prolonged indecision," MacArthur had said. "In war there is no substitute for victory." When we committed to Vietnam we should have gone in to win, or we should not have gone in. But, then, as Dean Rusk said, now "[w]e are there—and we are committed."

NIXON WAS MOVING ahead with the Whalen draft and the speech was scheduled for taping on Saturday, March 30. On the Ray Price "2nd Draft," however, Nixon had recoiled at the tone. "Talk about Hope," he wrote at the top. "Defeatism bad." Following the line in the draft "Unless a start is made soon in a new direction the war will be lost, and this would set in motion a chain of events the results of which would be catastrophic," Nixon wrote emphatically: "Can be won." Where the draft read, "I do not charge the President with lying," Nixon struck the line out and scribbled in "Adm officials are devoted to peace." After the draft quoted Martin Luther King that America was "the greatest purveyor of violence in the world today"—without identifying King as author of the words— Nixon scribbled again, "President—loyal—Rusk." He was ordering his writers not to challenge the decency, loyalty, or desire for an honorable peace of America's leaders. In his memoir, RN, he would describe Dean Rusk as "one of the ablest and most honorable men ever to serve as Secretary of State."

Where Whalen had written, in obvious reference to the "secret plan" imbroglio, "There is no gimmick, no 'plan,' no push-button solution that can magically end this war and win the peace," Nixon wrote a new introductory clause, "As I have repeatedly said." This signaled that the Boss's enemies had drawn blood when they distorted his words in New Hampshire to say he had a "secret plan" to end the war. And he felt the wound.

At the end of the 22-page draft, Nixon wrote a new close in longhand with truncated words: "We can end the war in Vietnam in a way that will enable us to win the peace in the Pacific and in the world. This is the goal to which I am committed—and this is a goal which I believe can and will be achieved by a new administration."

Nixon's edits, though seemingly minor, say much about the man. In dealing with a war now producing 200 to 300 American dead every week, Nixon was determined to be responsible. He wanted his opponents treated with respect. He was more of a historical optimist than Whalen or I. Thus he would turn to Price for what some of us called his "blue sky" speeches. He was far more deeply engaged in the writing and editing of his most important speeches and statements—on Vietnam, crime, or civil rights—than any other political figure for whom I have written. He was as well informed on the issues as those who worked for him, in some cases better informed, though the Nixon writing and research staff of 1968 was the most able I have ever seen in a campaign.

With this March 30, 1968, speech, Nixon would rule out escalation or intensification of the war effort. I thought this a major political and strategic mistake. That morning Price, Whalen, and I were at the Nixon apartment, where we had spent the week. Nixon was to tape at 2 p.m. The phone rang. I picked it up. It was Frank Shakespeare, the ex–CBS executive who was our TV man. Johnson had just asked for airtime to address the nation Sunday night. For me, a deus ex machina. Nixon immediately canceled his speech.

"I SHALL NOT SEEK, AND I WILL NOT ACCEPT . . ."

On Sunday, Nixon asked me to be at LaGuardia's private terminal when he returned after an appearance in Milwaukee. He would be coming in late and wanted me to monitor Johnson's speech and brief him, so he would be prepared to comment if the press was waiting for him at the terminal. I was sitting in the limousine on the tarmac with Nixon's black driver, listening to the radio as LBJ gave his address. As I had predicted in Nixon's apartment Saturday, Johnson was not going to escalate but impose a limited bombing halt and push for negotiations with Hanoi. Then President Johnson came to the close:

> With America's sons in the fields far away, with America's future under challenge right here at home, with our hopes and the world's hopes for peace in the balance every day, I do not believe that I should devote an hour or a day of my time to any personal, partisan causes or to any duties other than the awesome duties of this office—the presidency of your country.
>
> Accordingly I shall not seek, and I will not accept, the nomination of my party for another term as your President.

The driver went wild. "I knew it. I knew it! I predicted it!" I was stunned. Right about then, Nixon's plane came in. I told the driver to move as far down the tarmac and get as close as he could to the plane, which was taxiing up to the private terminal. I got out, ran to the plane, got there before the press, and climbed aboard as soon as the steps came down. Nixon was still in his seat. "He's not running!" I said. "Johnson's not running!"

Nixon sat stunned, pondered a minute, then went to the open door, came down, and said to the press, "This is the year of the dropouts. First, Romney, then Rockefeller, now Johnson." Nixon would regret the remark, writing in his memoirs that in Johnson's case this was flippant and unfair.

We got into the limo and talked all the way into the city about the implications. This was worrisome. The Democrats might not be divided in the fall between the antiwar Kennedy-McCarthy wing and a hawkish wing backing a war President and detested by the Left. For Hubert Humphrey, the beneficiary of Johnson's withdrawal, *could* unite the Democrats. And if he did we were in trouble. For, like the Army of the Potomac opposite Lee's Army of Northern Virginia, the Democratic Party was twice the size of ours.

Nixon now realized the risk he would take in any definitive statement on Vietnam, when Johnson could move swiftly and leave him stranded. He declared a moratorium on speeches on Vietnam until the effect of Johnson's partial bombing halt and offer to negotiate with Hanoi became clear. Two days later, our spirits soared when Nixon rolled up almost 80 percent of the primary vote in Wisconsin. Not only was the primary turnout the largest in Wisconsin history, Nixon had won a larger share, 31 percent, of the total vote of both parties than he had in 1960 when Humphrey and JFK had battled it out in Wisconsin. And as John MacIver noted, "The voters of Madison—the most dovish, pro-McCarthy area in the state—voted 57–43 against a Vietnam withdrawal."

When I told Nixon that Republican governors were now reportedly uniting to stop us, Nixon, perhaps remembering that Cleveland governors' conference of 1964, was contemptuous. They do this every four years, Nixon scoffed. "They'll be eating each other before this thing is over."

Nixon was right. They never united. Ambition, the desire of big-state governors to be seen by Nixon as an attractive running mate, thwarted any united front against us—and for Rockefeller. When the governors were to break together for Rocky, only one did: Ray Shafer of Pennsylvania. This caused one wag to plagiarize the beer commercial of that day: "Shafer's the one governor to have—if you're having only one."

A NIXON-REAGAN ENTENTE

On April 4, two days after the Badger State primary, Nixon dictated a "Dear Ron" letter to Reagan thanking him for "using your influence to discourage some of your more enthusiastic supporters who understandably wanted to launch a major campaign in your behalf" in New Hampshire and Wisconsin. This sounded as though Reagan had agreed to give Nixon a clear shot in the first two primary states, and Nixon was now thanking Reagan for having honored their agreement. A blind copy of the letter to Reagan went to Lieutenant Governor Bob Finch, who was like a younger brother to Nixon.

Six days later, Reagan wrote back to congratulate Nixon on his wins in New Hampshire and Wisconsin, adding, "I'm especially happy to know that you understand the touchy position I'm in at this time maintaining a neutral stand while running as California's Favorite Son." Again, this read as though an understanding had been reached that Reagan would neither authorize nor promote activity on his behalf in the first two primaries that might siphon off conservative votes from Nixon. There clearly seemed to be a Nixon-Reagan entente here, directed against the Rockefeller-Romney alliance.

Six months earlier, in a *Human Events* column, November 18, 1967, Ralph de Toledano, whose ties to the Boss went back to the 1940s, wrote unequivocally that just such an arrangement had been made:

Mr. Reagan and Mr. Nixon are working under a tacit agreement. Gov. Reagan has let it be known he is leaving the field open to Dick Nixon and will continue to do so unless and/or until there is a marked change in Mr. Nixon's [fortunes]. . . .

In practical terms this sets up a date for any play by Governor Reagan. If Mr. Nixon sweeps the New Hampshire and Wisconsin primaries, then the Reagan "candidacy" will fade and the governor will make it clear that he intends to pass up this chance for the presidential nomination.

If, however, Mr. Nixon falters—or if he tears his political pants between now and April 2—when the Badger State shows its preferences—then Mr. Reagan can be expected to push ahead. . . .

According to a highly reliable source, in fact, Mr. Reagan and Mr. Nixon have agreed to the strategy outlined above.

Then, in a startling sentence that I underlined (I put "RN—Note" on the column I sent to Nixon), de Toledano wrote, "[I]t can be flatly stated that both men have explored the consequences of this strategy and discussed it—if only in those carefully noncommittal terms that are the linguistic coinage of the political world."

De Toledano was saying Nixon and Reagan had agreed that Nixon would get first crack in the primaries, but if he had not taken the measure of Romney by Wisconsin, Reagan was free to make his move. That Nixon returned the de Toledano column to me with a check mark, but no comment at all on such explosive material, attributed directly to him, told me that, most probably, he had been Ralph's "highly reliable source." De Toledano was spreading the word to the Right. Reagan has agreed: Nixon bats first.

On May 20, 1968, Rose got a call from Finch. Bill Clark, Reagan's chief of staff, had just phoned Bob, knowing it would be transmitted instantly to us, that in New Orleans, Rockefeller, who had arrived around midnight, had contacted Lyn Nofziger, a Reagan aide, to say he wanted a private meeting with the governor. Nofziger put him off. Early the next morning, Rocky showed up at Reagan's suite while he was getting dressed, started in talking about how the two were not that far apart on philosophy, then switched to how they had to collaborate to stop Nixon. The notes Rose took from Finch, reporting what Bill Clark said, then read as follows:

> Then he [Rockefeller] turned into an out-and-out Stop Nixon movement and Reagan put him off more abruptly. They spent a total of eight minutes together and they had Rockefeller go out the back door to avoid the photographers that had followed him up there.
>
> Nellie [Rockefeller] had a press conference—said he had a nice visit with Reagan—that they talked philosophy and that there were not as many differences in their philosophies as some people have said.

Confirmation of the Reagan depiction of the New Orleans meeting came from Hillings, whose source was a "personal friend . . . a member of the Reagan staff." In a memo to RN and Mitchell, Hillings wrote, "Reagan was upset and annoyed when Rockefeller stopped by his room in New Orleans last week and got him out of bed. He did not want to talk with Rockefeller and feels Rockefeller took unfair advantage."

The source, Hillings went on, said, "Nancy Reagan is utterly opposed to the Governor's taking a Vice Presidential nomination," and Reagan "is telling staff he thinks the V.P. spot is a great waste." The governor was said to be showing his staff clippings of how Vice President Humphrey had been promised an "influential role" in the White House that had "turned out to be false. . . . Our informant quotes Reagan as saying, 'See, see . . . all of this doesn't mean anything.'"

Again it appeared that Reagan wanted to get the message to Nixon that he had had nothing to do with the Rockefeller intrusion, that it had been unwanted and repulsed. Nevertheless, we continued to monitor closely the increasing activity on Reagan's behalf, some of which looked tied to his staff in Sacramento. Nixon urged me to pull together the information we had on Reagan's political activity and recent travel schedule and get it to the press.

Should Nixon have challenged Reagan's favorite-son designation? As he was looking to unite the party for November, Nixon had stood down to let Reagan arrive in Miami Beach as the Golden State's favorite son. But by the spring of '68, California was Nixon country. In the Muchmore State Poll of May 20, 1968, 56 percent of California Republicans said they favored Nixon for the nomination, 32 percent said Rockefeller. Only 8 percent said Reagan.

KEMPTON ON KENNEDY

Immediately after Johnson declared that he would not run again, Bobby Kennedy fired off a telegram to the President, congratulating him on his act of statesmanship: "Your decision regarding the presidency subordinates self and country and is truly magnanimous. I respectfully and earnestly request an opportunity to visit as soon as possible to discuss how we might work together in the interest of national unity." Murray Kempton's take:

> Sen. Kennedy managed to look yesterday about as appetizing as any man could who had just offered "to work together for national unity" with a President he had accused the week before of calling up the darker impulses in American life. . . .
>
> In the required new key he radiated something of that gentle compassion which overcame him in West Virginia at the sight of the defeated Hubert Humphrey whom he had instructed Franklin D. Roosevelt, Jr., to accuse of draft-dodging. . . .
>
> After enduring Sen. Kennedy yesterday, it seemed sensible to go to his office and pick up his recent campaign speeches before they are burned.

CHAPTER 8

Assassinations and Anarchy

VIOLENCE IS AS American as cherry pie.
—H. RAP BROWN (1967)

O N FEBRUARY 29, 1968, the National Advisory Commission on Civil Disorders, established by Johnson after the
Detroit and Newark riots in the summer of '67, with Illinois
governor Otto Kerner, Jr., presiding, issued its report. Responding
to LBJ's request to identify the root causes of the days and nights
of shooting, looting, and burning, the commission reported back.
"White racism" had divided the nation, and America was "moving
toward two societies, one black, one white—separate and unequal."

Nixon's response—the Kerner commission "blames everybody
for the riots except the perpetrators of the riots"—was well received
by a nation whose patience with people justifying their criminality
by pointing to the disadvantaged circumstances of their lives had
run out. Americans, black and white, had gone through tougher
times in the Depression and people had not resorted to rioting,
fire-bombings, and looting.

The following night, March 7, in a radio address to the nation,
Nixon pledged "to meet force with force, if necessary, in the cities."
He urged the government to contain and control "the planners of
violence," called for rapid "retaliation against the perpetrators of
violence," and wanted the response to be "swift and sure." For the

"violence being threatened for this summer is more in the nature of a war than a riot. A riot, by definition, is a spontaneous outburst, a war is subject to advance planning."

By the spring of 1968, the days of tragedy and triumph of the civil rights movement were history and Martin Luther King was long past his glory days. The Montgomery bus boycott, after Rosa Parks refused to move to the back of the bus, was over a dozen years in the past. Klan violence was also history: the beating of the Freedom Riders; the assassination of Medgar Evers; the bombing of the 16th Street Baptist Church in Birmingham; the murder of the civil rights workers Schwerner, Chaney, and Goodman in Philadelphia, Mississippi; and the police beating of John Lewis at the Edmund Pettus Bridge in Selma.

Middle America was moving on. Talk of race had turned to black incendiaries like Stokely Carmichael and H. Rap Brown, to Black Panthers like Huey Newton and Eldridge Cleaver, whose autobiographical book *Soul on Ice* told of raping white women as racial revenge, and to Black Muslims whose charismatic Malcolm X had been assassinated by a rival Muslim a year after Malcolm had chortled over JFK's assassination: "[C]hickens coming home to roost never did make me sad, they made me glad."

Dr. King's address at the Lincoln Memorial during the March on Washington for Jobs and Freedom, which I witnessed, had been delivered five years before. His Nobel Peace Prize had come in 1964. The Civil Rights Act and Voting Rights Act had been on the books for years. King had lost much of his constituency in 1967 by denouncing America as the "greatest purveyor of violence in the world today." He had charged his country with moral culpability in the deaths of a million children in Vietnam. Because of King's ties to former Communist Party leaders Stanley Levison and Hunter Pitts O'Dell, the Kennedys and President Johnson had directed the FBI to wiretap him and keep him under surveillance. King had moved so far out of the mainstream that black columnist

Carl Rowan had penned an attack on him in *Reader's Digest*. Bill Buckley wrote that King was becoming "the Harold Stassen of the civil rights movement." That there would be a national holiday for King was unimaginable in that spring of '68, as would be the claim by twenty-first-century conservatives that Dr. King was somehow one of us.

Hence few were paying attention to a sanitation workers' strike in Memphis when word came the evening of April 4 that King, who had gone to stand with the strikers, had been shot on a balcony of the Lorraine Motel and had bled to death. The assassin was said to be a white male. Within hours, riots broke out in a hundred U.S. cities, including the capital. All involved arson, pillage, bloodshed, deaths, troops. In Washington, DC, federal troops were being called out. I was phoned by a friend who told me the fires were spreading up 7th Street, where Griffith Stadium stood, and along the 14th Street corridor up to Mitchell's sports store, where in the '40s and early '50s we bought bats, gloves, and catchers' equipment for our CYO teams. By Palm Sunday, Washington was an occupied city.

At headquarters we argued over whether Nixon should go to the funeral. Nixon stepped out front by flying to Atlanta and going to see Coretta King before the funeral. Was this enough? At Key Biscayne he decided to attend the funeral and told me later that at the service he and Gene McCarthy had agreed they would march part of the way with the funeral procession carrying King's coffin to the grave site, then peel off. He later told me his being seen on the cover of magazines marching behind the mule train cost him heavily in the South.

Yet, while the nation was moving right on crime, Hollywood was moving left, embracing and exploiting a culture of increasingly graphic violence, a decision that would sustain the industry for the next half century. At the Academy Awards just days after King's assassination, *Bonnie and Clyde*, the romanticized story of a pair of psychopaths who murdered their way across Depression-era

America, was runner-up for Best Picture and got ten nominations. Warren Beatty, who played Clyde Barrow, was nominated for Best Actor; Faye Dunaway, who played Bonnie Parker, for Best Actress. *In Cold Blood*, the film version of Truman Capote's indulgent profile of two ex-cons who brutally murdered four members of a Kansas family, was nominated for four Academy Awards. Author Tom Wolfe called Capote's book "Pornoviolence."

THE LONG HOT SUMMERS

It is hard to overestimate the damage these riots did to race relations in America. They had begun six years earlier. Almost no national attention had been given to it, but racial violence had erupted in Washington, DC, on Thanksgiving Day, 1962, after the city title football game between Catholic League champion St. John's and the public school champion, Eastern. The largest sports crowd in DC history, 50,000, had attended the game at the new stadium, now called RFK. After St. John's rolled to an easy victory, Eastern fans poured out of the stands and stormed across the field to attack the people on the St. John's side. Drew Pearson described what happened:

> Immediately, Negro spectators descended from the grandstand, swept across the field like an angry army, and with fists, knives, rocks, pieces of pipe proceeded to beat up white spectators. . . . Simeon Booker of *Ebony* Magazine stated frankly: "The explosion of hate stemmed mostly from my own people."

"This was the worst race riot Washington has seen since the riots immediately after the end of World War I over 40 years ago," said Pearson. National coverage was almost nonexistent. But Moscow's *Izvestia*, in the article "Bloodshed in Washington," said the riot "revealed that racial hatred flourishes in American society." I learned about it from family who had been at the game. Pearson

compared the rampage at the DC stadium to the white riots at Ole
Miss, when Governor Ross Barnett sought to block the desegregation of the school only two months earlier.

When Barnett had gone to the University of Mississippi to prevent the admission of James Meredith, declaring that rather than
allow a Negro in Ole Miss he was "prepared to go to jail," I wrote
the editorial in the *Globe-Democrat* urging that the governor of
Mississippi

> be cited for contempt in supporting his rabid racial policies
> and denying what have been interpreted as Meredith's con-
> stitutional rights. If the Governor would prefer to go to jail
> rather than abide by this decision, we hope that prompt steps
> will be taken to accommodate him.

The pattern was set. Violence by whites resisting integration
merited national coverage and thunderous condemnation. Black-
on-white violence called for reticence and perspective, an understanding of the "root causes," exactly the position Pearson had
taken in his column.

The next race riot took place in Harlem in the summer of '64
with a rampage that lasted five days and required 6,000 cops to
contain. America's "long hot summers" would not end until after
the summer of '68. These riots burned up much of the goodwill in
Middle America toward the cause of civil rights—and they contributed mightily to the discrediting of liberalism and the election of
Richard Nixon.

END OF THE OPEN-HOUSING DEBATE

On March 5, after Romney dropped out, I outlined for Nixon what
I thought should be our position on the open-housing bill moving
through Congress. Nixon should favor ending the filibuster and

letting the Senate work its will. But he had always "felt that the principle of open housing was best . . . and most effectively implemented at the state and local level because of the differences in racial progress and racial tension in the various sectors and communities of the country." Yet a federal law "can have value in breaking down psychological barriers to acceptance of the principle of open housing."

On March 22, I got an "urgent" memo from Bill Timmons, our man on the Hill. It began and ended, "Help, Help, Help!" There were reports in the *Times*, the *Washington Post*, and papers across the South that Nixon had phoned party leaders in the House to urge adoption of the Senate's "Civil Rights–Open Housing legislation."

"Not only are 'kooks' and diehard conservatives upset," Timmons wrote, "so are members of Congress from the South who have stuck their necks out for our candidate." Timmons mentioned Strom Thurmond and Albert Watson. "Did [Nixon] call the leadership on this matter?" Timmons asked.

I sent Timmons's memo to Nixon. He wrote back, "Just keep the lid on as long as possible. RN has only asked Ford et al. to get a bill—& remove the issue—he has not told them what bill." The bill that had moved through the Senate was stalled in the House when King was assassinated on April 4. Johnson moved to demand its passage and the Civil Rights Act of 1968, the Fair Housing Act, was signed April 10—with Nixon's support. Our statement said:

> This bill carried with it—whether justified or not—the hopes of many decent and hard-working Negro people. It carried with it the hopes of those leaders of the Negro community who have always counseled their people to seek change and progress through the law and not outside the law. Had we slammed this door in their faces, we would have weakened their leadership and armed the black anarchists in our society with another weapon to bring down the moderates.

Though the bill may have contradicted what Nixon thought was wise policy, and though it would hurt among conservative Democrats, Nixon had supported it to show solidarity with the civil rights movement. And I think he supported it because he believed it was the right thing to do, and that side of the argument was the right place to be. Politically, a divisive issue Wallace could have exploited was now off the table and settled.

And Reagan? In early 1968 he had switched and come out against repeal of the Rumford Act, the California fair-housing law. A man with his own dreams, the governor knew when to fold his cards.

THE CARDS FALL OUR WAY

In two months the world had been turned upside down. The Tet Offensive and heavy casualties in Vietnam had caused a national rethinking on the war. Romney had quit the race, leaving an unopposed Nixon to roll up huge victories in New Hampshire and Wisconsin. Gene McCarthy had humiliated Johnson, who had announced he would not run. Kennedy had plunged in. Rockefeller had dropped out. Now America's foremost black leader had been assassinated and every major U.S. city had been racked with racial violence. The war and the riots had become the issues. Vietnam and law and order were front and center in the politics of 1968.

Nixon, who had taken a tough line for two years on crime, violence, civil disobedience, and soft judges in national articles and was the Republican Party's expert and voice on foreign policy, was perfectly positioned. He had no opponent in the primaries, and the Republican nomination offered a clear path to the presidency, as the Democratic Party was in a three-way war, with McCarthy, Kennedy, and Humphrey, and this war would continue to the Chicago convention. We had only to move serenely toward the nomination in Miami Beach, as their party tore itself apart over the war and racial violence, and the causes and cures. Once again, Nixon was in the catbird seat.

That April, Nixon was invited to address the American Society of Newspaper Editors in DC. So, too, was Rockefeller. It was a face-off. In a meeting with his research and writing staff in the "Bible Building," as we called our new Manhattan headquarters that had housed the American Bible Society—"The Truth Shall Make You Free" was inscribed over the entrance—we discussed what Rockefeller would say. All agreed. Rockefeller would do the predictable and propose a big spending program for the cities we could not and would not match. If another Great Society program was the answer to America's social crisis, why did that crisis continue to deepen?

Rockefeller, true to form, in a long speech proposed $150 billion in spending on the cities over a decade. Nixon volunteered to be interrogated by the editors. It was among his finest performances. He was crisp and witty, joking about "Bobby," and the editors loved it. We walked out elated, everyone on the staff, and the Boss, too, knowing we had won this one.

During our meeting at the Bible Building we got a lesson in the new politics. Rose buzzed Nixon on the intercom and he irritably picked up the phone. He had told her he did not want to be interrupted when we were discussing ideas and issues to emphasize after the King assassination. After a pause, Nixon said to put the caller on. Nixon talked for a few minutes, then hung up. "That was Clem Stone," he said. "He just gave us five hundred thousand dollars." It was the largest contribution Nixon had ever received. W. Clement Stone of Chicago had built an insurance empire and admired Nixon's courage in coming back from repeated defeats. Like the rest at the meeting, I was jolted. All I could think was "That guy just bought twenty-five of me." I was earning $20,000 a year, more than twice what I had made at top Guild scale in St. Louis two years before.

Something else struck me, as I noted the presence of various aides at these meetings: Nixon had assembled a distant early warning system, his own DEW line. Ellsworth was a liberal Republican, Price was an establishment Republican, Garment was a liberal Jewish Democrat, and I was Catholic and conservative. As Nixon would discuss ideas, we were his antennae. Should one of us react negatively to a proposal, Nixon could be fairly certain this was how the elements of the electorate we represented would react. That Nixon was interested in hearing the reactions of all of us told me he did not fully agree with any of us, and was far less ideologically committed than any of us. In his campaign and White House, Nixon created a radar system that picked up and sent back signals from all points on the political compass, but ideologically, he was himself an eclectic.

AGNEW'S HOUR OF POWER

In Baltimore the rioting had begun Friday, April 5, and lasted a week. When it ended, 6 were dead, 700 injured, and 4,000 arrested, and parts of the city were in ashes. Troops were patrolling the streets. After the orgy of hate and what he regarded as the craven silence of civil rights leaders, Governor Agnew invited a hundred of them to the State Office Building in Baltimore—to a meeting with a press table, television cameras, and spectators.

Agnew had received a death threat the day before. He entered, state troopers fore and aft, and began reading a statement as blunt as any that any civil rights leader heard in that decade.

> Ladies and gentlemen. . . . I did not ask you here to recount previous deprivations, nor to hear me enumerate prior attempts to correct them. I did not request your presence to bid for peace with the public dollar. . . .
>
> Look around you and you may notice that everyone here is a leader—and that each leader present has worked his way to

the top. If you'll observe, the ready-mix, instantaneous type of leader is not present. The circuit-riding, Hanoi-visiting type of leader is missing from this assembly. The caterwauling, riot-inciting, burn-America-down type of leader is conspicuous by his absence. That is no accident, ladies and gentlemen, it is just good planning. And in the vernacular of today, "That's what it's all about, baby."

Agnew went into a depiction of how the black leaders had failed their community and failed Baltimore. He related an incident in which an agent of Stokely Carmichael had called Baltimore's police "the enemy of the black community":

Some weeks ago, a reckless stranger in this city carrying the credentials of a well-known civil rights organization characterized the Baltimore police as "enemies of the black man." Some of you here, to your eternal credit, quickly condemned this demagogic proclamation. You condemned it because you recognized immediately that it was an attempt to undermine lawful authority—the authority under which you were elected and under which you hold your leadership position. You spoke out against it because you knew it was false and uttered to attract attention and inflame.

When you, who courageously slapped hard at irresponsibility, acted, you did more for civil rights than you realize. But when white leaders openly complimented you for your objective courageous action, you immediately encountered a storm of censure from parts of the Negro community. The criticism was born of a perverted sense of race loyalty and inflamed by the type of leader who I earlier mentioned is not here today.

Then, writes Jules Witcover, author of *White Knight: The Rise of Spiro Agnew*, came the brutal phrase: *"And you ran."*

Speaking of the private meetings the civil rights leaders had had with Stokely Carmichael, which had been monitored by undercover cops, Agnew tore into them:

> You met in secret with that demagogue and others like him and you agreed, according to published reports that have not been denied, that you would not openly criticize any black spokesman, regardless of his remarks. You were beguiled by the rationalizations of unity; you were intimidated by veiled threats; you were stung by insinuations you were Mr. Charlie's boy, by epithets like "Uncle Tom." God knows I cannot fault you who spoke out for breaking and running in the face of what appeared to be overwhelming opinion in the Negro community. But actually . . . it was only the opinion of a few, distorted and magnified by the silence of most of you here today.

As one after another of the black leaders walked out, Agnew went on to praise Roy Wilkins, Whitney Young, and Dr. King, and condemn "agents of destruction" like Carmichael and H. Rap Brown, who "will surely destroy us if we do not repudiate them and their philosophies—along with the white racists . . . and their fellow travelers." Declared Agnew, "I publicly repudiate, condemn and reject all white racists. I call upon you to repudiate, condemn and reject all black racists. This, so far, you have not been willing to do."

For an hour after he read his statement, Agnew engaged the civil rights leaders who stayed to challenge what Witcover called his "insulting sermon." Part of Agnew's statement was reprinted in the *New York Times*. I clipped it, and sent it immediately on to Nixon.

Though hundreds of cities, including our national capital, had been wracked by racial violence, shootings, lootings, and arson, and though the National Guard and Army troops had been called out across the country, a moral paralysis seemed to have gripped the liberal establishment. Agnew was saying in language people understood what people believed and wanted to hear. If these civil rights leaders were real leaders, why were they not denouncing the criminality in their communities? Were black rioters exempt from the criticism all would have leveled had it been Southern white leaders who were silent as white mobs burned down buildings, looted stores, beat up black people, and shot at firemen and cops?

Agnew was no racist. As Baltimore County supervisor, he had won the governorship in 1966 by supporting open housing against George P. ("Your home is your castle!") Mahoney, whom Nixon had put in the same basket as Maddox and Wallace. Agnew had supported Scranton in 1964 and was the most visible governor in the draft-Rockefeller movement in 1968. But Spiro Agnew was a no-nonsense, tough-minded man who believed the rule of law was the bedrock of society and his duty was to enforce that law. Like Richard J. Daley, mayor of Chicago, who was now issuing "shoot-to-kill" orders to stop arsonists, and Frank Rizzo, police commissioner and future mayor of Philadelphia, Agnew was not afflicted with the guilt that immobilized so many during that decade.

Agnew had been radicalized the previous summer by what happened on Maryland's Eastern Shore. Caribbean-born Stokely Carmichael had succeeded John Lewis as chairman of the Student Nonviolent Coordinating Committee. After civil rights marcher James Meredith had been shot on a Mississippi highway in 1966, he abandoned nonviolence and converted SNCC to "Black Power," expelling all whites. "When you talk of black power," said Carmichael, "you talk of building a movement that will smash everything Western civilization has created." Carmichael fled to Guinea, changed his name to Kwame Ture, and was succeeded by H. Rap Brown, now serving a life sentence for murdering a Georgia sheriff's deputy. In the summer of '67, Brown ignited a riot in Cambridge, Maryland, on the Eastern Shore, declaiming, while standing on the trunk of a car, "If America doesn't come around, we're gonna burn it down!" Brown would be forever associated with his defense of mayhem, "Violence is as American as cherry pie," and with the Cambridge rioters' call to arson: "Burn, baby, burn!"

The day after the blaze, which gutted the black business district and a black elementary school, Agnew arrived in Cambridge to declare, "It shall now be the policy of this state to immediately arrest any person inciting to riot, and to not allow that person to finish his vicious speech." Out of the Cambridge riot, Rap Brown and Spiro Agnew surged to national prominence.

Agnew's reading of the riot act to the civil rights leaders who had gone silent in the face of wholesale violence in Maryland's largest city after King's death was a major factor in Nixon's choice of him for vice president. Here was a Republican with liberal credentials on domestic issues and a law-and-order temperament, a rare combination in those days.

GREENSPAN WEIGHS IN

After the Detroit and Newark riots of 1967, Alan Greenspan had written Nixon a memo, "The Urban Riots of the 1960s." One of several passages that Nixon underlined read:

> What is significant and dangerous about the implicit sanction given by liberal intellectuals to the riots is that it has morally disarmed the law-abiding, non-rioting segment of the Negro community who in decades past acted to keep the rebellious elements of the Negro ghetto in line.

Greenspan was not far from the Agnew position. In a single-page memo to Nixon, he wrote, "[T]he fundamental cause of the riots is the moral sanction given to the Black Power militants by the 'liberal' community."

They are being told their cause is just. But the Black Power militants are wrong. There is no conceivable moral justification for violence in a free society. This is not Nazi Germany or the Soviet Union. All citizens have the means to achieve their ends through political persuasion.

RFK is attempting to cash in on the tragic events of recent days by fostering guilt among the whites and accordingly presenting himself as a moral leader. He has deftly skirted the issue of whether violence is unequivocally wrong. He must be called on this. Does RFK consider violence in a free society morally justified or not?

Alan was regarded by the conservatives on the research-and-writing staff as one of us. In early May 1968, there was a mutiny when Glenn Olds, an academic brought in by Len, began to assert authority over the staff and talked of "doubling and tripling" its size. Olds was claiming he had been granted the franchise to staff the federal government and was discussing Cabinet posts. Four staffers came to me, and I relayed to Nixon that if Olds was put in charge of research and writing, our guys felt he would "Rockefellerize the staff," and they would walk.

The staff wanted Greenspan, who "will quit his job and go to work fulltime—to be named Director of Research–Domestic Policy." They wanted Olds out and Len to cease "floating" in their operation. I told Nixon this was the solution, as Alan was a "committed RN man, a hard worker, willing to give up his job. He has the confidence and support of everyone in research, and they like the guy." Nixon scribbled instructions at the top of my memo: "Mitchell: 1. Olds is personnel projects. 2. Len Garment out of research." Alan Greenspan took charge of domestic policy research.

Olds was a pleasant academic, but I have never met anyone in politics with less "savvy." When I showed him Nixon's office in our headquarters, Olds was aghast. Behind Nixon's chair on the wall was a print of a Southern mansion, a saddled horse, a rider, and a black servant holding the horse.

Get that thing out of here! Olds commanded. I started to explain that the Old Man liked the painting—then decided to do as Olds directed and tell Nixon that Dr. Olds had ordered me to remove his racist painting.

SETTING RACE AGAINST RACE

Nixon was sympathetic to the Negro cause but was no Great Society liberal. He shared a conservative skepticism on the wisdom of programs piled one on top of the other to bring about social progress in the inner city. After *Newsweek* produced a cover story titled "The Negro in America," its columnist Milton Friedman entered a rebuttal December 17, 1967, which I underlined and sent to Nixon. It came back with a message scrawled at the top: "Pat, This is excellent. Put this sentence by sentence indictment in my next speech on this subject—and in my briefing book." The passages Nixon marked included half of the column.

Negroes had made great strides over the previous century through a free market and their own efforts, Friedman wrote, but government had now arrested that progress and liberals were responsible:

> The drive for further legislative measures, and particularly the techniques adopted, have awakened the sleeping giant of racial prejudice among the whites in the North. The encouragement of unrealistic and extravagant expectations has produced frustration, outrage and a sense of betrayal among the Negroes in the North. Unwittingly, the liberals have set race against race.

Friedman listed the policies producing social disaster. Welfare had "weakened family structure and produced a permanent class of people on relief." Government schools were failing the Negro. The $1.40-an-hour minimum wage priced black teenagers out of a labor market where one in four were now unemployed.

> Public housing and urban renewal programs have destroyed more dwelling units than they have constructed. Concentration of the poor, many of them broken families, in public housing has reinforced despair and fostered juvenile delinquency. Urban renewal has destroyed viable neighborhoods, driven the poor from their homes to even less satisfactory and more expensive housing and created slums where none existed before. It deserves the insidious label of a "Negro-removal program."

Friedman had written what many of us had argued in editorials. Martin Anderson of our staff was the author of *The Federal Bulldozer*, the definitive work on what urban renewal had done to the black poor, which I had reviewed for the *Globe-Democrat*. But by the time we came to office, the Great Society was entrenched in a vast bureaucracy with an interest in sustaining it, and backed by a Democratic Party that controlled both houses of Congress. And on domestic policy, the Nixon White House was anything but counterrevolutionary. Nevertheless, the intensity of Nixon's visceral reaction to what Milton had written told me, as did much else that he said and scribbled in those days, that Nixon agreed with us.

Yet there was another side to Nixon. While law and order were indispensable to a civilized society, they were not enough. The month King died Nixon delivered his "Bridges to Human Dignity" speech, which was written by Ray, on national radio, and he introduced the idea of "black capitalism," directing private investment and loan guarantees into the urban areas of America. Contacts were made with Roy Innis and others at the Congress of Racial Equality, which had sent the Freedom Riders south and, in that Freedom

Summer of 1964, had sent Schwerner and Goodman into Mississippi, where they were murdered in Neshoba County.

ANARCHY IN ACADEMIA

The campus revolution of the 1960s began at Berkeley in the fall of 1964 with the Free Speech Movement. Led by Mario Savio, students declared they would henceforth refuse to have their freedom circumscribed by faculty or administrators, that there would be no limits accepted on where they could solicit funds for causes, and that the absolute freedom to say what they wished would now be the rule on the Berkeley campus of the University of California. Thousands held a police car and its occupants hostage for thirty hours. In a speech now famous to student radicals, Savio declaimed from the steps of Sproul Hall:

> There's a time when the operation of the machine becomes so odious—makes you so sick at heart—that you can't take part, you can't even passively take part, and you've got to put your bodies upon the gears and upon the wheels, upon the levers, upon all the apparatus, and you've got to make it stop. And you've got to indicate to the people who run it, to the people that own it, that unless you're free, the machine will be prevented from working at all!

The claim that students at the most prestigious school in the Golden Land were persecuted and oppressed was absurd. Americans looked at the Berkeley antics as the revolt of the overprivileged. Yet countless campuses in that decade witnessed student strikes, sit-ins, demonstrations, and protests over faculty, curriculum, rules of conduct, and the war in Vietnam. Faculty, fearful of falling behind a popularity curve, would vote "me too" with the students. In the lead editorial in the *Globe-Democrat*, "Campus Anarchists," I raised questions about the Berkeley uprising that would echo through the decade: Why did academics not stand up in defense of their authority, institutions, and traditions? Why did so many capitulate to mob rule? What was the matter with these people?

[W]hat kind of educational program is being offered at the University of California when the Academic Senate, comprising all the faculty with tenure, voted 824 to 115 to support the FSM students by urging no restriction be put on the "content" of speech but remained silent on the disorderly, disruptive "sit-in"?

If there is so much restriction of freedom of speech on the campus, how is it that a few yards from Sproul Hall the Young Socialist Alliance has a poster complaining of "American aggression in The Congo" and urging students to "support the Congolese rebels"?

Thus, when the worst campus riot of the 1960s occurred a few miles north, at the university from which I had graduated six years before, it came as no shock. Hamilton Hall and Low Library at Columbia were ransacked. A dean was taken hostage. Administration offices were occupied by hundreds of black and white radicals led by Mark Rudd. The siege lasted for days. A student was photographed sitting at the desk of university president Grayson Kirk. After a week of this nonsense, the NYPD was called in and retook the buildings, clubbing scores. After the cops cleared the radicals out, Columbia closed for the semester. I drafted a blistering statement Nixon issued about the riots and the occupation of campus buildings, calling this a "national tragedy and a national disgrace." These disorders, said Nixon, are

the first major skirmish in a revolutionary struggle to seize the universities of this country and transform them into sanctuaries for radicals and vehicles for revolutionary and political goals.

A university is a community of scholars seeking truth. It is a place where reason reigns and the right of dissent is safeguarded and cherished. Force and coercion are wholly alien to that community and those who employ it have no place there.

Some staffers thought this response far too strident. But soon came vindication. In an Oregon poll that asked whether campus protests "had been handled too harshly, too easily, or just about right," 2 percent had said "too harshly," and 80 percent "too easily." By forty-to-one, Oregonians thought campus radicals were being coddled. What did Oregon Republicans think should be done with "students who seriously interrupt university activities—or use violence—or invade buildings?" Two percent said they should be "forgiven because they had good reason to protest." Thirty-seven percent said they should be expelled. The rest thought they should be turned over to disciplinary committees.

When Nixon headed out on the road in early May, I sent him a memo warning he might be confronted by students for his remarks on Columbia. I suggested he respond by citing the words of a scholar I admired, Sidney Hook. At a party given for him on his recent retirement as chairman of the philosophy department at NYU, Hook had said the real victim of the student revolt would be the academic freedom he had defended all his life:

We need more than a defensive strategy safeguarding the intellectual integrity of the teaching profession. We need to counterpose to the revolt of the emotionally committed the revolt of the rationally committed. I do not want to identify this with the revolt of the moderates. There are some things one should not be moderate about.

On April 30, Nelson Rockefeller, who six weeks earlier had asked the nation to take his declaration of noncandidacy seriously, and not cynically, declared his availability for the Republican nomination. The filing deadlines for Indiana, Nebraska, and Oregon had passed. Rocky had ducked an open-primary fight with the man he and his staff had for years been calling a loser. But the day of his announcement, he pulled off a coup.

With a write-in vote in the Massachusetts primary, where Governor John Volpe, a Nixon supporter, was running as favorite son, Rockefeller narrowly beat Volpe and captured all 34 delegates. It was a brilliant raid and gave Rocky a good launch. Nixon was miffed. And that our political operation in Washington failed to see this coming suggested it needed buttoning up.

By the end of May, Rockefeller was denouncing Nixon's attack on the Columbia radicals as "unjust," and praising their "spirit of protest." Which was fine with me. On no issue did America agree with us more. Left, right, center, hardly anyone seemed to sympathize with college students raising hell and breaking rules. The same Oregon poll confirmed Nixon's response to the black riots in DC and a hundred other cities after King's death. Seven in ten Oregonians believed there were legitimate grievances behind black anger—inequality, poverty, lack of education. Yet a plurality felt the riots had to be put down decisively by police. Republicans by two-to-one said police decisions not to use force to halt the riots after King's death, even if it meant shooting looters, had been a mistake. A plurality of Democrats and independents agreed.

Thus did Nixon's new ideas for social and economic progress like "Black Capitalism," married to his tough stance toward lawbreakers in the inner city and on college campuses, track almost exactly the thinking of the nation.

"THROW CLARITY OFF THE PLANE!"

On May 7, Nixon swept Indiana. But the big news was the victory of Robert Kennedy over Governor Roger Branigin, who was a stand-in for Humphrey, and over Gene McCarthy, who ran third. Kennedy followed with a victory in Nebraska on May 14. Nixon carried the state the same day with 65 percent. Reagan, who had not campaigned, got 21 percent. If we had a problem ahead in winning this nomination, that problem was not Nelson Rockefeller

Oregon was the last major contested primary for Republicans, as California, which held its primary a week later, on June 4, was committed to Governor Reagan as favorite son. Nixon had declared a policy of not challenging favorite-son governors, be it Romney in Michigan, Rockefeller in New York, Rhodes in Ohio, or Reagan in California. We were running our campaign in such a way as to ensure a sufficient number of delegates on the first ballot to capture the nomination, without alienating or humiliating any of our rivals.

Thus Nixon was stunned when James Clarity of the *New York Times*, after a press conference with Nevada governor Paul Laxalt in Carson City, wrote, "Tanned and smiling, Mr. Nixon told a news conference at the governor's mansion here, 'I've already won the nomination, now I want to win the election.'" In saying that he had "won the nomination," Nixon was referring to 1960. Every reporter took it that way. But when the quote appeared in the *Times* under Clarity's byline, it gave Rockefeller an opening to attack Nixon for arrogantly asserting that he had the '68 nomination locked up. Whatever Nixon may claim, Rocky declared, this race remains wide open.

Nixon was seething over the story and Rockefeller face-slap, but I did not know how angry he was until I got aboard our plane for the midnight flight out of Oregon after a day of campaigning across the state. Nixon was sitting deep in the rear of the plane and I was told he wanted to see me.

"This plane is not taking off," Nixon growled at me, "until you throw Clarity off the plane." I was dumbstruck. Nixon repeated the charge. "Did you hear me! We are not taking off until *you* throw Clarity off this plane."

Having no idea what I was going to do, I walked to the front of the plane where the door was still open, and told Clarity we had to talk. Glancing outside, I could see only darkness. I told Clarity how angry Nixon was, and justifiably so. He did not disagree or protest. He was contrite. He admitted he had blown it. I went back to Nixon to say Clarity realized he had made a mistake and was anxious to make amends.

"I told you to throw him off this plane!" Nixon said.

I trudged back to the front of the plane. Clarity was still at the door. Was I supposed to order him to get off, and shove him through the doorway and down the stairs if he resisted? I wasn't about to do it. The traveling press were now alert that something was amiss. Then, Bob Ellsworth, having apparently received identical orders from Nixon, was soon beside me.

All I could think of was that if I told Clarity to get his butt off our plane somewhere in the wilds of eastern Oregon, it was going to be no small story if and when Clarity ever reconnected with civilization.

Ellsworth and I talked to Clarity for ten minutes. He agreed that as soon as we arrived in South Dakota, after our overnight flight, and Nixon held a press availability, he would stand up, state what he had written in the *Times*, and let Nixon correct the record in public. And Nixon's correction would be fully reported in the *Times*. We could not ask for more.

We went back and explained to Nixon the offer Clarity had made.

Nixon thought silently, then blurted, "Okay, let's take off."

When we got to South Dakota, Clarity rose and asked his question. The press knew it was a setup. But Nixon was no portrait in magnanimity. He held Clarity's head under water and let him and his colleagues know what a blunder he had made. I felt badly for Clarity, a likable guy who had made an egregious but understandable mistake. There was no malice there.

Late that afternoon, a morose Clarity was playing bridge in the bar with Jayne Brumley, Don Irwin, and Ward Just. When Clarity left for the men's room, his colleagues rearranged the cards in the deck so that when Clarity was dealt his next hand, his thirteen cards would be the ace, king, queen, and jack of spades, and the ace, king, and queen of the other three suits.

As each player sorted his cards, I watched Clarity from the next table. For fifteen seconds he stared at his hand and slowly sorted his cards by suit. Then, realizing he had the most perfect bridge hand ever dealt, he threw down his cards and yelled, "You sons of bitches!"

Nixon and a couple of us took the Lear from South Dakota to Key Biscayne. Clarity flew on the prop plane three more hours to New York.

ABOUT NIXON AND the traveling press of 1968 a word needs to be said. While a large contingent of political reporters came to New Hampshire for Nixon's announcement, first press briefing, and maiden speech in Concord—Novak, Broder of the *Washington Post*, and Jules Witcover of the Newhouse chain—only a handful of reporters traveled with us regularly from New Hampshire through the Oregon primary on May 28.

They included Hal Bruno and Jayne Brumley of *Newsweek*, Ward Just of the *Washington Post*, Don Irwin of the *Los Angeles Times*, Bob Semple of the *New York Times*, Mike Wallace of CBS, and Herb Kaplow of NBC. By the time the primaries were over, most of us regarded them as friends with whom we had gone through a bit of history together. We did not look on them as the enemy. We got together after campaign events, drank, argued, talked, and laughed into the early hours. As for Nixon's relationship with the traveling press in the primaries, the Clarity incident was the exception to the rule. We were covered fully and fairly.

Indeed, in the final hours of the Oregon primary, Ward Just of the *Washington Post* fully echoed the chagrin of our staff that Nixon was not getting the credit or recognition he deserved. "The Nixon campaign has been almost flawless," wrote Just:

> What is the trouble with Richard Nixon? He wins the presidential primaries in New Hampshire, Wisconsin, Indiana and Nebraska by staggering majorities—in each case by more than 70 percent of the vote. He forces George Romney out of the race, then lures Nelson Rockefeller into an in-out-and-in-again performance so indecisive and amateurish Adlai Stevenson looks in retrospect like Napoleon. . . .
>
> [Nixon] must be America's only major political figure who can win 70 percent of a state's vote and have the analysts talking about his opponent's 23 percent. Yet it happened in Nebraska with Gov. Reagan.

"If Robert Kennedy or Hubert Humphrey had done what Nixon has done," everyone would be calling him "The Winner," wrote Just. "Why then are there still so many doubts about Nixon?"

The frustration gnawed at Nixon. Once, he began to recite to me the objections to his nomination and how he had dealt with them. Called a loser, he had entered and won every primary. Told Rockefeller was stronger, he took the lead from Rocky among independents. Told he could not win the fall election, he was showing up in the Gallup polls as the strongest candidate. Yet still came the carping that the Republican Party must turn to someone else.

"What the hell are we supposed to do!" Nixon exploded in exasperation. "Paint our asses white and run with the antelopes!"

AFTER OREGON, THE relationship with the press changed. This was in part a function of numbers. Our traveling staff grew, as did the press corps, for Nixon was now a near-certain nominee and potential President. We did not know many of the new reporters who came aboard, and they did not know us. They brought their own impressions of the old Nixon and their cynicism about the new, and we had all heard from Nixon that final verdict: "The press is the enemy." We had to be circumspect in what we said, as these folks were not friends but strangers. Haldeman and Ehrlichman had arrived after Oregon and a curtain fell between the candidate in the front of the plane and the staff and press to the rear. Occasionally, a reporter would be brought forward on the plane for an interview with the candidate, then escorted back.

Yet it needs to be said: Despite what happened to our relationship with the press after Oregon, the last major primary, the coverage of the comeback of Richard Nixon from January 1966 to May 1968 was as good as we could have asked for, or had any right to expect, given the wretched history of Nixon and the media. My files listing hundreds of columnists, cartoonists, publishers, editors, newspapers, and magazines contain countless letters from Nixon thanking these folks for fair, friendly, and even favorable coverage and commentary. The Nixon haters in these files are outnumbered five- or ten-to one.

Our coverage in the fall was another story, fault for which must lie in part with us. Some of the arriving journalists declared themselves to belong to what they called "the adversary press." I took them at their word. And with America dividing on cultural and racial lines, and with the riots and hundreds of U.S. dead coming home every week from Vietnam, they took their side and we took ours. It was never the same. Years after the Oregon primary, the traveling press and the small Nixon staff from those days before the curtain fell got together for a reunion on Martha's Vineyard one Memorial Day weekend. But there was a tenseness and testiness that had not existed in those early months of 1968.

How bad did it get? During that fall, through an error, the luggage of Rowland Evans of Evans and Novak was sent to the wrong city. It took days to retrieve. Evans was enraged and we apologized. But soon we were all laughing about it. And until election day, whenever Nixon heard of any negative comment by a reporter, columnist, or commentator on our plane, he would issue the command, "Lose his luggage!" We did not comply, but "Lose his luggage!" became an inside joke with the Nixon traveling staff.

THE FIRST KENNEDY DEFEAT

As we campaigned in Oregon, Reagan's name was on the ballot, and while he did not campaign, his people paid for the television airing of a film about the governor. Rockefeller, who had defeated Goldwater in Oregon in 1964 on the slogan "He cared enough to come"—Rocky had campaigned hard in Oregon that year—declined to return to the state. Mayor John Lindsay of New York came out instead to campaign for Rocky. So we ran an ad declaring, "He cared enough to send John Lindsay. Write in John Lindsay."

On the Democrat side, though he was riding victories in Indiana and Nebraska, Kennedy here hit the wall. Oregon was not a good fit for Bobby. The Democrats were not Catholic, blue-collar, or black but suburban liberal. And five days before the primary Drew Pearson and Jack Anderson reported that, as Attorney General, Kennedy had authorized the FBI to wiretap the now martyred Dr. King, a blow to both King's and Kennedy's reputations and Kennedy's hopes to rally Adlai Stevenson liberals. The wiretaps on King had become known in December 1966. Kennedy denied then he had been aware of them, a denial J. Edgar Hoover called "absolutely inconceivable."

The *Times*'s James Reston found Kennedy either noncredible or noncompetent in 1966, writing, "[I]f Mr. Kennedy didn't know, either he wasn't doing his job or Hoover was going beyond his instructions. If he did know, he was condoning what he now condemns."

We were at the Benson Hotel in Portland that election night, and by early evening it was clear that Nixon had won the Republican primary going away. He would win 73 percent to Reagan's 23 and Rockefeller's pathetic 4 percent. He and Mrs. Nixon went down to the dining room to celebrate.

For me Kennedy's loss, 45–39, was startling, the first defeat of a Kennedy in an election since JFK came home from the war to win his seat in the 80th Congress in 1946, a generation earlier. Now Nixon had won his primary and Jack Kennedy's younger brother, who aspired to be Nixon's rival in 1968, was flying up from California to accept his defeat.

I wanted to see this. Shelley and I stationed ourselves at the front door of the Benson. When Kennedy arrived with Teddy White and Freckles, his dog who traveled with him, the commotion was tremendous. We went to the ballroom where he was to make his concession speech and stood in front of the stage where he was to speak. His graciousness in conceding defeat and congratulating Gene McCarthy was impressive. He told his followers another great contest was coming a week later in California. The man in front of us seemed more like brother Jack than the "Ruthless Robert" of renown. I had seen JFK up close at a wedding in Palm Beach in 1958 and at his State Department press conference in 1962, where he had congratulated John Glenn on being the first American to orbit the earth. This was the first time I had seen Bobby in person. He could not have shown himself better in victory than he did in defeat that night.

"BOBBY KENNEDY'S BEEN SHOT"

It was 3 a.m. when the phone in my apartment on East 50th Street rang. I picked it up to hear the grim voice of Jeff Bell from the Bible Building.

April 4, 1968. Dr. Martin Luther King lies mortally wounded on the balcony of the Lorraine Motel in Memphis, as aides point to where the shot was fired. Nixon flies to Atlanta and marches in the funeral parade. *(Joseph Louw/Getty Images)*

Stokely Carmichael succeeded Selma bridge hero John Lewis as chairman of SNCC. He abandoned nonviolence, converted SNCC to "Black Power," expelled all whites, and was an instigator of the Baltimore riot of April 1968 that vaulted Governor Spiro Agnew to the nation's and Nixon's attention. *(Robert Abbott Sengstacke/ Getty Images)*

May–June 1968. After King's assassination ignited the worst riot in D.C. history, a Resurrection City was set up on the Mall and a Poor People's March begun by his successor Ralph Abernathy, who said, the "promise of a great society was burned to ashes by the napalm of Vietnam." *Above:* Coretta Scott King at the White House gates protesting the war. *(Courtesy of the LBJ Presidential Library—Robert Knudsen)*

April 1968. The worst campus riot of the '60s as Columbia University explodes in violence. Nixon's statement, written by me, called this the "first major skirmish in a revolutionary struggle to seize the universities of this country." It divides the Nixon staff and is denounced by Rockefeller, who now enters the race. *(AP Photo)*

June 5, 1968. An elated Robert Kennedy proclaims victory in California around midnight at the Ambassador Hotel. Minutes later, RFK was shot and mortally wounded in the hotel kitchen. *(Bettmann/CORBIS)*

June 25, 1968. At the breaking news that Chief Justice Earl Warren was resigning and Justice Abe Fortas would be nominated to replace him, I urged Nixon before a press conference to oppose LBJ's lame-duck packing of the Supreme Court. (NEW YORK DAILY NEWS/*Getty Images*)

Nixon and his staff watch the nomination roll call in Miami Beach. *Counterclockwise from Nixon:* me, Rose Mary Woods, Herb Klein, Ray Price, Dwight Chapin, and Bob Haldeman (*back to camera*). Famed war photographer David Douglas Duncan took this photograph. *(David Douglas Duncan/Harry Ransom Center, the University of Texas at Austin)*

Nixon and his running mate, Governor Spiro Agnew of Maryland, after Agnew turned back the Romney challenge for the vice presidential nomination. *(Wally McNamee/CORBIS)*

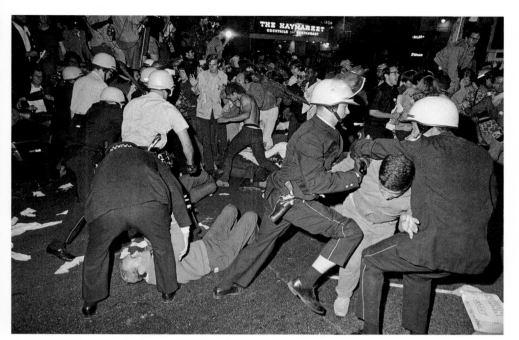

August 1968. Outside the "Comrade Hilton" from whose nineteenth floor Norman Mailer and I witnessed "the Battle of Chicago" that tore the Democratic Party apart and imperiled Humphrey's chances. *(Bettmann/CORBIS)*

Nixon on the hood of a limousine, giving his famous victory sign. We began the fall campaign 15 points ahead of Humphrey. *(Courtesy of the Nixon Presidential Library)*

Alabama Governor George Wallace, "the Wild Card" in the three-way race and a demon campaigner who was at 21 percent in early October and would carry five Deep South states and almost cost Nixon the election. *(AP Photo)*

On the road, with Ehrlichman, Haldeman, and Marty Anderson in the background.

Shelley Scarney, a veteran of Nixon campaigns, with future First Lady Pat Nixon aboard the *Tricia*. Shelley and I would marry in D.C. the weekend of the 1971 May Day riots, where the 82nd Airborne was deployed and 12,000 rioters were arrested and penned up near RFK stadium.
(Arthur Schatz/Getty Images)

October 16, 1968. Vice President Humphrey, President Johnson, and Nixon at the Al Smith Dinner where Hubert shone, but, as all too often, went on too long.
(New York Daily News/*Getty Images*)

A weary Nixon, in his bathrobe, in his Waldorf Astoria suite, as the networks call his victory, making him the thirty-seventh President of the United States. *(Courtesy of Dwight Chapin)*

Nixon's inauguration on the East Front of the Capitol, after which the limousine taking him to the White House would be showered with debris. *(Courtesy of the Nixon Presidential Library)*

"Bobby Kennedy's been shot!" Jeff said, and gave me the details as he had heard them over television from Los Angeles.

Nixon was awake when I phoned and told me David and Julie had been watching the returns from California of Kennedy's victory when the news came in. Within twenty-four hours, Frank Mankiewicz was on the hood of that limousine at the hospital announcing that Senator Kennedy was dead. We had already declared a moratorium on all campaigning. Nixon edited the statement I drafted describing Kennedy as "a man of tremendous energy and vitality" whose death was a "tragedy both for a family and a nation which have known too many such tragedies in recent times."

"While the Kennedy children are stricken with sorrow today," Nixon said, "as they grow up they will know their father was a young man of great courage who already had left his mark on history."

Nixon attended the funeral mass at St. Patrick's before the casket was taken to the train for the slow eight-hour trip to Washington, then to the site at Arlington where President Kennedy was buried. It was a sickening time, reflective of the poisoned character of our public life. Yet we were not yet at midpoint in a year that had seen the 77-day siege of Khe Sanh and the Tet Offensive, the assassinations of King and Kennedy, the worst race riots in our history, anarchic violence at Columbia and other campuses, and a President broken by a faraway war that was bringing home 200 to 300 Americans in body bags and caskets every week. America seemed to be a country coming apart. Four years before, fresh from his 44-state landslide, Lyndon Johnson exulted, "These are the most hopeful times in all the years since Christ was born in Bethlehem." It had not turned out that way.

YET EVEN WITH a victory in California, I had not seen Kennedy taking the nomination from Humphrey. And if somehow he did,

I had not seen him as a formidable opponent. In no contested primary had he won a clear majority of the vote. He had little of his
late brother's charisma, few of his brother's natural gifts. And Robert Kennedy as nominee would have made Johnson a silent partner
of Nixon, so great was the animosity between him and RFK. That
animosity dated to Robert Kennedy's resistance to Johnson's selection as vice presidential nominee in 1960, and RFK's contemptuous treatment of "Uncle Cornpone" during his brother's presidency.
Some Kennedy loyalists saw Johnson as a usurper, an illegitimate
heir to the martyred JFK. And LBJ's animosity could only have
been deepened by Bobby's having fallen upon him in his moment of
maximum vulnerability after New Hampshire, when RFK piled on
and accused the President of calling up "the darker impulses of the
American people." Nor did Gene McCarthy bear any great love for
his fellow Catholic who had lacked the courage to take on Johnson
until he, McCarthy, had wounded the President in the Granite State.

SCRAMBLING ON THE GUN ISSUE

On June 9, the day after Kennedy was buried, Maryland senator
Joe Tydings went on *Meet the Press* to launch a preemptive strike on
Nixon—for cowardice on the gun issue.

> Richard Nixon just several weeks ago issued a white paper on
> crime. It took six pages of fine print in the *Congressional Record.*
> He talked about everything and he conspicuously avoided any
> mention whatsoever of gun control. . . .
>   If we have that kind of leadership and timidity and fear of
> the gun lobbies, we are never going to get a responsible legis-
> lative program.

The next day I sent Nixon a memo quoting Sears as saying that
"the GOP, the law and order party, should not let the Democrats

grab the ball and run on Gun Control." I told Nixon that Martin Anderson was working on a "strengthened RN position on guns." Gun control was suddenly an issue ablaze. Nixon replied instantly: "Let's get the position out—& get Harlow to get some House members to push it. . . . Is there a new approach—no one has thought of? (like the adoption of a model state law)."

I attached to my memo a transcript of the answer Nixon had given to a gun control question in our Oregon telethon a week before Kennedy was shot. Nixon had replied to a questioner that while we needed to enforce state laws more effectively, "as far as federal law is concerned what should be required is simply an affidavit so that any individual who happens to buy firearms by mail has to indicate that he has complied with state law." The way to stop the proliferation of guns, Nixon had added, is to deal with crime, "because that's the reason a lot of people are purchasing firearms."

This was weak and Nixon knew it. Two days later, when I sent him Anderson's recommended position, Nixon wrote at the top, "Buchanan: Develop a way for RN to get out of his Oregon telethon position—perhaps a statement by Klein—answering a press inquiry?—and then add to it."

Anderson wrote that "recent polls show that about 85% of Americans favor more gun control legislation." Attorney General Ramsey Clark and Rockefeller were now piling on Nixon. Two weeks before Robert Kennedy's death, Rockefeller had called him a "carpetbagger" who "seems able to change his rhetoric as fast as he once changed his residence." Now Rockefeller was offering himself as natural successor to his fallen idol. "With [Kennedy's] death," said Rocky, "a strong hand has fallen from the torch of freedom." But, fortunately, Rocky's hand was there to catch it.

On June 12, forty-five U.S. newspapers, including the nation's largest, ran full-page Rockefeller ads targeting Nixon. On June 13, the *Times* carried a major story on a Rockefeller challenge to Nixon to a series of debates. The Rockefeller ads declared:

Our cities can be saved but they will not be saved by a gospel of do-nothing. . . .

They will not be saved by men who read rousing speeches about crime control—and say not a word about gun control.

They will not be saved by men who choke hope in the name of law and order—and then turn to undermine our highest court of law.

That morning I memoed Nixon again: Do not engage Rockefeller, do not get into a quarrel with him on gun control only a week after Robert Kennedy was shot.

Rockefeller's approach—rather the only way he can get news coverage of any kind—is to attack RN. His hope would be to force an angry response, and this is partially why he is gradually distorting RN's position on the Supreme Court, on gun control, on the draft. Our counteroffensive should be coming from our people on the Hill—who should accuse him of lying, of distortion, of dividing the party, of playing crass partisan politics in the wake of a national tragedy, or selling out the party's chances, etc.

Beside that recommendation, Nixon scribbled "OK." On June 14, I memoed Nixon again: "On gun control Bryce [Harlow] said if RN does not move Hubert will chew him up":

My own thinking is that perhaps the thing can be finessed. The NRA types are red hots, and if we can find a strong position in the public mind which is not a set anti-NRA position, I would take it . . . [but] Bryce thinks this is a gut issue.

Marty Pollner, our crime expert, had urged Nixon to adopt the LBJ-Clark line on guns, saying good politics and policy dictate it.

On June 15, I wrote Nixon endorsing Pollner: Hit LBJ hard for holding up the omnibus crime bill, which has gun control measures in it, and endorse LBJ's call for a follow-up gun bill. I told Nixon I was going to Washington to talk this over with Bryce and, at dinner, with Bill Loeb and the head of the NRA.

On the 17th, Nixon released a statement demanding that LBJ sign the crime bill, which had "90 percent of the gun control features the President asked," including controls on interstate shipment of handguns. Nixon's statement said he would extend these to mail-order rifles and shotguns to keep them out of the hands of minors, convicted criminals, and those with a history of mental illness. The statement got a terrific ride with UPI's lead: "Richard M. Nixon says President Johnson should 'cease dragging his feet' and sign the anti-crime bill if he is 'interested in vigorous national action against crime.'"

On June 20, after Johnson signed the bill, we clipped him again, saying the President and Attorney General Ramsey Clark had "proved more of an impediment than an impetus to the strongest provisions of the anti-crime bill," and both seemed "reluctant conscripts" in the "national war against crime."

On June 24, I sent Nixon 1,200 words on our revised position. He had supported controls on mail-order pistols in the crime bill, endorsed the crime bill itself, and now urged controls on mail order shotguns and rifles like the one Lee Harvey Oswald used. As for licensing and registering guns, that was not a federal responsibility. Alaska is not New York. LBJ's statement had read: "Automobiles, boats, dogs and even bicycles in many communities are commonly registered. Our citizens must get licenses to fish, to hunt and to drive." RN's response should be: "Fishing and hunting and driving licenses are the responsibility of the separate states." My memo concluded:

The political advisable position for RN is to appear before the public to be in favor of good gun control measures—but not to be in favor of those particular pieces of legislation which are going to send a million individuals into angry disgust over RN's position.

The great danger is that between now and November some prominent American is going to be shot to death by a rifle or pistol and then the hysteria will begin again—and we may be the target of it.

On June 30, courtesy of a *Washington Star* editorial, we came up with another idea. Nixon should say, "Why don't the states of this country pass laws which carry a mandatory jail sentence for any unlicensed person carrying a weapon—and a mandatory prison sentence for anyone using a gun in the commission of a crime." Nixon replied, "Good. Get it Out."

On July 3, I replied, under my own name, to an inquiry from the Emergency Committee for Gun Control, laying out the elements of Nixon's position while declining the committee's invitation to have the former vice president join their organization.

A month after Kennedy was shot, the storm died down. This terrible and unanticipated event had thrown us on the defensive and tested our ability to react. All on Nixon's staff knew the Oregon telethon position on guns was no longer tenable. We had to move. Our adversaries were seizing on Nixon's stand in the emotion of the moment to paint him as soft on gun violence and undermine his tough-on-crime stance. We had taken some hits, I thought, but succeeded.

In September, I received from an aide to Ed Brooke, Alton Frye, a letter explaining the senator's proposed National Firearms Inventory Act. Every manufacturer, importer, dealer, pawnshop, or individual gun owner that sold or transferred any gun would be required to send to the Treasury Department, as well as to local law enforcement, the name, address, age, and Social Security number of the recipient. Goal: a national registry of all gun owners and all guns. "[W]ith surveys showing approximately 70% of the population in favor of strong firearms legislation," Frye wrote, "we believe it is very important for the ticket to have a positive stance on the problem."

I have no record of a reply to Frye. And while fending off attacks on the law-and-order issue, we had launched one of our own in a place of special vulnerability for Johnson, Humphrey, and the Democrats generally—the town where they lived, the town where they ruled: Washington, DC.

"D.C. SHOULD NOT STAND FOR DISORDER AND CRIME"

"I have noted with concern the rising spiral of crime and terrorism in the District of Columbia," Jeff Bell, one of the youngest members of our research-and-writing team, began his memo of June 10, two days after the Kennedy funeral. Bell made his case with statistics. Crime had risen 24 percent in DC in the last year, housebreakings were up 43 percent, murders 67 percent. Bus drivers were going on strike to demand police protection. Roving gangs were shaking down businesses. Jeff put it into historical context:

> Throughout history, the first sign of a great nation's decay has been its failure to keep order in its own capital. . . . The first great republic in human history—Rome—became a dictatorship when mob violence in its capital became the rule instead of the exception. Much of the disorder and revolution in Europe for the last three centuries—from the first French Revolution, to the Bolshevik Revolution, to the Hitler takeover, to the present—could have been averted had the threatened governments been able to maintain order in their own capitals.

Bell suggested that Nixon issue a statement on crime in our capital city and place blame on the administration for doing nothing. I thought it a terrific idea. By June 17, I had expanded Jeff's memo to 1,200 words and sent the draft to Nixon as a Buchanan-Bell collaboration. "Good," Nixon wrote back. "See if [Bill] Safire might have any sharp phrases to add. Why not go with it when I am in D.C. Saturday. Release while RN is there."

In the writing process, references to Rome, Paris, St. Petersburg, and Berlin, where crime and violence in a capital city had presaged the fall of the Weimar regime, were dropped. But Safire had come up with a line we inserted into the text: "D.C. should not stand for disorder and crime."

On Saturday, June 23, Nixon was to address the GOP congressional candidates in DC and I came home to oversee distribution of our statement. It was a ten-strike. The *Washington Post* put a photo of Nixon at the top of page one alongside its story, which ran beneath the two-column headline "Nixon Labels D.C. a 'Crime Capital,' Blames Johnson." The lead said that Nixon was charging that the "disorders and violence here 'are more than a national disgrace— they are a cause for acute national concern.'"

"In the capital of the world's greatest democracy, freedom from fear must be re-established," said Nixon, "and the current Administration has not been equal to the task."

> If it is proved necessary to double the number of police in this city and to triple the number of court and prosecution personnel to effect a radical change here—then that is what must and will be done. I pledge that a Nixon Administration will sweep the streets of Washington clean of these marauders and criminals and remove from this city the atmosphere of apprehension and fear that hangs over it.

In that Sunday edition the *Post* published Nixon's statement in full below a four-column photo of him with GOP congressional leaders. We could not have gotten better coverage if I had been sitting in Ben Bradlee's chair. The *Star* ran an editorial praising the statement. The two-week project on the DC crime statement showed Nixon's team at the top of its game. Where he saw an opening to score, Nixon moved decisively.

SORRY END TO A CIVIL RIGHTS ERA

In 1967, Dr. King had planned a Poor People's Campaign, which, at his death, was taken up by his friend and successor Ralph Abernathy. In early May 1968, thousands came to Washington to set up a Resurrection City of tents and shacks on the Mall. Residents used this 15-acre mudflat as a base camp from which to launch sit-ins and civil disobedience in the Capitol and at Cabinet departments. The press reports were largely negative.

Abernathy was said to be residing at a posh downtown hotel while conditions at Resurrection City deteriorated. Girls coming to camp out in solidarity with the cause were allegedly being assaulted in their tents. I was on a shuttle coming from New York when the pilot tilted the plane coming down the Potomac so everybody could see the now-famous Resurrection City. Many of the passengers broke out laughing.

It was the wrong place and the wrong time. Washington was still smoldering from the fires of the worst riots ever to hit DC, after Dr. King's death. Bobby Kennedy was murdered one month into the protest. And Abernathy's demands for a "freedom budget" of billions were absurd when a Democratic Congress was calling for $6 billion in cuts in LBJ's "guns-and-butter" budget and the administration was looking favorably on the request.

Andrew Young wired Nixon to ask him to condemn Agriculture Secretary Orville Freeman for not transferring $200 million in customs receipts "to feed starving people." Then came an invitation from the widow of Dr. King and Abernathy for Nixon to join a Solidarity Day march from the Washington Monument to the Lincoln

Memorial, June 19, "to evidence your concern for the disadvantaged and dispossessed of our society." Nixon would be introduced from the platform.

I did not think this a good idea. Nixon declined. Nelson Rockefeller, Gene McCarthy, and Vice President Humphrey showed up. Rockefeller and McCarthy were cheered. Humphrey, who had launched his national career at the 1948 Democratic Convention with a blazing speech for civil rights, delivered in the face of a Dixiecrat walkout, and who had floor-managed the Civil Rights Act of 1964, was booed.

The AP reported, "The speeches were bitter." One wonders how LBJ, his record on civil rights unrivaled since Lincoln, reacted when he heard that Abernathy had declared that "the promise of a great society was burned to ashes by the napalm of Vietnam, and we watched the Johnson administration perform as the unwitting midwife at the birth of the sick society."

Abernathy said he would stay in Washington and engage in civil disobedience "until justice rolls out of the halls of Congress." But it was over. After June 19, the residents of Resurrection City were swiftly gone. Five years after this writer had stood on the steps of the Lincoln Memorial as King gave his "I Have a Dream" speech, the movement was guttering out—on the same spot.

That weekend, Rockefeller flew to the Stamford estate of Brooklyn Dodger legend Jackie Robinson and stood mute as Robinson, who had endorsed Nixon in 1960 over John F. Kennedy, volunteered:

Take a good look at the record. If Nixon is nominated I am a Democrat. The same people who supported Goldwater support Nixon today. If Nixon is elected president, we Negroes are in serious trouble; we would, in my opinion, be going backward.

We ignored "42." Bill Buckley, in a column he sent Nixon, noted Robinson's endorsement in 1960 and asked what had changed, as

"Mr. Nixon has backed every single civil rights bill written and unwritten."

Rockefeller had helicoptered over from his estate in Pocantico Hills to bring along the press to witness Robinson's smear that Nixon planned to roll back advances in civil rights. We ignored Robinson. If this was the best that Rocky could do, we had no worries on that flank.

"THE FORTAS FILM FESTIVAL"

A week after the Kennedy funeral, we received a clipping from the *Philadelphia Inquirer*. Earl Warren had "confided to friends" he was going to resign. The last paragraph read, "[T]he Chief Justice is said to feel that Richard Nixon—regarded as the GOP's likely Presidential nominee—would be bound to appoint a new Chief Justice pledged to overturn recent court decisions guaranteeing constitutional rights of criminals." Nixon sent the clipping back to me with a note: "Buchanan: Why doesn't Thurmond send this to Southern papers—opinion leaders?"

The *Inquirer* story was well sourced. Within days, Warren resigned, contingent upon the confirmation of a successor. Johnson moved swiftly to name Justice Abe Fortas, a longtime crony, to Warren's seat, and Appellate Court Judge Homer Thornberry, another crony, to Fortas's seat. This smelled like what it was, an insiders' deal cooked up to lock in liberal control of the Supreme Court before the nation, chafing under fifteen years of imperious Warren Court rulings, could speak to the issue in November.

On June 26, the day Fortas was named, I was with Nixon at LaGuardia, where he urged Johnson not to fill the Warren seat and start a "political donnybrook" where "the new chief justice would go in under a cloud." When we got to Michigan, Johnson had named Fortas, and Nixon dialed it back: "Although he [Fortas] is likely to be approved, it would have been better to have waited. . . . Now the matter is in the hands of the Senate and I am not going to interfere."

Some of us wanted very much to interfere. Senator Bob Griffin of Michigan had stepped out front and declared he would not vote to confirm anyone in 1968, that any nominations should be made by the President elected in November. On June 22, I had memoed Nixon that he might at least say that Griffin's stand was a "good idea" and we should look for a "new Learned Hand in the Federal System."

While I was urging Nixon to sign on to the Griffin position, fifteen GOP senators, including Howard Baker, Dirksen's son-in-law, issued a statement that any vacancies on the court should be filled by the President elected in November, and, "with absolutely no reflection on any individuals involved," these senators would "vote against confirmation of any Supreme Court nominations of the incumbent President."

That day, June 25, I spoke with former attorney general William Rogers and conveyed Rogers's view to Nixon: "[T]his is a battle that is now in the Senate, and should be left to the Senate." Nixon, Rogers was saying, should stay out of the fight. Privately, Nixon wanted the Fortas nomination killed, but he did not want our fingerprints on the murder weapon.

"What to tell Baker is the problem," I memoed Nixon. If we quietly counseled Baker to vote against Fortas and Thornberry, it would surely leak that Nixon was leading the resistance. The next day Martin Anderson called to tell me that Senator John Tower's office said Dirksen had come out for Fortas and Tower's people wanted Nixon to intercede with Dirksen before he brought along his Republican loyalists. Again I talked with Rogers. Nixon's position should be, he said, "It would be inappropriate for RN to make any comment; it is now in the hands of the Senate; it should be left to the Senate."

In a memo on the 26th I warned Nixon that there were rumors that if Fortas made it, "[Justice Hugo] Black and [Justice William]

Douglas will then resign, and their replacements will be Kuchel and Goldberg." I added my thoughts: "Buchanan's advice is to have them in the Senate put up a fight—rather than take the [court] packing lying down." I noted that Percy and Ed Brooke wanted to avoid a challenge to the Johnson nominees. Then I drafted a statement for Nixon to issue that was anything but neutral, and urged him to take the lead and sink Fortas. The proposed statement read:

> In the decade past the Supreme Court has become the focus of increasing controversy. . . . In decision after decision, the Court has taken itself across judicial frontiers proscribed by the decisions of its predecessors. . . .
>
> The Supreme Court sits today in the eye of a hurricane of public controversy. It is vital that there be a visible Wall of Separation between its chambers and the rough and tumble of the political arena. President Johnson has lowered that wall with the appointment of two men—whose outstanding common attribute in the mind of the people of this country—is their decades of loyal service to the cause of Lyndon Johnson's political career.
>
> I urge the Senate to withhold confirmation. The naming of a new Chief Justice should be left to the new President who receives a new national mandate just four months from now.

In a cover memo I mentioned that, after a "lengthy discussion" with Sears and others, "it might be better not to do anything. Certainly, the holding of the fire right now is advised until the lines clear and the gains and losses from acting become more apparent." Nixon, after circling "holding of the fire right now," replied: "1. Yes. 2. Keep RN advised of change in attitude."

So we held our fire. On July 10, Rogers and I talked again, and I sent Nixon his latest advice: "Bill Rogers is concerned that if RN says anything, it may be taken as a thrust against the first Jewish

Chief Justice. The thinking of Rogers is that RN should hold to his present course, and leave it up to the Senate."

Congress departed for vacation and the two parties headed to their conventions. Resistance to Fortas grew. When hearings began, the first ever for a Supreme Court nominee, Judiciary Committee Chairman Jim Eastland said he had "never seen so much feeling against a man as against Fortas."

The culture war had begun. Strom's office came up with the idea of inviting senators to a closed room for a viewing of *Flaming Creatures*, a transvestite pornographic film that Fortas, alone of the justices, in *Jacobs v. New York*, had ruled did not violate obscenity laws. Senator after senator went to the room, watched the film, and emerged shaken, to vote against elevating to chief justice any jurist who regarded this a legitimate form of entertainment. I had no role in the enterprise, but did tell *Time*'s Sim Fentress that "the Fortas Film Festival" was going to nail the coffin shut on our aspiring chief justice. Fentress relished the phrase and asked if he could quote me. Wishing not to involve Nixon, I said, "No attribution."

On October 1, 1968, on the Senate vote to halt the filibuster of Fortas's nomination, the Democratic majority needed 67 votes. They got 45. Abe Fortas asked Johnson to pull his nomination. Thus did we get Warren Burger as chief justice and the Burger Court. In 1969, Fortas would step down from the court in a scandal.

"COURAGE AND HESITATION"

This Fortas episode disclosed a potentially fatal deficiency in the Nixon campaign. While masterfully, even flawlessly, run in the primaries, ours was a campaign that rarely took risks. And it had failed to capture the heart of the country. We had not bonded with the people, as happens in great fighting causes. Moreover, the liberal side of the Nixon staff recoiled at our taking populist or strong conservative stands. On July 12, the columnist Roscoe Drummond, citing these "Nixon supporters," wrote that they "are aware that the only man who can defeat Nixon is Nixon himself. That is why they shudder a little when their candidate gives the impression that he is speaking too hastily after he has read the morning headlines."

Drummond cited three incidents, in all of which I had been involved, either by urging Nixon to take a stand or by writing or clearing his remarks. Drummond wrote that the dissidents felt Nixon had blundered when he described as the "flying *Pueblo*" a U.S. military charter ferrying troops to Vietnam, which had intruded into Soviet airspace but had been released after forty-eight hours and a U.S. apology. Allen had drafted and I had approved the "flying *Pueblo*" statement. Nixon also erred, said Drummond, when he blurted out that he agreed with Republican senators—not Dirksen, who was backing Fortas—that a "lame duck" Lyndon Johnson should not be appointing a new chief justice. The "supporters" were also shaken by Nixon's comments in early May about the radical student takeover of Columbia.

> While he was in the midst of the Oregon campaign, Nixon let out with a blast at the student protesters at Columbia University. Some Nixon supporters, who have first-hand knowledge of the Columbia situation, told me they felt Nixon made much too sweeping an indictment and that, while student use of force should be condemned, Nixon did not show himself aware of the many legitimate student grievances.

Jeff Bell put his finger on our real deficiency in a 2,000-word memo I sent to Nixon. Comparing our campaign to Dewey's in 1948, and noting that we had stalled in the mid-30s, 6 or 7 points behind Humphrey in three Gallup polls, while Wallace was surging, Bell wrote:

Clearly, nothing catastrophic has occurred. No significant errors have been made by RN or his campaign—as everyone, including the press, has acknowledged.

Equally, though, it is clear that a campaign which doesn't make mistakes is not enough. The RN campaign has been run on a strategy of not taking chances—and it has failed to catch fire.

On those occasions when a controversial issue has been seized, the initial flurry of protests from the liberal press has often caused it to be modified—if not dropped. Examples: Columbia, the Supreme Court, crime itself.

"It's my feeling," wrote Bell, "that we will win this election, if we do, by a strong appeal to the middle class: Americans who make $6,000 to $15,000 a year. The group that Richard Scammon has called 'the unblack, the unyoung, and unpoor.'" Crime, riots, and the decline of America's prestige abroad were the issues that resonated with these Americans. We needed less emphasis on "think" speeches. "I don't think the staunchest admirers of the 'New Coalition' and 'New Democracy' speeches would argue that these did us the slightest good with the Gut vote"—Nixon underlined this passage.

Because to the Gut vote what is important and understandable is that which is specific: this American ship held by North Korea, that poverty grant that subsidized a gang, this college being disrupted by sons and daughters of their bosses, that trade agreement which helped Poland to make the ball bearings which killed our men in Vietnam, that American embassy that was burned.

At this point in the Bell memo, Nixon wrote, "Have Bell get R.N. 10 or 15 examples he can use in speeches." The memo went on: "Liberal commentators will accuse us of demagogy whenever we do something that is appealing. I think we must steel ourselves to that fact." Nixon scribbled "Right" in the margin. On Vietnam, Bell wrote:

> Rockefeller claims to be the only candidate with a viable peace plan. RN must become the only candidate with a viable war plan. . . . Hanoi is not the sort of adversary that agrees to reasonable terms unless it faces, as its only alternative, a grinding process of attrition that will lead to defeat. This is a hard course for RN to take. On the other hand—given his own position and his future credibility—it is also the <u>only position</u> he can take.

At the top of the memo Nixon wrote, "Buchanan, follow up on page 5," which contained Bell's specifics of how to reach the Gut vote. Nixon ordered the memo sent to Whalen, Ellsworth, Haldeman, and Dick Moore. Haldeman ordered it sent to Price and Garment. Bell was articulating the frustrations of the research-and-writing team—Buchanan, Whalen, Allen, Anderson, Khachigian, Huston, Bell. Our opposition was Garment, Price, Safire, Ellsworth, and the political types, who agonized over what the press would say about tough law-and-order articles and Nixon's blistering attack on the Columbia radicals.

As we had seized on the DC crime issue, we wanted to attack the cronies' deal by which Nixon's old enemy Earl Warren, Johnson, and Abe Fortas were maneuvering to lock liberalism into the high court for another generation. Yet Nixon often seemed to conclude that he could best win by being the man in the middle between Humphrey and Wallace and running out the clock. He seemed of two minds: One responded instinctively, viscerally, positively, in margin notes to what Jeff had written. That Nixon wanted a fighting campaign. But wary of a backlash, the other Nixon would heed the counsel of those who warned that he was risking becoming another Goldwater, that he was resurrecting the "old Nixon" of the McCarthy era and Helen Gahagan Douglas days. The battle for the soul of the Republican Party between a robust and rising conservative movement and a Rockefeller-Javits-Lindsay wing in eclipse was raging inside the Nixon staff of 1968. *Courage and Hesitation* was the title of a book novelist Allen Drury would write about Nixon in 1972. The title fit the candidate of 1968.

ABOUT THIS TIME, in late June, there arrived at my office in the Bible Building, anxious to enlist, a young aide to Bronx congressman Paul Fino—of "Leftkowitz, Fino, and Gilhooley" fame, the 1961 mayoral ticket I had covered in journalism school. Within minutes of talking to Kevin Phillips, I realized he knew more about ethnic blocs and voting patterns of the 435 congressional districts right down to the county level than anyone in our campaign. Kevin had completed the first draft of his 1969 seminal work, *The Emerging Republican Majority*. He gave me a memo on dealing with the Wallace challenge. I sent it straight to Nixon—with this cover memo:

> This is a memo from an amazing creature in Fino's office who wants to work for RN—and who has enormous depth and breadth of knowledge of the American electorate and voting patterns. He has told me he would be willing to be quizzed by our four top people on his ability. Attached is a copy of memo prepared by him at Len's request <u>in ten minutes</u>.

After reading my memo and Phillips's memo, Nixon wrote back, "RN agrees. . . . Haldeman—Let's hire this guy." Phillips was aboard. Having read Phillips's book, Jeff Bell wrote me on July 12, "In terms of a grasp of national voting patterns and issue identification, right down to county level, I doubt if anybody in the country knows more." But rather than bring him into the research-and-writing operation, Haldeman assigned Phillips to John Mitchell, who had management of Nixon's overall campaign. Once aboard, Kevin sent me a note:

> Jeff Bell says that you give credence to the strategy of RN's winning Wallace Protestants and Humphrey Catholics. I expect that you will largely concur with the sociopolitical theory of the enclosed state strategy memoranda—New York, Illinois, Missouri, New Jersey and Connecticut—which I have prepared for Messrs. Mitchell and Flanagan. My principal emphasis, as you will see, is on garnering Catholic support.

The conservatives in the Nixon camp had gained a persuasive and well-positioned ally to press the strategy of a fighting campaign on the Gut issues, both to win the presidency and to realign national politics for a generation.

"GUESS WHO'S COMING TO BALTUSROL"

On July 8, Nixon hosted delegates to the GOP convention at the prestigious Baltusrol club in Springfield, New Jersey, where he was a member, though he had not golfed there in two years. Two days later, the New Jersey chapter of the ACLU charged Nixon with "participating actively in discrimination against Negroes and Jews" and demanded that the Justice Department investigate Baltusrol for violations of the 1964 Civil Rights Act.

Nixon was in Cleveland and the reporters were all over him, but he fought back effectively. Baltusrol did not have a policy of discriminating against Negroes or Jews and had Jewish members, Nixon said. Moreover, there were Jews and Negroes in the delegation he brought to Baltusrol and his Jewish partners at Nixon,

Mudge had played at the club. Nixon fell back on the "working-from-within" defense, declaring that he thought members of clubs who deplored their restrictive policies should vote within the club to integrate them and bring guests of all races and faiths in to enjoy the facilities. And that is what he did, and had done.

"Are there any Negroes in the club?" Nixon was pressed.

"There are no Negroes in the club," Nixon responded tightly.

With that, voice dripping with sarcasm, Nixon went on the offensive, leading with a pair of sentences that told those who knew him well that he was just below the boiling point.

> But let me make one thing very clear. Let's be quite candid about it. I hope . . . the press could perhaps render an unusual service for the press, that is adopt a single standard. Perhaps the press should ask all the presidential candidates to list all their clubs. Perhaps the press then should see what presidential candidates might adopt as a policy to get clubs to adopt a non-discriminatory policy. . . .
>
> Anyone who belongs to country clubs is quite aware of the fact that the major block is not religious. It is the color line. Whether it is a Jewish club or . . . a non-Jewish club . . . the color line has not been crossed in hardly any private clubs in America.

Nixon was asked what he had done himself to change the situation at Baltusrol.

> What I will do is actually what I have done, to bring people in as guests and then when the opportunity is presented by vote of the membership, to use my influence that way. I would trust, too, that Vice President Humphrey, Governor Rockefeller, Senator McCarthy, would do the same thing . . . if they are members of clubs of that type.

Nixon was virtually assigning the press to cover Rockefeller, too. Two weeks later came a delicious headline in the *New York Times:* "Rockefeller Quits Criticized Club." James Farmer of CORE, leader of the Freedom Riders of 1961, had demanded that Rockefeller resign from the Knickerbocker Club because of its discriminatory policies. Confronted by the press at his Harlem headquarters, after his Negro supporters demanded it, Rocky had announced that he was resigning from the Knickerbocker, as it refused to drop its policy of discrimination: "They are not ready to change their policies, and therefore I'm dropping out." There was some confusion as to whether the governor's letter of resignation had yet been received, or even sent. The governor said the matter had been handled by aides. The *Times* noted that Rockefeller was reviewing his membership in his other clubs on a "case-by-case basis." *Who's Who in America* listed Rocky as a member of the Century Association and the Dartmouth Club in New York and the Cosmos Club and Metropolitan Club of Washington. "The Knickerbocker problem was made more complex," said the *Times*, "by the disclosure that the club is housed in a building, at 62nd St. and Fifth Avenue, that is owned by a trust of which 4-year-old Nelson A. Rockefeller Jr. is the ultimate beneficiary."

Nixon lived at 62nd and Fifth Avenue. Weeks later, Nixon headed for Baltusrol for a round of golf. As Len Garment chortled, "Guess Who's Coming to Baltusrol," walking the course with Nixon was 7-foot ex–NBA star Wilt Chamberlain. Six months later, Jim Farmer was assistant secretary of health, education, and welfare in the Nixon administration. Revenge is a dish best eaten cold. What Murray Kempton once observed was true of some of us on staff when it came to Nelson Rockefeller: We had "reached that point in life when one's greatest pleasures lie in the misfortunes of others."

After Rockefeller's resignation from Knickerbocker, I put into Nixon's briefing book an answer to a question as to whether he would follow suit and resign from Baltusrol. "No, I'm not going to resign," but work from within, as we did at that delegates' gathering of "Jews and Catholics and Negroes and Protestants. The only discrimination was against Democrats."

> As for Governor Rockefeller I was rather surprised that he suddenly decided to resign from clubs in which he had a part ownership as I recall—such as the Knickerbocker—and where he has been a member for some twenty years at least according to the news stories. I am delighted that he suddenly saw the light after all these years—and is now following in the straight and true path. It's good to see the Faith come to one in his advancing years like this.

This last paragraph was written to amuse Nixon, who was enjoying the governor's discomfort as much as I.

On integrating private clubs, Nixon had a record and a commendable one. As a seventeen-year-old he had arrived at Whittier College, helped form the Orthogonians as a rival club to the elite Franklins, had become its first president, and brought in as a fraternity brother William Brock, a black star on the football team who called himself Nixon's "buddy" and would ever after, though a Democrat, vote for Richard Nixon.

PROTESTANTS, CATHOLICS, AND JEWS

In July also, a Gallup poll came out showing Humphrey at 40, holding the lead he had held since May, with Nixon at 35, his low point. Nixon had almost no support among Negroes and Jews and was winning 27 percent of Catholics against Humphrey, a Protestant, and 30 percent against Catholic Gene McCarthy. Yet, inside our political and press shops, the talk was all about how we had to increase our share of the black and Jewish vote or lose.

In a July 13 memo, politically incorrect even for that time, I wrote Nixon in exasperation, "[A]ll this endless talk we have been getting about RN losing unless he gets the Negro and Jewish vote is a pile of crap. We have let ourselves be sold a bill of goods."

> I have already documented the quintessential importance of RN winning the Wallace Protestants—the other wing of RN's victory is the Humphrey Catholics. . . . [They] have half of our victory and the Protestants of George Wallace have the other half. If we get one of these two halves back, we win; if we get them both, we can win a landslide—and the two objectives are not mutually exclusive.

Using statistics on the population of Catholics, Jews, and Negroes, I noted two statistical truths. The Catholic vote was nearly two and a half times the Negro vote and eight times as large as the Jewish vote. And as Jewish and Negro voters were more deeply Democratic in their loyalties, winning over Catholics was an easier proposition. Simply raising Nixon's Catholic vote from 27 to 35 percent, by 8 points, would add as many votes to Nixon as raising his share of the black vote by 20 points, which was hugely improbable, or raising his share of the Jewish vote by 60 points, an impossibility.

History was on my side. In 1960, John F. Kennedy, the first Catholic on a national ticket since Al Smith, won 78 percent of the Catholic vote. In 1964, Lyndon Johnson carried 76 percent. But with the social upheaval of the 1960s, Catholics had started to move. The 75 percent of the Catholic vote Democratic candidates for the House had won in the off-year election of 1962 had fallen to 65 percent in 1966. The three-to-one Democratic margin among Catholics had dropped to two-to-one. Political result: a Republican resurgence. The Democratic coalition had suffered a compound fracture. Not only was the Wallace vote gone in '68, another of its largest and most reliable blocs was breaking off. Besides Kevin Phillips, the Nixon aide who understood the Catholic opportunity best was Bill Gavin, who had grown up Catholic and conservative, his views and values shaped by family, faith, and friends, as he related in his splendid book *Street Corner Conservative*.

Tom Huston wrote me about the memo saying, "I don't think we have a chance to win in November unless we cut significantly into the Wallace vote and pick up a big chunk somewhere else (the Catholics, for instance)." But Huston thought my memo too raw:

> I fear that you state your case too strongly. Your conservative bias shows through so clearly that I am afraid the Boss may discount the merit of your arguments by dismissing them as the fears of a dogmatic rightist. Of course, I think you are 100% correct. . . . I hope you're still on the payroll by the time this arrives.

My prediction to Nixon: "Hubert Humphrey will be looking for a Catholic . . . to put on that ticket with him." Humphrey did exactly that seven weeks later with Senator Ed Muskie. Among my recommendations: If we were to make targeted appeals on issues and at events, the Catholic community should take precedence. On foreign policy: "It might be in RN's interest to begin to say what intelligent men are already saying—that when it comes to the Middle East or anywhere else—that an American statesman's first duty is to place America first, and not any other country, no matter how strong our ties or our commitments."

That July 13 memo ended, "The Irish, Italian, Polish Catholics of the big cities—these are our electoral majority—they, and the white Protestants of the South and Midwest and rural America. That way lies victory."

And so it would be for the next quarter century, from 1968 to 1992.

CHAPTER 9

The Wild Card

MY GOD, the galoots are loose!
—BRITISH REPORTER AT WALLACE RALLY,
American Melodrama (1968)

ON JANUARY 14, 1963, a newly elected Governor George Corley Wallace of Alabama delivered his inaugural from the portico of the State Capitol, the exact spot where Jefferson Davis had been sworn in as first president of the Confederate States of America. The historical fact was noted in his address, when Wallace declared, "In the name of the greatest people that have ever trod this earth, I draw the line in the dust and toss the gauntlet before the feet of tyranny, and I say segregation now, segregation tomorrow, segregation forever."

On June 13, 1963, Wallace, who had pledged to stand in the doorway and block any black student from entering the University of Alabama, did exactly that. The event had been choreographed. He stood in the doorway of Foster Auditorium in Tuscaloosa and defied a U.S. court order to admit Vivian Malone and James Hood. Nicholas Katzenbach, the deputy attorney general on-site, called the President. Kennedy immediately federalized the Alabama National Guard. Wallace stepped aside. The two students entered. The governor and the President both benefited. Kennedy had shown he would stand up for civil rights. Wallace had kept his word. Unlike at Ole Miss, there was no violence. It was a rehearsed one-act play on a national stage.

Years later, Wallace and I became friends, and I would visit him in Montgomery after he had been crippled in the attempt on his life in Laurel during the 1972 Maryland primary. He told me that while he accepted federal supremacy, he did not believe federal judges had the power they were asserting over states' rights. Had a law been enacted by Congress and signed by President Kennedy, ordering desegregation of the university, Wallace told me, he would have acted differently.

Three months after he stood in the doorway, on Sunday, September 15, 1963, three Klansmen planted nineteen sticks of dynamite outside the basement of the 16th Street Baptist Church in Birmingham. The blast killed four black girls, eleven to fourteen years old, injuring twenty-two others. Two months later, just days before that fateful day in Dallas, Wallace, not yet one year in office, declared for the Democratic nomination for president. Running in the Wisconsin and Indiana primaries, he drew huge crowds, winning a third of the vote against stand-ins for President Johnson, who was cobbling together a congressional coalition to pass the Civil Rights Act of 1964. In Indiana, Wallace ran strongest, wrote David Broder, "in the lower-income Polish districts around Gary." Against Senator Dan Brewster in the Maryland primary, Wallace won 47 percent of the vote, 15 of the 23 counties, a majority of the white vote, and a landslide on the Eastern Shore, which we in DC knew as "a little slice of Mississippi." In Milwaukee, Gary, and Baltimore, Wallace's support came from the ethnics: the Italians, Irish, Greeks, Poles, and other Slavs who saw their neighborhoods and schools imperiled by open housing and compulsory integration. His print ads in Maryland targeted the Catholics and ethnics of Baltimore and the steelworkers of Sparrows Point.

ONE WEEK AFTER Nixon declared his candidacy in New Hampshire in 1968, Wallace announced he would seek the presidency, but this time as a third-party candidate. He would not enter any Democratic primaries as he had in 1964, but would be on the November ballot. Wallace was a mortal threat to us and the last best hope of the Democratic Party to hold the White House.

In November 1967 I had done an electoral vote breakdown of a Nixon-Johnson race, without Wallace in. Nixon would carry upper New England, and 9 of the 11 Southern states, with Texas and Arkansas undecided. He would hold Indiana and Iowa, and sweep the plains and mountain states. My conservative estimate was that without Wallace in the race, Nixon had 196 electoral votes locked up, needing only 76 more from a trove of states that included California, Ohio, Illinois, Texas, Pennsylvania, New Jersey, Michigan, Wisconsin, Oregon, Washington, Missouri, and New York. Without Wallace in the race, we were the winter-book favorite to win the White House.

America had had its fill of the Great Society, the soaring crime rate, the riots, the inflation, the campus radicals, the war, and was ready to be rid of the party and President that had presided over it. If Nixon, a centrist, was the sole alternative to four more years of LBJ, he would win. The Wallace threat was that he gave alienated America a way to express its resentment at what LBJ and his party had produced, without replacing LBJ and his party.

Wallace was an ideal backlash candidate. He had been for five years America's most outspoken opponent of integration. He had denounced the hippies, rioters, and campus anarchists with a populist rhetoric Nixon could not match. He was a demon campaigner with a brutal but effective humor. Everywhere he went the crowds were big and excited. While he had only 9 percent of the national vote in a Gallup poll in April, by July, he was at 16. With his "Stand Up for America!" slogan and his charge against Humphrey and Nixon—"There's not a dime's worth of difference between them!"—Wallace was stealing our votes. And he had singled out Nixon, charging him, along with President Eisenhower, with having "put bayonets in the backs of the people of Little Rock" when Ike had sent in troops to integrate Little Rock High in 1957.

In early June I wrote Nixon a memo calling for "hard decisions with regard to where RN is going to get his Democrats to form his majority coalition." He could, I wrote, seek them in the Negro community that had gone 94–6 for Johnson in 1964. But black Americans were the most loyal of Democratic voters, especially with Humphrey, the civil rights hero of the '48 convention and floor manager of the 1964 Civil Rights Act, as nominee. "No one would disagree with going after these votes," I wrote. But even if we could raise the GOP share of the Negro vote from 10 percent to 30 percent, a monumental task, that would add only 1 million votes to Nixon's total.

On the other hand, Wallace's poll numbers, translated into ballots in November, meant he had already corralled 12 million votes, more than twice the entire Negro electorate. If we could peel away just 8 percent of the Wallace vote, that would add a million votes to Nixon's total.

"Which is easier for RN to accomplish?" I asked Nixon: for us to capture 20 percent more of the Negro vote or 8 percent of the Wallace vote?

You go hunting where the ducks are. We had to find our Democrats on the side of the pond where the Democrats were already telling pollsters they were swimming away from the party. Our problem: The "new Nixon" of the primaries—the mature, reasoned, relaxed, centrist-conservative of 1968, who was "cool" in a McLuhanesque sense—could not compete with Wallace as the Nixon of 1950 might have. I wrote Nixon a memo urging a "little more passion on the Boss's part, a determination to keep hitting on those gut issues in phrases which stick in the mind of the average voter," especially disaffected independents and Democrats. Nixon wrote back: "1. RN thinks this is very perceptive. 2. Discuss with Whalen, Haldeman and Safire as to: 1. Sharp phrases. 2. Media program in South."

Yet within the Nixon household there was a deep divide over ideas, issues, strategy, and the future of the party. FDR had put together a coalition that had ended seven decades of Republican dominance. To me the goal was always a new majority that would require cracking up this coalition. From 1860 to 1932, there had been thirteen Republican Presidents and two Democrats: Grover Cleveland and Wilson. From 1932 to 1952, FDR's coalition had won five straight elections. Eisenhower, who would have won on either party ticket, interrupted a generation of Democratic rule. But under Ike, the GOP atrophied, and after Ike had come Kennedy, Johnson, and a Democratic majority that controlled both houses of Congress for all of the eight years they were in office.

The crucial elements of the new majority I had in mind were the solid centrist GOP base that had stood by Nixon in 1960, the rising conservative movement, to which I belonged, the "northern Catholic ethnics" of German, Irish, Italian, Polish and other East European descent, and the Southern Protestants, who saw themselves as abandoned by a Democratic Party moving leftward. I had grown up in something of a Catholic ghetto. My mother's family was 100 percent German Catholic from the Mon Valley of southwest Pennsylvania. My father was the son of an Irish-Catholic mother of potato famine stock and a Scotch-Irish veteran of the Spanish-American War from Okolona, Mississippi. The guys I grew up with were from Democratic families. Yet most believed as I did. I had little in common with the liberals and moderates in Nixon's New York–centered campaign. While all of us were loyal to Nixon, we argued constantly over issues and the direction of the campaign.

In 1964 Wallace was a Democrat running in Democratic primaries. His movement had its greatest appeal in the old Confederacy, all 11 states of which had gone for Wilson and FDR all six times they ran. His strength in the North was among the German, Italian, Irish, Polish, and East European working-class and middle-class Catholic and Orthodox ethnics in the cities, who belonged to the Democratic Party of their fathers.

In mid-May Nixon devoted one of his national radio speeches to the "new majority" he hoped to lead. Safire had written it and I had not seen it. "A New Alignment for American Unity" described an "exciting, healthy development" in national politics about which observers had been unaware, a quiet gathering of disparate tribes on new common ground. The elements of this "alliance of ideas" were the Republican Party, the New Liberals, the New South, the Black Militant, and the Silent Center.

Repeating "new alignment" a dozen times, Safire was hoping to coin a phrase for the history books like New Freedom, New Deal, and New Frontier. But the coalition he described was an absurdity. James Reston called it a canvas painted by Jackson Pollock. Nelson Rockefeller scoffed that "incongruously pretending to merge new Southern leadership and the new black militants . . . is an exercise in political fantasy." Reston and Rockefeller had more than a small point. What caused the heart to sink was not the risibility of white Southerners, black militants, and Eastern liberals joining a congregation led by Pastor Nixon, but that Nixon could have delivered such a speech. For it was impossible to believe he believed this, from the incisive comments he was making on our strategy memos.

A NIXON-REAGAN TICKET

By now, members of the writing-and-research staff who understood what was happening beyond the Hudson—Whalen, Huston, Allen, Bell, Phillips—had concluded that while Nixon battled Humphrey for the center, we had to battle Wallace for Texas, Florida, the upper South, and the Catholic working-class and middle-class wing of the Democratic Party. At 16 percent, Wallace had locked up most of the Dixiecrat states that had gone for Goldwater—South Carolina, Georgia, Alabama, Mississippi, Louisiana. Four of these had gone for Strom Thurmond in 1948. The battle for the remaining six— Texas, Florida, North Carolina, Virginia, Tennessee, Arkansas— would likely be between Nixon and Wallace. We needed help on the Southern front and it had to come from our vice presidential choice. In an urgent memo to Nixon, I wrote,

> the Nixon campaign is confronted with the old German problem—the two-front war. . . . We are going to have to stave off the assaults of Wallace from the right, to keep him from making any further inroads, and we are going to have to defeat the challenge of Humphrey in the center of American politics. It is almost impossible for one candidate to do both of these things well at the same time.

Ronald Reagan on Nixon's ticket would free us of "the burden of fighting Wallace, a burden we would otherwise have to assume totally, a burden which would necessarily cost us in the center." During the primaries, I wrote, a conservative campaign to win a majority of the Republicans had been the sound and successful strategy. But in the fall, with both fronts active, it would be far different. "We are going to have to be bold to win this one," I wrote, and "I can currently think of nothing bolder than to put the hero of Bedtime for Bonzo on the ticket."

As Whalen relates in *Catch the Falling Flag*, Dick Allen had reached the same conclusion. Establishment hostility, Allen wrote, would block us from further gains at Humphrey's expense in the center. We needed to peel away Wallace votes—and Reagan was the man to do it. Not only was he a tremendous campaigner, wrote

Allen, "with him there is no crude appeal—his 'old-time religion' is founded on the very elements which are missing today: law, order, patriotism, thrift—and in language which the common man can understand." Whalen argued that Nixon needed a vice president to "take the heat and lightning in order to spare and conserve the prestige of the man in the White House." Our arguments pointed straight to Reagan.

I urged Nixon to treat Wallace with the respect the press denied him. If asked, "Mr. Nixon: Do you consider Wallace a racist?," I told Nixon he should reply, "Governor Wallace, by his own admission, believes in segregation and I oppose segregation." Not calling Wallace vile names, treating him with decency, would make Nixon more acceptable to Wallace voters when they abandoned his candidacy to choose Nixon or Humphrey. Moreover, it was the right thing to do. We did not know what was in George Wallace's heart. Years later, I came to know and regard the governor as a friend. In *Nixon on the Issues*, our campaign compendium, Nixon is quoted thus:

> I don't buy the line of some of the professional liberals in the press and television that Wallace's vote is entirely racist. Of course, he does appeal to this element. However, it is not all racist if the polls are right and 21% or 15 million people are considering voting for him. Many of these are union members, white collar people and the like—good, honest, decent Americans who are concerned about law and order, and concerned about the fact that our foreign policy has brought us a lack of respect around the world. These people are concerned about issues that George Wallace is hitting very effectively, yet in a very simplistic way.

When Howard "Bo" Callaway, the ex-congressman who had lost the Georgia governor's race to Lester Maddox in 1966, and our

1968 Southern chairman, said he would welcome Wallace's support and Wallace belonged in the Republican Party, and on "our team," Rockefeller landed on us. Wallace is a racist, railed Rockefeller, and Nixon is running a "Southern Strategy." He demanded that Nixon repudiate Callaway.

In Nixon's "Briefing Book," which was done in Q & A style and which I kept constantly updated, I put in four questions about Rockefeller, Callaway, and Wallace. I urged that Nixon say that he would not engage in "verbal swordplay" with Rockefeller, as that might imperil the Republican unity that we had achieved. But Bo Callaway was "not a racist."

"As for Mr. Wallace himself, we have not sought his backing— and after reading a few of his comments about me, we're not counting on an early endorsement." As to the Rockefeller allegation we were running a "Southern Strategy," I urged Nixon to reply, "[W]e're not writing off any state, South or North, East or West. As a matter of fact—with Governor Rockefeller carrying the ball for us up there in the Empire State—I think we can take New York from Hubert Humphrey this fall." To the questions "Mr. Nixon: Do you agree Governor Wallace belongs in the Republican Party? Do you agree with Governor Rockefeller that Mr. Wallace is a racist?" I recommended this answer:

> I am not going to set myself up as a one-man credentials committee of the Republican Party. . . . Mr. Wallace is running on the American Independent Party ticket—and up to very recently, he has been a Democrat—like Arthur Schlesinger— so I don't think that is a problem that is really of any pressing concern to the Republican Party. . . .
>
> As for whether or not I agree that George Wallace is a racist, let me say this. There is a gulf of difference between the positions of Governor Wallace and Richard Nixon on the issue of civil rights and other issues, there is no question about this.

> But I don't think it serves any cause at all for me to be calling
> him names—or to call any other candidate names. This coun-
> try is deeply divided and I don't think I would be serving the
> cause of unity by calling Mr. Wallace or anyone at this point
> in time "a racist."
>
> Walter Lippmann said recently that there is a desperate
> need in America to return to the "tradition of civility." I would
> endorse that statement.

This was the tone. If you wanted Wallace's people to come your
way, you did not insult the man. Some in the press suggested that
to treat Wallace with respect was an immoral Southern strategy.
Yet these same folks did not seem to object when Vice President
Humphrey, declaring, "I am happy to be in the presence of a good
Democrat," had walked arm in arm with Lester Maddox, who had
kept black folks from integrating his Pickrick Restaurant by bran-
dishing pick handles, forever after known as "Pickrick drumsticks."

"The Democratic Party is like a big house," said Humphrey,
standing beside Maddox. "There's room for all of us." Nor do I fault
Humphrey for being gracious to Maddox. At a huge indoor rally in
Marietta in 1996, when my presidential campaign was at apogee, I
had finished my speech and had started to leave, when I heard my
name called out by someone on stage behind me. I turned and saw
the outstretched hand and smiling face of the octogenarian former
governor of Georgia who had crossed party lines to endorse me.

CHAPTER 10

Montauk and Miami Beach

BUCHANAN, I THINK we've got ourselves a
hanging judge.
—RICHARD NIXON, MIAMI BEACH (1968)

O N JULY 18, President Eisenhower, at Walter Reed after
a fifth heart attack, wife Mamie at his side, summoned
reporters—to endorse Nixon for President. No one had
forgotten Ike's dismissive comment, eight years earlier, when asked
to give an example of a major decision where Nixon had played a
crucial role. "Give me a week, and maybe I'll think of one," Ike
quipped. Sander Vanocur of NBC, a press questioner in the first
Kennedy-Nixon debate, had thrown Ike's quote up at Nixon, taking
him by surprise, and ensuring 70 million Americans did not forget
what Ike had said. Now Ike was making up for it, saying of Nixon,
"He's a man of great reading, a man of great intelligence, and a man
of great decisiveness. He's had great experience over the years and
he's still quite a young man."

Hearing the news, Rockefeller was his usual gracious self:
"It would be an embarrassment for [Nixon] if he didn't" get the
endorsement, said Rocky, since Ike's grandson was about to marry
Nixon's daughter. "If my grandson was marrying Dick's daughter, I
think I'd endorse him myself."

WHALEN VS. BUCHANAN—ON VIETNAM

As the convention approached, Nixon assigned Whalen to write the Vietnam statement that he would deliver to the platform committee as his position on the war. From *Catch the Falling Flag*, the reader might conclude that Whalen thought I had signed off on what he had produced. I had not. When the July 28 "4th draft" was turned over to me, I sent Nixon four pages shredding it. Whalen's statement condemned LBJ for sending 500,000 troops to South Vietnam, which was far beyond the modest levels deployed by Eisenhower and JFK. Nixon seemed to be damning Johnson for an escalation of the war that he had himself advocated, supported, and defended. I wrote Nixon,

> It seems to me a bit demagogic to ram Johnson while praising Ike and JFK—since neither of the latter two had to contend with the type of guerrilla-overt warfare that LBJ was confronted with. Saying Ike and JFK kept our involvement within the scope of our aims again seems demagogic since there was no war going on. . . . RN has himself said our aim is to keep a non-Communist Vietnam which is in the <u>strategic national interest</u> of the United States. Is that no longer true? Or are 500,000 men [sent] to uphold those interests—to achieve those aims? . . . [If this is] only an "Asian war for self-determination"—then what the hell are we doing there in the first place?

In the Whalen statement Nixon was to say, "The next administration will reverse a fundamental error of the present one and reduce the military and political involvement in the war. I declare this aim of 'de-Americanizing' the war without reservation or qualification, for it is basic to the search for peace." Not only had Nixon supported this "fundamental error," the term "de-Americanizing" the war, I wrote Nixon, was understood by hawks and doves alike as code for getting out and letting the Vietnamese settle the issue. As of the summer of '68, that meant a Communist victory.

Whalen's draft continued, "I have refrained from a promise of 'victory' in Vietnam, for the ordeal inflicted on the nation by the present administration has drained that word of its meaning." This sentence, I wrote, represents "an awfully brutal attack on this Administration—it would seem to me the Viet Cong, the N Vietnamese and the Communist world is one hell of a lot more responsible for the 'ordeal' inflicted on Americans and South Vietnamese than anybody else." And ruling out victory seems a "sop to the doves" that will do nothing for us but "tick off some people who think RN will win a victory of sorts for the US."

Whalen had included in an earlier draft a line dating to the March speech: "The B-52 is an extremely costly and irrelevant weapon against the Vietcong terrorist armed with a knife." I had seen this line before and felt it nonsensical. The B-52s interdicted arms, troops, and supplies coming down the Ho Chi Minh Trail through Laos, and B-52s over Hanoi in 1972 and in the "Christmas Bombing" of that year would force Hanoi to sign the peace.

Yet what Whalen's statement, which I persuaded Nixon to gut, and the March 30 speech that had been aborted by LBJ's preemption said, loud and clear, was that Nixon's advisers were at odds on whether we should fight on in Vietnam. And as Nixon had been prepared to deliver the earlier Whalen speech, and was considering going with the Whalen draft to the platform committee, he was entertaining a new range of options on the Vietnam War, strategically and politically. And if this was apparent to Whalen and to me, as we had been wrestling over Vietnam since he came aboard, it was not lost on Moscow or Hanoi.

IN EARLY AUGUST, while the rest of the staff flew on to Miami Beach, Nixon brought Price and me out to Montauk, where he had holed up to write his acceptance speech. Here we encountered the Secret Service assigned after the assassination of Bobby Kennedy. As Price and I were walking up the drive to the house to meet with Nixon, I spotted a Secret Service man. To check his reaction, I picked up a stone and threw it high over his head into the woods beyond. It landed with a crunch. The Secret Service man went into a crouch, put his hand on his gun, and stared toward the woods. When I told him it was me he was not amused. Probably not a smart thing to do.

Nixon was cloistered for days. We rarely saw him. Once he phoned and said tersely, "Send me three paragraphs on crime," and hung up. The lines would be woven into his speech. I also drafted Nixon's statement on crime to be sent to the platform committee.

The great preventive of crime is respect for law and the rights of others, I wrote, "[b]ut when the homes and schools and churches of a free society fail in their role as commissioned watchdogs of those standards, then the people must fall back for their safety upon police and prosecutors and courts . . . the last defense of a free people." By 1968, the country had had enough of crime, riots, and campus anarchy and had heard enough about this being the inevitable consequence of what our oppressed youth and minorities had to endure.

About our nomination I was not in doubt. Even if we came up short on the first ballot, the favorite-son delegations would then be released, and there were Nixon loyalists in every one, including Rockefeller's New York, Romney's Michigan, and Reagan's California. We would go over the top on the second ballot. As for a Rockefeller-Reagan alliance, I did not see how it worked. Reagan's people would never accept the nomination of Nelson Rockefeller, who had damaged and then deserted Barry Goldwater. And to Rockefeller's people, Reagan was the Goldwater of 1968. My sense was that if Rockefeller started gaining traction, Reagan's folks would throw in with us. And if Reagan looked like he was about to stampede the convention, the moderates and liberals would panic and come to us. The Rockefeller and Reagan forces might be working together, but neither would accept the other's man. And neither Rockefeller nor Reagan would take second spot on the other's ticket. Had they thought this through to the endgame?

Indeed, if the two should stop Nixon and deadlock the convention, the delegates would be looking to a centrist candidate who could unite the party. This would bring them back to Nixon. Their dilemma: If they stopped Nixon they would get Nixon. The Boss was yet again in the catbird seat.

At Montauk, after talking with Ray Price, I realized that the choice of Reagan as running mate would risk a redivided Republican Party, which we had come so close to uniting. At dinner, I told Ray that the one candidate who could do the most to help us in the South, in the border states, and among working-class Democrats, and also in carrying California, was Reagan. Price objected vehemently and viscerally. The conversation became acrimonious. Ray seemed sympathetic to Lindsay. I told him Lindsay was intolerable. By the time we returned to our cabin we were barely speaking. Yet, as Ray reflected the thinking of the establishment, his reaction meant that Reagan's nomination for vice president could cause a liberal walkout in Miami Beach. But if the polls showed us still running behind Humphrey at convention time, I believed we had to roll the dice.

Where were the polls? Gallup was the gold standard, and we had been up and down that turbulent year. In mid-April, according to Gallup, Nixon had a 9-point lead over Humphrey, 43–34. By early May, the alarm bells had begun to ring. Nixon had lost 5 points and was only 3 ahead of the vice president, 39–36.

Wallace had gained what Nixon had lost. He had surged from 9 percent in mid-April to 14 percent in just three weeks, which explains Nixon's feeling that his presence at the King funeral must have hurt. We were now in a battle with Wallace for the votes of Democrats recoiling from what the Great Society had produced. And we were losing that battle. The conservatives in Nixon's writing-and-research shops began to argue that Reagan on the ticket might be the sine qua non of winning the White House.

By late May, Nixon had fallen to 36 percent and Humphrey was at 42. He had gained 8 points in six weeks. By the end of June, he was still 5 points ahead at 40 percent to Nixon's 35, and Wallace was creeping up, at 16 percent. The choice of running mate was now looking critical, if not decisive.

At Montauk, Nixon asked me to sound out Bill Buckley and James J. Kilpatrick, the popular conservative columnist, on whom they would like to see on the ticket. Both had been supportive since the breach with *National Review* was healed in early 1966. That they were both backing Nixon and not Reagan had sent a clear message to the conservatives. When I called "Kilpo," he was taken by surprise but volunteered the name of Howard Baker, the freshman senator from Tennessee.

"What about Reagan?" I asked.

"Can we get Reagan?" asked a surprised Kilpo.

Maybe, I said, if folks will start pushing him.

I called Buckley. His recommendation: John Gardner, LBJ's secretary of health, education, and welfare, who had presided over the creation of Medicare. I asked Buckley if he was joking. He stood his ground. Gardner was the man.

"Buckley said that!" Nixon said, astonished.

Five years later, in the final days of Watergate, I wrote Buckley a note: "How stands the Gardner for Vice President Committee?" Buckley shot back, "The Gardner for Vice President Committee believed in just enough law and order to keep him out of the Oval Office."

BATTLE OF THE POLLSTERS

On July 25, Lou Harris delivered what he surely hoped would be the coup de grace, a poll fairly screaming that if Republicans wanted to win in November they would not dare to risk nominating Nixon a second time.

"Despite his string of victories in the primaries," Harris wrote,

> the "loser image" still sticks with Nixon. Before he declared his candidacy, 55 percent of the nation's voters agreed with the statement that "he has lost too many elections." After the primaries . . . 52 percent of the electorate still views Nixon as a "loser."

As Lincoln said, they have a right to criticize who have a heart to help. And Lou had a solution to the party's Nixon problem. About Rockefeller's claim that "he is personally more popular than Nixon, the evidence tends to bear out the New York governor's claim," wrote Lou. Harris reported that after polling a "cross-section" of voters on characteristics they would ascribe to each of these two candidates, Rockefeller had won on being independent, strong, coolheaded, good-looking, straightforward, up-to-date, and exciting, and one who inspires confidence. Nixon led Rockefeller in the categories of being too clever, old-fashioned, weak, dull, and not his own man.

Rockefeller led Nixon among suburbanites and city dwellers, Jewish voters, Democrats, independents, Negroes, the college-educated, union members, voters outside the South, and those under thirty-five. Nixon led among Republicans, Southerners, small-town and rural voters, and people over fifty. Harris's head-to-head showed Rockefeller leading Humphrey 37–34.

But Harris had Rockefeller losing to Gene McCarthy, 38–32. This seemed to suggest that Harris had sampled rather heavily among Kennedy-McCarthy voters of the antiwar Left, who did not like LBJ's vice president either. Harris's survey and analysis seemed so slanted as to be devoid of all credibility. Yet by convention time such polls were Rockefeller's last best hope of stopping Nixon. However, if you live by the polls, you often die by the polls.

When Gallup's final preconvention poll came out on Monday, July 29, Nixon had received a new prognosis. Startlingly good news. Nixon had closed his 5-point deficit with Humphrey at June's end and moved into a 2-point lead, 40–38. That was a 7-point turnaround in Nixon's favor in July. Wallace was holding at 16 percent. In this poll, Rockefeller was tied with Humphrey 36–36, with Wallace taking 21 percent. Rockefeller was seen as not tough enough to take votes from Wallace. Harris's "Nixon-can't-win" argument had been torpedoed amidships. Gallup's message to Miami Beach delegates: Nixon is your strongest candidate. And as Nixon had won all of the primaries, was the favorite of the Republican rank and file, and now had America's most respected pollster saying he alone was beating Humphrey, there was no argument left for denying him the nomination.

Lou Harris swiftly produced a new poll that put Rockefeller up 6 over both Humphrey and Gene McCarthy, 40–34, with Nixon trailing both—behind Humphrey 41–35 and McCarthy 43–35. Our response: What else would you expect from "Lying Lou," whom Nixon folks viewed as a leftist who had been in the tank for JFK? When Gallup and Harris got together to reconcile their differences—Gallup had polled from July 20–23, Harris from July 25–29—the effect was to discredit both.

A HATFIELD BOOMLET

By the time we got to Miami, the major issue still undecided, if our delegate count held, was Nixon's choice of a running mate. Still, we were nervous that one or more of the convention speakers might go dovish on Vietnam, endorse a bombing halt, and cause a split the press could exploit. Of special concern was Senator Mark Hatfield of Oregon. Ellsworth and I argued with the senator over the speech he planned to deliver. Recollections differ as to how responsive he was, but his final draft presented no difficulties.

A liberal on foreign policy and a press favorite, Hatfield was thought to be on Nixon's short list. Whalen and others had signed a memo in Miami Beach urging Nixon to choose Hatfield as vice presidential nominee to signal the future of Vietnam War policy. I was adamantly opposed. Hatfield was an attractive man and candidate but a "Christian pacifist," I told Nixon, a dove on Vietnam. His selection would say that Nixon had given up all hope of victory. Our Tower-Goldwater-Thurmond flank would be imperiled. Reagan would have an opening. And what did Hatfield bring? With Gallup showing us ahead of Humphrey, the probability of any gamble—choosing Lindsay, Hatfield, Percy, or Scranton on the left, or Reagan on the right—was, I felt, gone. Nixon would, I believed, make a safe centrist choice like Governor John Volpe of Massachusetts, the Italian-American whose working-class and ethnic roots could help in New Jersey and Connecticut, or Senator Howard Baker of Tennessee, who might help in the border states.

"WE GOT THE BIRCHERS!"

While our delegate hunters and counters in Miami were fending off raiding parties, keeping Strom secure from the Reagan camp, the research-and-writing staff was working with the convention speakers like Governor Agnew, who was to nominate Nixon, and those who were to give the seconding speeches.

The Agnew speech nominating Nixon was our first collaboration. As Whalen relates in his memoir, Agnew had rejected a staff-written speech. It was then edited by his chief speechwriter, Cynthia Rosenwald, and rejected again. Whalen then wrote a draft Rosenwald returned, as the governor had said "it has too many long sentences." Whalen enlisted Price, whose speech was rejected as not sounding like Agnew. "Time was running out," wrote Whalen in *Catch the Falling Flag*. "We could, if necessary, impose a draft on Agnew but that would only cause bad feeling and guarantee a poor performance."

> Buchanan came to the rescue. "Let me have those papers," he said, scooping up the drafts and disappearing into his room. For an hour his typewriter rattled like a machine gun, and the prose came out in short simple bursts. This draft, sped to the governor, came back approved. Confident that we would shortly see and hear the last of Agnew, we turned to the only source of excitement at this cut-and-dried convention, Nixon's choice of his running mate.

The night of Agnew's speech and Nixon's nomination, a few of us were invited into Nixon's suite to witness his moment of triumph. Also invited, to record Nixon watching his nomination, was Mike Wallace with his CBS camera crew. The roll call began and was going as expected from what we had been told by Mitchell, Ellsworth, and Sears. But when Michigan was called and the chairman of the delegation rose to announce 44 votes for Romney, 4 for Nixon, I blurted out, "We got the Birchers!"—forgetting about the CBS cameras. We had expected that four hard-core conservatives in the Michigan delegation, possible Birchers, would abstain or vote for Reagan. No one had expected them to go for Nixon. Nixon looked at me, startled. A discussion was swiftly held with Wallace agreeing to excise my instant analysis from the tape that was later shown to the nation.

Wisconsin put Nixon over the top, which delighted him. John MacIver, who had delivered that state, was seen on CBS being pounded on the back by colleagues as Governor Warren Knowles announced that all thirty of Wisconsin's votes would go to the winner of the April 2 primary. After the roll call ended, Bob Finch came into the suite, tears running down his cheeks, and cursing. The tears were tears of joy that the Boss, whose failed 1960 campaign Bob had managed, had won. The cursing of the lieutenant governor of California was for the governor of California. Nixon put his arm around the shoulder of his former aide and devoted friend and walked him into another room so we would not see the tears. The two had shared moments of defeat that I had not known.

"TIRED OF NEGROES AND THEIR RIGHTS"

In his statement to the platform committee, Nixon took a stance on Vietnam that would be reflected in the policy he would pursue as President. He called for training and equipping the South Vietnamese to assume the burden of battle. "American troops can and should be phased out."

On crime and justice, Nixon's statement to the platform committee clashed with that of Mayor John Lindsay. "The root cause of most crime and civil disorder is the poverty that grips over thirty million of our citizens, black and white," said Lindsay. "If we are to eliminate crime and violence in this country we must eliminate the hopelessness, futility and alienation from which they spring." His remarks did not explain why there was less crime in the Depression than in the prosperity of the Soaring Sixties.

The Nixon statement was consistent with what we had written in *U.S. News* in 1966 and *Reader's Digest* in 1967. We laid responsibility for crime and violence on the perpetrators and a cowardly establishment that could not or would not unapologetically enforce the law.

> The people of this country want an end to government that acts out of a spirit of neutrality or beneficence or indulgence toward criminals. . . . Poverty, despair, anger, past wrongs, can no longer be allowed to excuse or justify crime or violence or lawlessness. We must cease as well the granting of special immunities and moral sanctions to those who deliberately violate the public laws—even when those violations are done in the name of peace or civil rights or antipoverty or academic reform.

Nixon was not here professing indifference to the grievances of black America, or denying that issues of poverty, peace, and civil rights needed to be addressed. He was saying these causes did not justify lawless methods or violent means and as President he would not tolerate, condone, or indulge the use of such methods or means. And the country had moved toward our view. By 1968 law and order was seen as the sine qua non of a civilized society, and the country had concluded that the real "root causes" of crime were criminals.

Between Humphrey, who had ruminated about "leading a pretty good riot myself," and Wallace, who told his roaring crowds no hippie better "lay down in front of my presidential limousine," we were perfectly positioned. Yet there was no doubt that on the law-and-order front the threat did not come from the Left or Hubert Humphrey.

SOMETHING NORMAN MAILER wrote in Miami Beach was reflective of how the mood of the country had changed from the early and mid-'60s—the days of desegregation of the Universities of Alabama and Mississippi and the atrocities against Medgar Evers and the girls at the 16th Street Baptist Church. With other reporters he had found it "unduly irritating" to be made to wait a good period of time for the scheduled arrival of Ralph Abernathy, Dr. King's friend and successor, at a press conference at the Fontainebleau:

> as the minutes went by and annoyance mounted, the reporter became aware, after a while, of a curious emotion in himself, for he had not ever felt it consciously before—it was a simple emotion and very unpleasant to him—he was getting tired of Negroes and their rights. It was a miserable recognition, and on many a count, for if he felt even a hint this way, then what immeasurable tides of rage must be loose in America itself?

"TWO DAUGHTERS"

Against few journalists did Nixon bear a greater or more justified grudge than James Wechsler of the *New York Post*. Wechsler had been a member of the Young Communist League in the 1930s who had split with the party after a trip to the Soviet Union and the Hitler-Stalin Pact. As a *Post* editor, he had broken the story of Nixon's "secret fund," which—though it turned out to be a normal political fund to pay for Nixon's travel on behalf of the GOP and its candidates—almost drove Nixon off the 1952 ticket and brought about the "Checkers speech."

In June 1966, Wechsler's daughter Holly was graduating from Finch College in Manhattan with classmate and friend Tricia Nixon. In a column, "Two Daughters," Wechsler wrote how he was determined to appear at Holly's graduation, lest "another father, older, busier and perhaps wearier," show up and shame him for his absence. Noting that Nixon "once used my name on a national TV broadcast in an effort to find Adlai Stevenson guilty of association with me," Wechsler described the ninety-minute ceremony:

312 PATRICK J. BUCHANAN

At the end we were admonished to remain in our seats while the "Recessional" took place. The students, lamentably attired in caps and gowns that no young woman should be forced to wear, filed out in pairs; one from the left side would find a companion from the right.

From the left came Patricia Nixon, a lovely animated blonde young woman; from the right came Holly, whose beauty was plain in the eye of the beholder. And through the accident of such arrangements, they arrived at the same starting point at the same time and they walked the same steps of this sentimental journey together with unforgettable smiles. I trust they were not laughing at their feuding fathers.

At that moment all political combat seemed remote and irrelevant. I have no way of knowing whether Richard Nixon knew Holly's identity . . . [yet] we were joined together in the fatherhood of man. . . . I winced at the recollection of some things I had written.

Wechsler finished his column by saying that when he got back to the office, he signed off on an editorial attacking Nixon's speech on academic freedom. In a personal letter Nixon responded that same day:

While we have disagreed on some major issues over the years, there is obviously one subject on which we are in complete agreement—both Holly and Tricia are lovely young ladies!

I, of course, understand the necessity for your running the editorial on my speech at Rochester. I would not respect you or your associates on the editorial staff if you had allowed our "academic truce" to affect your editorial policy.

Four days later, Wechsler wrote back: "Many thanks for your gracious note. . . . Perhaps the friendship between our daughters

says something more important about our country than the differences we have had. Holly was also delighted with your letter."

While not the Christmas truce in the trenches of 1914, this gesture, across a near-unbridgeable ideological gulf, spoke well of both
men and of their generation. And it underscored the priceless asset
Nixon had in his daughters. At Miami Beach, Mailer, another New
York Jewish intellectual, writer, and man of the Left, was taken
aback by Julie and Tricia, their poise, and their devotion and defer-
ence to their father:

> The arrival of the girls [Tricia and Julie] and covert scrutiny
> of them by the reporter [Mailer] produced one incontestable
> back-slapping turn-of-the-century guffaw: a man who could
> produce daughters like that could not be all bad. The remote
> possibility of some reappraisal of Richard Nixon was now
> forced to enter the works. . . .
>
> Nothing in his prior view of Nixon had ever prepared him
> to conceive of a man with two lovely girls. (Since the reporter
> had four fine daughters of his own, he was not inclined to look
> on such matters as accident.) And, indeed, later that night, the
> voice . . . of one of Nixon's daughters was heard for a fragment
> of dialogue on radio. No, she was saying, their father had never
> spanked them.
>
> "But then," the girl's voice went on, simple clarity, even
> honest devotion in the tone, "we never wanted to displease
> him. We wanted to be good." The reporter had not heard a
> girl make a remark like that about her father since his own
> mother had spoken in such fashion thirty-odd years ago.

In future first lady Pat Nixon, and Julie and Tricia, and Julie's
fiancé, David Eisenhower, Nixon sent a message to the country in a
way more compelling than words, in that decade of social and political revolution, that he represented the America many had come to

fear they were losing forever. The contrast with the "kids" I saw at the Pentagon and would see in Grant Park could not have been more stark.

"A HANGING JUDGE"

The nomination secure, Nixon moved to the question of a running mate. Having solicited the thoughts of party leaders, he then held meetings of the writing and political staffs, and with the heavyweights like Thurmond, Tower, and Goldwater. At the meeting of staff, I cannot recall any discussion of Agnew, nor was there any consensus on a candidate.

But when Nixon went down the next morning to tell the press the vice presidential nominee would be Governor Agnew of Maryland—"Spiro Who?" to an astounded press—Mike Wallace went off. This is an outrage, he yelled at me; you guys have just lost the election. A charge of "racist" was made, traceable to Agnew's handling of the riots after King's assassination. While elated with Nixon's choice—I had marked up and sent Nixon the clippings on Agnew lacerating the civil rights leaders who had refused to denounce Stokely Carmichael and company—Mike's reaction was representative of the press corps. He was no Nixon hater. In the Nixon camp we looked on Mike as a friend. He was the reporter whose chartered flight to Waterville, Maine, on November 4, 1966, gave Nixon his opening to respond on national television to Johnson's legendary outburst against our criticism of the communiqué that LBJ signed in Manila in late October. So close had Mike become to many in the campaign he had been sounded out on becoming Nixon's press secretary. And if Mike was cursing mad now, feeling almost betrayed, he accurately reflected the sentiments of most of the press corps that just heard Nixon's announcement.

It was in response to Mike's question at that Hilton press conference that Agnew answered, "I agree with you that the name of

Spiro Agnew is not a household name. I certainly hope that it will become one in the next couple of months." It would—for the next five years, and beyond.

After Nixon announced Agnew, he went back to his suite and invited me in to watch as Agnew met the press. No one else was there. And Governor Agnew handled himself with poise and grace. Facing a hostile audience, he was unintimidated, crisp, tough. After watching for ten minutes, Nixon turned to me and said with a look of satisfaction, "Buchanan, I think we've got ourselves a hanging judge."

Agnew was nominated that night, but only after Romney allowed his name to be put in nomination by liberals enraged at the selection of Agnew. In the roll call vote, Romney was crushed. The anti-Agnew forces had wanted to put up Lindsay. But he stood aside, and seconded Agnew's nomination. The Eastern Establishment that had once dictated nominees to the Republican Party had been routed a second time at a national convention. It would not be the last. Though the party had suffered a humiliating defeat in 1964, it had crossed that sea of fire to a new place. Now, to be a liberal like Romney, Rockefeller, Percy, Hatfield, or Lindsay meant you could not muster a majority at a Republican national convention. The center of gravity had shifted. Nixon was the party nominee because he had seen where the power had gone and he had recognized that Rockefeller, with whom he had negotiated the Pact of Fifth Avenue in 1960, was yesterday.

GAVIN'S MOMENT

In 1967, Nixon received a remarkably bold letter from a high school English teacher in Pennsylvania: "May I offer two suggestions concerning your plans for 1968. 1. Run. You can win. Nothing can happen to you, politically speaking, that is worse than what has happened to you."

Quoting Spanish philosopher José Ortega y Gasset, author of *Revolt of the Masses,* Bill Gavin wrote, "'[T]hese are the only genuine ideas; the ideas of the shipwrecked. The rest is rhetoric, posturing, farce. He who does not really feel himself lost is lost without remission.'"

You, Gavin told Nixon, "in effect are lost. That is why you are the only political figure with the vision to see things the way they are and not as Leftist or Rightist kooks would have then. Run. You will win." Recommendation 2 was to use television to have "live press conferences" in his presidential campaign. "People will see you daring all, not answering phony questions made up by your staff."

Gavin, a conservative of the heart who put ideological purity on a shelf below the values of faith, freedom, family, work, and neighborhood, was soon aboard.

Nixon's acceptance speech was well delivered and well received by the nation, if not the national press. To those of us who had traveled with him from the winter in New Hampshire, almost all of it was familiar. But part was fresh and came from the heart. Toward the close, as he described the tragedy of a child with dreams in America, who is denied their realization by the conditions of his birth, Nixon began to speak of another child:

But this is only part of what I see in America.

I see another child tonight. He hears the train go by at night and he dreams of far away places where he'd like to go. It seems like an impossible dream. But he is helped on his journey through life.

A father who had to go to work before he finished the sixth grade, sacrificed everything he had so that his sons could go to college. A gentle, Quaker mother, with a passionate concern for peace, quietly wept when he went to war but she understood why he had to go. A great teacher, a remarkable football coach, an inspirational minister encouraged him on his way. A courageous wife and loyal children stood by him in victory and also defeat.

And in his chosen profession of politics, first there were scores, then hundreds, then thousands, and finally millions worked for his success. And tonight he stands before you— nominated for President of the United States of America.

You can see why I believe so deeply in the American Dream.

After midnight Nixon returned to the hotel and entered the lobby, where a big party was under way. He walked over to Bill Gavin, who had suggested this close and helped craft it, put his arm around him, and pulled him away. The whole crowd watched. For minutes, Nixon had his arm around Gavin's shoulders and was speaking to him quietly. He was not only thanking Gavin but making sure everyone in the room knew how deeply he appreciated the contribution of Gavin to one of the most important speeches he would ever give. It was as gracious a gesture of gratitude to a staffer as I have witnessed in politics. Four decades later, on a panel of Nixon speechwriters, Gavin recalled that moment, which I remembered as well as he.

The first Gallup poll after the Miami Beach convention, in mid-August, put Nixon up 45–29, a margin of 16 points over Humphrey that Nixon had never known before. Wallace was at 21, closer to Vice President Humphrey than Humphrey was to Nixon. Our media men cut up the tape of Nixon's speech at Miami Beach and began to use segments as campaign ads.

WHALEN'S DEPARTURE

From Miami we flew to Texas, where Nixon helicoptered to LBJ's ranch. From there it was on to Mission Bay near San Diego, where the campaign bivouacked and where, to the astonishment of some of us, we discovered that John Mitchell's political team had put together the program without consulting the writing team. Among the meetings set up was one between Nixon and Republican mayors to discuss the urban crisis. When we saw the roster of attendees we were stunned. The largest city represented was Indianapolis, by new mayor Richard Lugar. Absent was John Lindsay of New York, who had seconded Agnew's nomination and whose presence at Mission Bay would have shown Nixon as a leader who reached across the spectrum for counsel. We protested, and an invitation went out to Lindsay.

We were seething over the omission and the exclusion of the writing staff from contributing to the schedule, and Whalen was seething more than the rest of us put together. One night, Price, Whalen, Anderson, and I were drinking after dinner at the restaurant when Mitchell ambled over. "What are you boys up to?" he said in an amiable way. Whereupon Whalen gave him both barrels in the face, relating what a mess Mitchell's team had made in putting together the invitees lists to Mission Bay, and demanding to know why the writers had not been consulted. Mitchell was jolted, and his mood darkened. He retorted in kind, then shuffled off. The next morning Whalen gave Shelley letters of resignation to deliver to Nixon and Haldeman—and headed down the long driveway, bags in hand.

Whalen was a talent, a strong writer, and his loss would blow a hole in our writing staff. I went to Nixon and urged that he call Whalen and ask him to reconsider. Nixon quickly vetoed the idea. We're going to have collisions in this campaign, he said. And if Whalen will walk when things don't go his way, better he walk now when few are paying attention, rather than quitting in the heat of battle, when his resignation could damage us badly in the press. We can't take the risk, Nixon said: Let him go.

In mid-August Arthur Burns called me. He had been trying to get through to Nixon. He conceded Whalen was "temperamental," but said people with brains usually are, and people with brains are hard to find. He wanted Nixon to call Whalen, stroke him, invite him back, and tell him that in the future, if things were fouled up, come to Nixon, don't walk off. Price and I seconded Burns, saying we could put Whalen in the New York office, not on the plane. Nixon remained adamant. There would be no reprieve.

To fill the void, we recruited the president of the Ripon Society, Lee Huebner, who had traveled with Nixon in 1964. To maintain ideological balance, we also brought in Jeff Hart, the Reagan speechwriter, *National Review* contributor, and professor of English literature. Bill Kilberg, a student at Harvard Law who had been working at Nixon, Mudge, moved to our research-and-writing shop. Bill wrote the endorsement of Nixon in the *Ripon Forum*, which included a spirited defense of Agnew. He described Nixon's running mate as a progressive on civil rights who had enacted the first open-housing law south of the Mason-Dixon Line and championed gun control and a graduated income tax—in other words, as a law-and-order liberal. Many of Bill's colleagues in the Ripon Society were taking a hike on the Nixon-Agnew ticket.

THE CRUSHING OF THE PRAGUE SPRING

The day Nixon and I returned from Israel in June 1967, Johnson met with Soviet Premier Alexei Kosygin, who had come to the UN to deal with the Mideast crisis, at a summit at Glassboro, New Jersey, equidistant from the White House and the UN. From their three-day meeting had come "the Spirit of Glassboro." By August 21–22, just days before the Democratic Convention, the Spirit of Glassboro was suddenly dead. Warsaw Pact armies, 250,000 strong, led by 2,000 tanks, had plunged into Czechoslovakia to crush "the Prague spring"—the easing of controls over politics, speech, and the press under premier Alexander Dubček. The invasion was a less bloody affair than Khrushchev's brutal crushing of the 1956

Hungarian Revolution. But it was Moscow's declaration that the captive nations of Europe, control of which had been ceded by Roosevelt and Churchill to Stalin at Yalta, would remain forever captive. The man who ordered the Warsaw Pact armies in, Soviet Communist Party boss Leonid Brezhnev, proclaimed what would soon be called the "Brezhnev Doctrine": Once a nation has been brought into the Communist camp, it can never leave.

The invasion came as no great surprise to me. I expected it. Dick Allen had predicted it in a June memo to Nixon. On May 28, I had alerted Nixon to a C. L. Sulzberger column warning that the May Day student uprising in Paris was the perfect distraction to cover a Soviet move against the Czechs. In the cover memo I wrote:

> Sulzberger makes an extremely cogent point in that the chaos in France is precisely the Western discomfort and attention diverter that might induce Moscow to step in and slap down the Czechs with dispatch.
>
> From this vantage point it seems to me difficult to see how the Soviet Eastern European empire can survive the kind of challenge that the Czech revolution throws up to it.

On July 28, Allen wrote Nixon again: "If Moscow does not act against the Czechs, it runs the risk of having the liberalization movement spread like wildfire throughout the rest of Eastern Europe, and even into the Soviet Union." Brezhnev could not tolerate having Prague slip peacefully out of the Soviet bloc, or the stampede would be on. Yet Moscow's crushing of the Prague Spring made ludicrous the notion there had ever been a "Spirit of Glassboro." This humiliation, like the Soviets' complicity in the recent Mideast war, exposed anew the fatuousness of the administration's belief in a detente with Moscow. The invasion torpedoed Johnson's plans to meet with Kosygin in Geneva to talk disarmament.

At a midnight meeting August 20–21 at the Nixons' apartment

with Allen, Ellsworth, Price, and me, LBJ phoned Nixon, spoke with him for twenty minutes, played to his patriotism, and sought to persuade him not to take a tough stand against the White House. Nixon acceded. As Allen wrote in notes from that night, Nixon's statement expressed "mild outrage."

When Benjamin Welles of the *New York Times* reported, on September 22, that a Johnson summit with Kosygin would have a grave psychological impact in Western Europe, I asked Nixon if he wanted me to write a statement for him warning Johnson against going. His written reply: "No. I have told LBJ (through Rusk) that a trip would be a mistake— If he does it—I will hit him over it— But I feel I should give him time to react." Clearly, Nixon had a back channel to Johnson and Dean Rusk of which some of us were unaware.

With the administration's Soviet policy in a shambles as great as its Vietnam policy, the unhappy and divided Democrats headed for Chicago.

CHAPTER 11

At the "Comrade Hilton"

NOBODY WHO WAS at the corner of Michigan and
Balboa on that Wednesday night in August of 1968
will ever forget it.
—HUNTER S. THOMPSON, *THE GREAT SHARK HUNT*

WITH GEORGE MCGOVERN we wouldn't have
Gestapo tactics on the streets of Chicago!
—SENATOR ABE RIBICOFF, CHICAGO (AUGUST 1968)

AT MISSION BAY I had suggested to Nixon that while he
was at Key Biscayne during the Democratic Convention—
it was then a tradition that a candidate stay out of the news
during his opponent's convention—I go to Chicago to be his "eyes
and ears." I sensed history would be made there. And whatever
came out of the Democratic Convention, it would surely be a more
dramatic event than the recent coronation in Miami Beach.

Nixon approved. The campaign got me a room and the party
paid for a hospitality suite. Both were on the 19th floor of the hotel
we would soon be calling the Comrade Hilton. Humphrey's suite
was several floors above, McCarthy's several floors below. Our
hotel was ground zero for the armies of the night. Across Michigan Avenue was Grant Park, base camp of the radicals who had

come to denounce the candidate, disrupt the convention, and show their contempt for conventional politics and what it had produced. Between the protesters and hotel entrance stood long lines of men in blue. Richard J. Daley's finest had their game faces on.

Walking the lobby of the Hilton I saw the familiar faces—senators, congressmen, governors, journalists, candidates—coming and going. The first friendly face I saw coming up the steps of the Conrad Hilton on Monday was that of Spencer Oliver. He and I had grown up in the same neighborhood of DC. In the early 1950s, we had gone to many of the same parties and played on opposing teams in the Wilson Night League. Spencer, whose phone at the Democratic National Committee would be the only successful wiretap in the Watergate scandal, was now national chairman of the Young Democrats.

"What are you doing here?" he asked in amazement.

"Just observing, Spencer." I smiled.

Bill Timmons of Congressman Bill Brock's staff was running our suite and Bill Safire had come out. We took pains to show we were not there to disrupt. When we ran into reporters or columnists in the lobby, the halls, or restaurants, we would give them the number of our suite and invite them up for a drink. We're open night and day, we said. Many came up to get a Republican take on the events. We hosted news conferences and brought in Republican stars like Governor John Love of Colorado and the young suburban Chicago congressman Donald Rumsfeld. Our motive in inviting journalists and holding press conferences was basic: Get our points and quotes into the Niagara of news pouring out of Chicago.

My first night there, I went down to the street and crossed through the police line into Grant Park. Around me was as nasty a crowd as had been at the Pentagon in 1967 when the MPs had charged and driven them down the steps with clubs. I was in coat and tie standing off by myself, when several pointed me out and started calling, "(Bleeping) FBI!" just as the crowd at the Pentagon had. The Catholic college dress code gave me away. Years later, when I was having breakfast in the White House mess with Pat Moynihan and the head of a Catholic university who was there to discuss aid to Catholic colleges, Moynihan asked aloud, "What has Fordham ever produced—but a long gray line of FBI agents?"

The protesters didn't make any overt move and I seemed a distraction from their business that night—cursing, insulting, taunting the cops standing in the street. Most of the protesters seemed in their twenties and their vocabulary was as filthy as they could make it, women as well as men. After twenty minutes, I walked back to the hotel, surprised at the patience of the Chicago cops. Looking at them, I sensed that just standing there and taking it was not how they had wanted to respond.

The next day I was a few blocks north of the hotel when I caught the scent of tear gas. As I trotted back along Michigan Avenue, it got worse. I was choking and trying to get into any hotel to get clear of the gas, but the bellmen blocked the entrances. After coughing for blocks I made it to the Hilton, flashed my room key, and was let in. When I got to the men's room on the lower floor to wash out my eyes, which were stinging, I noticed beside me, choking, the liberal columnist for the *New York Times*, Tom Wicker. He had been gassed as well.

Often that week, the Boss, who was with Bebe at Key Biscayne, would call to ask what was going on. I would relate what I had seen and heard and monitored on television. One night as the crowds had grown huge in front of the hotel, I was trying to sleep, when Nixon called, after midnight.

"What's going on now?" the familiar voice asked.

"You want to know what's going on, sir?" I replied. "Listen." I held the phone to the open window of my room. From 19 floors below came the howling of repeated chants "Dump the Hump! Dump the Hump!" and "F——— you, Da-ley! F——— you, Da-ley." Pulling the phone back, I said, "That's what's going on, sir."

Wednesday, the evening of the nominating speeches, the battle broke out right in front of our hotel that would cost Humphrey any convention bounce he had hoped for and be a subject of political and generational division for years. Fifteen minutes before the violence exploded, there had sauntered into the suite I was manning alone, looking for a drink, Norman Mailer, who had won a Pulitzer for *The Armies of the Night*, describing the confrontation at the Pentagon. With him was a tough-looking Puerto Rican whom Mailer introduced as José Torres. Torres had been the light heavyweight champion of the world. Mailer and I were talking, near 7 p.m. and still daylight, and he was explaining to me how he was a "left-conservative," when loud noises drew us to the window.

The protesters in Grant Park were continuing their stream of insults in front of the Hilton. But to our left at the corner of Michigan and Balboa, a parade of marchers heading south for the convention center had been halted. The mule train of the Reverend Abernathy's Poor People's March had been allowed to pass. The rest were blocked. Now up Balboa came a column of cops that halted briefly. Stand-off. Then the cops pulled out their clubs, broke ranks, and tore into the protesters and radicals, who scattered and ran into the park.

The cops did not stop. They chased and clubbed them, wrestled them to the ground, dragged them to vans. On and on it went. Mailer was silent, transfixed, as was I. Torres, watching each takedown, was cursing the cops in heavily accented English, "Sons of bitches! Sons of bitches!" This, wrote Mailer, was "the evening when the Massacre of Michigan Avenue occurred, an extraordinary event: a massacre equal on balance to some of the old Indian raids, yet no one was killed." In *Miami and the Siege of Chicago*, he describes the scene we witnessed from that 19th-floor suite:

> The police attacked with tear gas, with Mace, and with clubs, they attacked like a chain saw cutting into wood, the teeth

326 PATRICK J. BUCHANAN

of the saw the edge of their clubs, they attacked like a scythe through grass, lines of twenty and thirty policemen striking out in an arc, their clubs beating, demonstrators fleeing. Seen from overhead, from the nineteenth floor it was like a wind blowing dust, or the edge of waves riding foam on the shore.

But we were not down on the street. We were 200 feet above and we did not see the cops directly below us, who, according to Jack Newfield of the *Village Voice*, went for the spectators observing the battle, driving them through the plate-glass window of the Hilton. The cops then stormed after them into the Haymarket Inn restaurant on the first floor. Describing what we witnessed, Mailer saw its significance as did I. For the Democratic Party, the great coalition, Mailer wrote, this

was a great and solemn moment, as if indeed even the gods of history had come together from each side to choose the very front of the Hilton Hotel before the television cameras of the world and the eyes of the campaign workers and the delegates' wives, yes, there before the eyes of half the principals at the convention was this drama played, as if the military spine of a great liberal party had finally separated itself from the skin, as if, no metaphor large enough to suffice, the Democratic Party had here broken in two before the eyes of a nation like Melville's whale charging right out of the sea.

That night Senator Abe Ribicoff used his nominating speech to denounce the Chicago cops: "With George McGovern we wouldn't have Gestapo tactics on the streets of Chicago!" The cameras caught a bellowing Mayor Daley, hands cupping his face so the cameras could not pick up his words, cursing Ribicoff. That night, NBC News switched back and forth between film of the crowd outside the Hilton being beaten by cops and the festivities over Humphrey's victory in the convention. In the lobby and halls of the Hilton and on the elevators, the beaten and bleeding were being tended. The Democratic Party was coming apart, for both cops and protesters, Ribicoff and Daley, and those shouting at and cursing one another that night, inside and outside the convention and in the streets and hotels, belonged to one and the same party. Departing Chicago, I was quoted by columnist Robert A. Hoving, who had stopped by to visit our "infiltration squad":

> [T]he young idealists who are following Gene McCarthy got their noses bloodied and finally realized they couldn't buck the old-fashioned machine politics as epitomized by Hubert Humphrey. . . . [T]hey now know they can't fight city hall.
>
> This convention has cracked wide open the old Roosevelt-inspired coalition of intellectuals, labor, the Negroes and the South. The Democrats left this convention as the party of Daley-Bailey-Humphrey—and they can't sell that to the American people.

What was the national reaction? Tom Wicker wrote, "These were our children in the streets, and the Chicago police beat them up." But a Gallup poll reported that the majority of Americans supported the cops.

Returning to New York, I wrote several memos to Nixon. "Thoughts on Strategy" urged that "RN must tie Humphrey" to the "Chicago circus" that "appalled and . . . frightened" the people. He should contend that if the "Power Elite" of the Democratic Party "cannot even run an orderly convention, how can they create the conditions of order in the nation?"

> The caveat is that we don't want to imply or say that the great majority of Democrats or that the Democratic Party is in turmoil. It is just the tiny knot at the top, who have lost touch

with their rank and file; who ignored the will of the rank and
file, who chose, instead, the Hand picked Heir Apparent of the
Reigning Disaster.

"Any ritualistic denunciation of the Chicago police (which I was
confident other aides were urging on Nixon) will get us absolutely
zero in support," I wrote. "It will get us in hot water with some of
our own people." Nixon might concede that "some of the police"
in Chicago had "overreacted to the provocations," but should add,

> I think that it is really wrong to paint this in black and white—as
> some have done—with the police the devils beating up innocent
> children. A balanced presentation would include the disgusting
> and vulgar conduct of many of the demonstrators, their delib-
> erate attempts to provoke the police and national guard, their
> deplorable conduct toward the president and Mr. Humphrey.

Nixon should then defend Chicago by saying "an injustice has
been committed to the reputation of the city by reports in the foreign press and even in some of our domestic press, because of this
one incident," even as the reputation of Dallas had unjustly "suffered because an itinerant Marxist committed his atrocity there."

Nixon might add that while there is a "definite need to train our
police in the handling of provocateurs and demonstrations, a need
pointed up here in Chicago . . . there is an equal need on the part
of our opinion leaders to step up and condemn unequivocally those
demonstrators who think they have a right to insult, to provoke,
and to trample all over the rules and regulations of a city—because
they think their cause is just."

In a second memo, August 31, on Nixon's speech on his forth-
coming trip to Chicago, I wrote, "I would use the demonstrators,
the worst of them . . . as a foil for RN's arguments. I would allude
again to the Silent Majority, the quiet Americans whose cause is

just. They have a right to be heard." Nixon underlined "Silent Majority" and "quiet Americans." I then suggested this paragraph:

If someone in this room went out in Grant Park and used obscene remarks about the President, and cursed the police standing by, he would be wrong—and he would be arrested—and I think that simply because four thousand people do it at once—that doesn't make it right or just or good—simply because it is done in the name of some cause.

I urged that Nixon, in his first speech, which would be in Chicago, show strength: "The American people are frightened and confused—and they want a man with some steel in him—let's leave Garment and Shakespeare to the Next Door Neighbor's Boy stuff." Garment, Frank Shakespeare, and Harry Treleaven, known in the issues shop as the "holy trinity," were running the ad campaign and emphasizing the soft appeal.

The Democratic Convention was historically significant. With the party now split three ways—the McCarthy-Kennedy-McGovern antiwar third, the Middle American Catholic and conservative Democrats who backed the war their sons were fighting, and the Wallaceites who numbered nearly 15 million and were on our side of the social-cultural divide—how could Humphrey conceivably unite America?

He could not. Our party was one-half to two-thirds the size of the Democratic Party. But as a center-right party we could create and craft a new majority by annexing the center-right of the Democratic Party, with minimal losses on our left wing. Bringing in the Daley-Rizzo Democrats of the North and the Tower-Thurmond-Wallace followers in the South might yield another benefit: Not only would this constitute a new governing majority, displacing FDR's, but liberal Republicans, finding themselves in a party no longer defined by Rockefellers, Scrantons, Romneys, Javitses, and

330 PATRICK J. BUCHANAN

Lindsays, might drift away. And if they did, they would leave behind a party more antiestablishment and populist. Remaking the GOP into the party of anti-elitists and outsiders, of forgotten Americans and Middle Americans, was what some of us had long had in mind.

Chicago was a disaster for Humphrey. He looked like the candidate of the bosses who had been nominated only because Bobby Kennedy had been shot, and his handpicked delegates from non-primary states had controlled the floor as tightly as Mayor Daley had controlled the city.

After the Republican Convention, Nixon had opened a 16-point lead over Humphrey, 45–29. After Chicago, Humphrey narrowed it to 12, with Nixon falling to 43 and the vice president rising to 31. By mid-September, however, Gallup was showing Nixon holding at 43, but Humphrey falling to 28, his low during the year, with Wallace climbing to 21 percent.

Our problem? Only in the aftermath of our convention, from which a candidate customarily receives a bump, had we touched 45 percent. Now we were back to 43. In May and June, Humphrey had been that high when we were at 37 and 35, with little more than one-third of the nation saying they wanted Nixon for President.

To me the polls were saying loud and clear: This race is not over. If the Democratic Party, half again or twice as large as the Republican Party, comes together, if only for the election, we lose. And as I could not believe that Humphrey, once the *beau ideal* of the liberals and now the choice of the establishment, would end up with only half the share of the vote that LBJ had won in 1964, our lead must shrink. The only remaining question: When would the gap begin to close and how far would closure go?

After I got back from Chicago, I sent Nixon 13 pages of Q & A on how to deal with Chicago questions when we arrived in the city. To press questions about police "brutality," I urged him to respond thus:

[T]he city of Chicago was given a black eye . . . that it does not deserve. . . . [I]t is slanderous and unjust to be comparing Chicago to Prague. . . .

[B]efore making any final judgments on whether the police should have acted as they did . . . . we ought to look at what provoked them to act at all. From what I read these men were working twelve hours a day—they were subjected to filthy insults and provocations most of those twelve hours; they were harassed by demonstrators who somehow felt they had the run of the city; they were commonly referred to as Fascists and Pigs. . . . If they did get out of hand in dealing with these demonstrators, I don't say that is right, but I do say we ought to at least have a full representation of the balance sheet, which I have yet to see.

Should the press follow up this answer by demanding to know if Nixon was "condoning" what the Chicago cops did, I urged he respond thus:

No, I am not. I find it regrettable that some innocent people were injured; I find it regrettable that newsmen were injured in the line of duty. But I also think it is time in this country that we recognized that police officers are human beings behind the uniform they wear, that they have personal dignity and respect, and that if you badger and insult and provoke them long enough, they are liable to act like badgered and insulted and provoked men.

Tom Wicker had come down on the side of the crowd in Grant Park. Having been in Grant Park and observed his crowd close up, I thought we belonged on the side of Mayor Daley and the Chicago cops. That was where our interests and future lay. It was where the politics of the day pointed us. And it had the ancillary benefit of being the right side of the issue, in every sense of that word. Nixon would follow this line and, on election day, Illinois, the last state to report, would, unlike 1960, fall into the Nixon column.

THE CRISIS OF THE OLD ORDER

Chicago was the crescendo of the decade. Mailer had witnessed it as had I. Not only was the Democratic Party disintegrating, liberalism was being rejected as a failed ideology. It had been tried and found wanting. What had taken place in the 1960s was not simply a rebellion of the young against the authority of their elders. It was a revolution that would break the nation's establishment. On elite campuses, protesting students were not arguing for reform, they wanted to overthrow the system. They were saying to administrators and faculty, and parents who had sent them to the finest schools, "Take your American way of life and shove it! We have no wish to live your American dream of a home and family in the suburbs, two cars, and three weeks' vacation. We want no part of your 'dirty, immoral war' in Asia. We want no part of your Cold War." They burned draft cards, used a *k* in spelling "Amerika," hung posters of Che Guevara in dorm rooms as fellow students defied U.S. law and traveled to Cuba to laud Castro's revolution. But if they detested the beliefs and values of Middle America, their sentiments were reciprocated by a Middle America turning its back in disgust on an establishment too pusillanimous to deal with their anarchism. Johnson had seemed to understand that while the radicals might raise hell, the real danger came from elsewhere. "Don't pay attention to what those little shits on the campuses do," he told George Ball. "The great beast is the reactionary elements in the country. Those are the people that we have to fear." Johnson was right. As he spoke, that "great beast," a full fifth of the nation, was indicating its preference for George Wallace for President.

Liberals seemed paralyzed when confronted with the accusations and anarchic violence of black rioters. After a decade of court rulings and federal laws that had enshrined equality of rights, and of Great Society programs to raise people up and level the playing field, how did they explain these outbursts of hatred against the very progressives who had produced the reforms?

The sixties had been, in Professor James MacGregor Burns's phrase, "The Liberal Decade." Democrats had controlled the White House and Congress from JFK's inaugural in January 1961 to Johnson's departure in 1969. By 1965, Democrats held twice the number of seats in Congress as Republicans and twice the number of governors' chairs. The federal bureaucracy had been built up in the New Deal, Fair Deal, and Great Society, and was deep-dyed Democratic. The Warren Court, the most liberal in U.S. history, had been imposing the progressives' agenda for years. Hollywood, academia, and the national media were solidly in the liberal camp.

And Vietnam was Liberalism's War. In his inaugural Kennedy had declared, "Let every nation know, whether it wishes us well or ill, that we shall pay any price, bear any burden, meet any hardship, support any friend, oppose any foe, in order to assure the survival and the success of liberty." From that inaugural stand it was a direct flight to the jungles and rice paddies of Vietnam. When Ike left office there were 600 U.S. advisers in South Vietnam. At JFK's death, 16,000. When LBJ left, there were 500,000 U.S. troops in Vietnam, and more on the way, with 30,000 dead and no end in sight to the war.

The crisis of liberalism was that the social revolutions tearing America apart were contained, almost entirely, inside the Democratic Party. The antiwar movement was led by students from elite campuses who were of the Democratic Left. After Goldwater's nomination, black America had gone Democratic 16–1. Yet it was out of black America that the soaring crime and the urban riots were coming.

334 PATRICK J. BUCHANAN

Walter Lippmann, dean of liberal columnists for decades, saw it clear: Liberalism had run its course. It was being rejected by a nation that could not now be united by "Lyndon Johnson's creature." Humphrey could offer "no genuine prospect of a coherent government." America had become "the most violently disordered of the world's industrial nations. . . . [D]iscipline and authority and self-reliance had to be restored." Conservatives were the men to do it. Thus the title of Lippmann's column: "Nixon Is the Only One."

"To say that liberalism collapsed beneath the assault of leftist extremism was an understatement," wrote Richard Whalen of that time. "[I]ts nerve failed and it came apart."

> When campus radicals and black militants bit the hand that had spoon-fed them, liberals apologized and offered the other hand. When abysmally ignorant New Leftists, who made Birchers look like scholars, screamed obscene abuse of "the Establishment," liberals pleaded guilty. And when self-appointed black avengers leveled the mindless but morally devastating charge of "racism," liberals sank to their knees under the weight of other people's alleged sins.

"Wasn't that a time?" sang Peter, Paul, and Mary. Yes, it was. And out of that time, *mirabile dictu*, came President Richard M. Nixon. Hunter Thompson was not entirely wrong when he wrote, "Richard Nixon is living in the White House today because of what happened that night in Chicago."

CHAPTER 12

Hearing Footsteps

THE MOOD ON the plane was subdued—little gaiety,
no exuberance . . . from the most apprehensive,
Buchanan and Finch, to the most confident, Haldeman.
—THEODORE H. WHITE, *The Making of the President* (1968)

CHICAGO HAD BEEN a disaster for the Democrats. The early-September polls showed Nixon holding a double-digit lead, Wallace surging, Humphrey stalled at around 30 percent. After Labor Day, the Nixon game plan, long in its preparation, began to unfold. Motorcades through Chicago, San Francisco, and Philadelphia and an appearance at Billy Graham's Crusade for Christ in a Pittsburgh stadium received huge and friendly receptions.

Our advance men, schooled in 1966 and the primaries of '68, were the most experienced and best in the business. Our research-and-writing staff, together a year, operated smoothly. We had all gone through a four-month shakedown cruise from New Hampshire through Oregon that the Humphrey team never did. We would start the fall campaign performing at midseason levels. Dick Allen led the foreign policy research staff in New York and Alan Greenspan the domestic team. Price, Safire, Dick Moore, and I were on the candidate's plane, where the latest communications equipment had been installed and new IBM Selectric typewriters had been bolted to the desks.

Three planes carried the candidate, staff, and press. They had been christened *Tricia, Julie,* and *David.* The *David* was the "zoo plane," as TV technicians and cameramen were aboard and the liquor flowed freely. Among Nixon staffers it was felt we had more friends among these folks than among the print or TV media. Yet access to all media was freer and more open than in 1960. The national press remarked on the contrast. There did indeed seem to be, many wrote, "a new Nixon."

The candidate was not overworked, as he had been in 1960. There were fewer events, and they were better prepared and better run. Among the reasons things went smoothly was that Nixon's staff and the press both believed that they were traveling with the next President of the United States. Our September campaign had the look of a winner.

Nixon's "speech" was lifted from his acceptance speech in Miami Beach, itself a compendium of lines, phrases, and paragraphs honed in the primaries. Nixon would first describe what we all had witnessed in 1968, then ask if this was truly the destiny of our republic:

As we look at America, we see cities enveloped in smoke and flame. We hear sirens in the night. We see Americans dying on distant battlefields abroad. We see Americans hating each other; fighting each other; killing each other at home. And as we see and hear these things, millions of Americans cry out in anguish: Did we come all this way for this? Did American boys die in Normandy, and Korea, and in Valley Forge for this?

With the audience nodding assent that the country we loved did seem to have lost her way, Nixon identified those to whom America must turn with hope—"the forgotten Americans."

Listen to the answer to those questions.

It is another voice. It is the quiet voice in the tumult and the shouting. It is the voice of the great majority of Americans, the forgotten Americans—the non-shouters; the non-demonstrators. They are not racists or sick; they are not guilty of the crime that plagues the land. They are black and they are white—they're native born and foreign born—they're young and they're old. They work in America's factories. They run America's businesses. They serve in government. They provide most of the soldiers who died to keep us free. They give drive to the spirit of America. They give lift to the American Dream. They give steel to the backbone of America. They are good people, they are decent people; they work, and they save, and they pay their taxes, and they care. . . . This I say to you tonight is the real voice of America. In this year 1968, this is the message it will broadcast to America and to the world.

You are the real America, the true America, Nixon was telling his audience. He was speaking of what would become famous as the Great Silent Majority. Then Nixon framed the conclusion that these "forgotten Americans" were reaching about how to save their country:

And this is their answer and this is my answer to that question. When the strongest nation in the world can be tied down for four years in a war in Vietnam with no end in sight; when the richest nation in the world can't manage its own economy; when the nation with the greatest tradition of the rule of law is plagued by unprecedented lawlessness; when a nation that has been known for a century for equality of opportunity is torn by unprecedented racial violence; and when the President of the United States cannot travel abroad or to any major city at home without fear of a hostile demonstration—then it's time for new leadership for the United States of America.

Hard to disagree. As Nixon pounded home that line, "it's time for new leadership," the crowd would rise. And before, during, and after the convention, he would invoke an even more powerful image in his litany:

> And I say to you tonight that when respect for the United States of America falls so low that a fourth-rate military power, like North Korea, will seize an American naval vessel on the high seas, it is time for new leadership to restore respect for the United States of America.

The line scanned perfectly and was the "cheer line" of the campaign. Every American knew North Korea had boarded and seized the *Pueblo* outside the 12-mile limit and taken its crew hostage, an egregious insult to the U.S. Navy and the United States. And Kim Il-Sung had acted with impunity. Yet every American also knew that the nation that had reduced the Japanese empire to rubble in less than four years would never have tolerated such an outrage. What has happened to us, how did we descend so quickly to this, were questions Americans were asking.

This, then, was the message Nixon carried into September: Things we Americans never dreamed would happen are happening. Yet the heart of the country—"the forgotten Americans"—remains strong. And these are the folks who can take America back by electing new leadership to come to grips with her troubles.

This, then, was the indictment of Johnson and Humphrey. They had plunged us into a war in Asia they knew not how to end or win, in which 28,000 Americans had already died. They had promised a Great Society but produced a society where violent crime set records every year, urban riots had broken out in every great American city, and elite campuses had been reduced to anarchy. And if that party could not even unite itself in Chicago, how could it reunite the nation? Time for a change, time for new leadership.

The case seemed unassailable and we should have won by 10 points. But we were not running solely against the candidate of the party that had presided over the disaster, but also against a Southern populist with an appeal to folks whose hostility to Great Society liberalism was even more visceral. Wallace could reach voters at a gut level that Nixon could not. Had Nixon dared to try, he would have crippled himself with his base of centrists and independents.

The dilemma of 1968 was that during the fall campaign, opposition to the Great Society and the return of the Johnson-Humphrey Democrats to power reached 60 to 65 percent of the electorate. But Wallace claimed a slice of that majority. And if he won enough of it, a Democratic Party that a national majority wanted gone would be returned to office. Yet, how that party of Johnson, Humphrey, McCarthy, and McGovern could, should it prevail, continue to govern this sundered country escaped me.

Serenely in September we sailed along. We observed a moratorium on speaking about Vietnam, as we did not know what was being decided in Paris or what the situation would be when the next President took his oath. We did not want to lock ourselves into any policy, or rule out any option, or take any stand that could leave us exposed to a sudden White House shift. Having been at Ike's side when he announced in 1952, "I shall go to Korea," then seen Ike wrap up the war in six months with a veiled threat of escalation to nuclear war on the Chinese, Nixon did not want to lock himself into any course. Should he win, he wanted a free hand.

It was hard not to be overconfident that September, but I managed it. I was many times more nervous than I had ever been in the previous three years. Things were going too well. I did not believe the nominee of a majority party that had held the White House with that massive popular vote margin in 1964, over 60 percent of the electorate, was going to end up with 30 or 35 percent in 1968. Often I would compare the Democratic Party to the Army of the Potomac. If Lee and Jackson did not keep their adversary divided, there was a danger that, in a set-piece battle, the sheer numbers of men and guns would prevail. And in November 1968, they almost did.

Moreover, not only had we been running behind Humphrey in the summer, we had never broken 45 percent, even after our successful and united convention in Miami Beach, even after spending millions on TV ads in September while Humphrey was dark. We seemed to have hit our celling in the low to mid-40s. Was that enough to win?

To an alarming degree, this depended on George Wallace, who was now breaking 20 percent and pulling Northern votes in the millions. My fear was that if Wallace's numbers fell, Northern Catholic and ethnic Democrats would go back to the party of Harry Truman and the Kennedys, not to Richard Nixon, who had spent his career warring with those Democrats.

Were Wallace not running, we would easily carry all the Goldwater states of the Deep South (South Carolina, Georgia, Alabama, Mississippi, Louisiana) and probably sweep the upper and outer South (North Carolina, Virginia, Tennessee, Arkansas, Florida, and Texas). But there was no way Nixon and Agnew were going to take the Deep South from Wallace, and his strength in the upper and outer South could siphon off enough populist and antiliberal votes to deny these states to Nixon and throw them to Humphrey.

While our strategy had been thought through and we were executing the plan, I did not believe it could last. Our programmed and professional campaign was also our weakness. How would we react should Humphrey, a passionate liberal and excellent campaigner, catch fire? We were like a basketball team sitting on a lead, taking no risks, freezing the ball, running out the clock, as our floundering opponent remained so far behind he could never catch up. But what if Hubert got it together?

There was a world of difference between this September campaign and those we had run in '66 and the primaries. In the three years before the fall election of 1968, Nixon had traveled with a tiny staff. We reacted swiftly to events. When attacked, we gathered with the candidate, responded in the next news cycle, and quickly went back on the offensive. By the fall of 1968, while we were still running a professional campaign, it was a programmed, repetitious, and boring campaign.

The great question was where would the folks indispensable to our new majority—primarily Northern Catholics who had gone in landslides for JFK and LBJ in 1960 and 1964, and whose fathers and grandfathers had given FDR and Truman five victories—come down? Should the Wallace tide recede in the North, would they go to Nixon, JFK's adversary, and a Republican partisan in the late 1940s and early 1950s, ripping up Harry Truman and Adlai Stevenson?

A TILT TOWARD ISRAEL

Nixon, however, made his first play in September not for the Catholic vote but for the Jewish vote, which was a tiny fraction of the Catholic vote.

Safire was pushing hardest for Nixon to call for a U.S. tilt to Israel, and I was urging that we maintain a posture equidistant between our Arab and Israeli friends. On a television show in Chicago, an interview on the plane, and in a speech to B'nai B'rith, on September 9, Nixon called for a shift in U.S. Middle East policy to a virtual Israel-first policy. "Nixon Calls for Military Supremacy for Israel," ran the headline in the *Jewish Press*, September 13. The *JP* story began:

> Richard M. Nixon went further than ever this week in committing his party to a total support of Israel's defense when he declared before the B'nai B'rith triennial convention that the balance of power in the Middle East "must be tipped in Israel's favor. . . ."

The candidate went beyond the proposition that Israel should get enough arms so that it might achieve military balance in the region. Nixon declared that "I support a policy that would give Israel a technological military superiority margin to more than offset her hostile neighbors' numerical superiority."

If superiority meant sending Phantom jets to Israel, "we should supply those Phantom jets," Nixon was quoted as saying. "Israeli officials present at the convention expressed deep satisfaction with the Nixon speech." At the bottom of the article, which Safire sent to me, he scribbled, "Pat, It is this kind of press coverage that will deliver New York City, Chicago, L.A., etc. to us and insure both our ability to win and our ability to govern." Dick Allen sent me a column by John Cooley of the *Christian Science Monitor* with the headline "Arabs Accuse Nixon of Impeding Mideast Peace." It began:

> Richard M. Nixon's pro-Israeli remarks September 9 have dimmed Arab hopes that the United States would help achieve what they consider a just Middle East settlement.
> Many Western observers here share the Arab view that the Republican presidential candidate has virtually ended any chances of regaining lost American influence in the Arab world.

A Beirut columnist described as "the Arab world's Walter Lippmann" wrote that the vision of U.S. leaders is "so blurred they cannot tell black from white. This led to a disastrous U.S. involvement in Vietnam and would probably lead to a similarly disastrous U.S. involvement in the Mideast." Cooley said the Arabs, seeing Truman as representing the Democratic view and

Ike as representing the GOP position, "tended to view the Republican Party as more fair and objective on the Middle East than the Democrats."

In a September 11 editorial, the *New York Times* ripped into Nixon, saying his pledge to Israel to maintain its military edge was "a promise to scrap the existing American policy of trying to maintain a rough military balance between Israel and the Arab states and apportioning arms aid accordingly."

Nixon was inviting an arms race, said the *Times*, and warned of an escalation of Soviet military aid to the Arabs. "The American commitment to Israel's security is clear and outside political debate," said the *Times*. "But Mr. Nixon now seems ready to go well beyond that basic pledge to project a new, dangerous, open-ended and ultimately self-defeating commitment."

The *Jewish Press* rose to Nixon's defense, hailing his "famous speech calling for F-4 Phantom jets to Israel," and describing the *New York Times* as "the voice of the Russians in Arab dress."

My view on Israel as being on America's side in the East-West conflict had been formed before the Six-Day War. Yet I also felt, along with the U.S. envoys we spoke with on our trip and Lord Home, that the moderate Arabs holding the line against Nasserism should be accorded equal respect.

Half a century after Nixon tilted the GOP to Israel, a former CentCom commander of U.S. forces in the Middle East, General James Mattis, told an audience in Aspen, "I paid a military security price every day . . . because the Americans were seen as biased in support of Israel." General Mattis echoed his CentCom predecessor General David Petraeus. Today, as America is executing a long retreat from the Middle East after too many wars, the U.S.-Israeli relationship has reached a nadir. How did it work out with the Jewish vote in 1968? Nixon got 17 percent to Humphrey's 81 percent.

THE DETAILS MAN

A veteran of twenty-two years of campaigning, Nixon knew more about its aspects than his aides. On September 24, he sent a memo to his writers indicating dissatisfaction with the speech excerpts we had been dropping off for local coverage. These statements and excerpts, he wrote, must be made more "meaty and quotable," more current and "livelier," nothing "cute or gimmicky," none longer than a page and a half. Anything on agriculture could be put out without his seeing it, if cleared by Bryce Harlow:

"The national press couldn't care less about what we say on Karl Mundt's pet REA project nor on our repeating our agriculture program." We should try to drop a fresh statement at every stop, with a local angle to ensure local coverage:

> Just read the advance information sheets and if you see that some place cares about Indians—put out a little statement that we care about Indians, etc. A case in point was the statement Pat Buchanan prepared reacting to the Yippies that broke up the Catholic mass in Milwaukee. . . . [T]hat statement deserved even a national play. I hope it got out in time to get not only the local press but also to be circulated among our national press.

Two excerpts a week, Nixon directed, should hit the law-and-order theme, one or two the spending theme. Two or three should hit the respect-for-America theme. Nixon's directions, specific, detailed, went on for a thousand words. "I think we can make some mileage, too, out of everybody reading the press excerpts that Pat Buchanan sends in to me and then having our excerpt directly relate to one of those provided we are not simply answering Hubert."

Nixon was referring to the "news summary" he demanded every

day. Agnes Waldron would clip the early editions of the *Washington Post*, *New York Times*, and *Baltimore Sun* that were out and on the street by 10 p.m. in the East, and send them by a form of fax to our campaign stops. I would get these copies and designate the paragraphs to be typed up by Rose, Shelley, Marge Acker, Linda Underwood, and others on heavy bond paper. The thick pile of paper would be sent in to Nixon every day. We had the system down cold. I recall complimenting a surprised Bob Semple of the *Times* one night in California on his story about a Nixon event, which was datelined the next morning, but already out in the bulldog edition back east.

Nixon's advice went down to the minutest detail. When on the road, "never pass a men's room without going in," he advised me, which I found to be sage counsel. Once, when a congressman put in the *Congressional Record* remarks insulting to Nixon, I wrote a letter that was just short of challenging him to a duel. Nixon told me to drop it. "Ignore him," Nixon said. "He's a congressman." What he meant was that an ex–vice president does not engage a congressman. That would diminish us and elevate him. When we engage, it should be with the President, as it was with the Manila questions. "Never shoot down!" said Nixon. Challenge the champion, not some club fighter. Apollo Creed made that mistake when he took on Rocky Balboa.

Nixon sought constantly to keep the focus on our main message. In September 1968 we had released a statement raising the issue of genocide against the Ibo people of Biafra in the Nigerian civil war. This elicited a sharp retort from Senator Ed Brooke, who said that he knew of no evidence of genocide and believed the Nigerian regime was behaving responsibly in ending an Ibo secession that would produce a million dead. He asked that Nixon "clarify" his position. Nixon wrote in the margin of Dick Allen's memo on Brooke's letter, "Buchanan—let's stay out of these 'borrow trouble issues' in future."

CALM BEFORE THE STORM

Humphrey was having a hellish September. After the festivities at the Conrad Hilton and Grant Park and the Democratic Convention's rejection of the peace plank by two-to-one, Gene McCarthy had declined to endorse him. The Left, disconsolate over the death of Kennedy and seeing in Humphrey a sellout who had carried the brief for Johnson's war, wanted no part of him. By mid-September, Humphrey was down to 28 percent in Gallup with Nixon holding a 15-point lead at 43. Wallace was only 7 points behind Hubert. Together, Nixon and Wallace had 64 percent of the national vote. Not only was Humphrey floundering, he was turning nasty, crossing lines that Nixon would never have gotten away with. About his rival, Humphrey said, "[Y]ou can't trust a man who has a vacuum where his principles ought to be," and "Nixon and his party have chosen to join forces with the most reactionary elements in American society."

Watching the TV clips from the Humphrey campaign, I almost felt sorry for him. For his entire career he had wanted to be President. Now he was being robbed of his opportunity in a way that seemed un-American. Wherever he went, even campaigning with Teddy Kennedy in Boston, he was shouted down by hecklers who cursed him for Vietnam and denied him the right to be heard with constant chants of "Dump the Hump!" Every day they bedeviled him. Every evening that was the story of his campaign. With this coverage there seemed no possibility Humphrey could convince a nation, two-thirds of which got its national news from the networks, to elect him.

In his home state of Minnesota in late September, Humphrey issued a cry from the heart. These people "are not just hecklers," he said, but "highly disciplined, well organized agitators. . . . Some of them are anarchists, and some of these groups are dedicated to destroying the Democratic Party and destroying this country." Hubert had begun to echo us, if not Wallace.

As our campaign moved magisterially, the contrast with the anarchy around Humphrey's campaign was unavoidable. If Americans were to ask which of these men had a better chance of uniting the nation, the evening news gave the answer. We were the beneficiaries of what was being done to Humphrey. We were winning—by default. Yet some of us wondered: What if the disruptions stop, what if Humphrey brings his party together, what if he gains traction and begins to move? We had a forbidding lead, but not once had we risen above 45 percent. From mid-May to mid-July, Humphrey had consistently led us by 5 points.

Observing those hate-filled shouters deny Humphrey his right to speak, and deny the thousands in his audiences their right to hear him, I thought the term "fascist," tossed at the Chicago cops, was better applied to this crowd. Yet when the disruptions took place, we would invariably hear the idiotic retort, "This is what the First Amendment is all about!"

To me the First Amendment was about freedom of speech as practiced in the House of Burgesses, in New England town meetings, and in Philadelphia, where the dissenters were conceded the right to be heard. Every American was concerned about Vietnam in 1968 and had an opinion. Yet these people behaved as though their position were so righteous it alone should be heard.

SALT LAKE CITY

By September's end, Humphrey was at the end of his tether. He had nothing like the money we had or the organization we had built up over two years. Before Johnson's decision not to run, six months earlier, there had not even been a Humphrey campaign. Meanwhile, Nixon had labored ceaselessly to make himself acceptable to all wings of the party and he had succeeded in uniting the Rockefeller-Romney and Goldwater-Reagan wings. Hubert's party was split three ways. And thus, with nowhere else to go, Hubert decided to follow his instincts and his heart. He would cut the umbilical cord to Johnson and come out in favor of a halt to all U.S. bombing of North Vietnam.

When, on September 30, I heard this, I thought it ominous. The candidate of the majority party was about to tell his disaffected left wing, the Kennedy-McCarthy-McGovern Democrats, that, at heart, he was with them, that he, too, favored winding down and ending U.S. involvement in the war, that, under a President Humphrey, the first step, a complete bombing halt of the North, would be taken. While he hedged his statement with qualifiers, at its core was a declaration heard round the political world:

> As President, I would be willing to stop the bombing of North Vietnam as an acceptable risk for peace. . . . I would move . . . towards de-Americanization of the war. . . . I would propose once more an immediate cease-fire . . . and supervised withdrawal of all foreign forces from South Vietnam.

For Humphrey, victory in Vietnam was no longer an option. He had gone over to the peace camp. No longer a hawk in the aviary of LBJ, he was now sharing a nest with the doves who had sought to dump Johnson with the candidacies of McCarthy and Kennedy. Humphrey had taped his speech for airing on national TV from Salt Lake City, and the contents were on the AP wire. I ran into Phil Potter of the *Baltimore Sun*. He told me he thought the speech the quintessence of cynicism. This was stunning. Potter was of the Left but had sharply criticized the shallow coverage of the war and opposed, recalling Czechoslovakia and China, any coalition government. "Your old friend, Phil Potter, seems to be quite a hawk," I had memoed Nixon in May. Nixon read the piece I sent him on

Potter's speech at Johns Hopkins and dictated a note, praising Potter and asking for the full text.

Thus, I went to Nixon's suite and told him what Potter had said and urged that he take on Humphrey and say of his bombing halt north of the 17th parallel, "It is not Hubert Humphrey who will be taking that 'risk for peace,' it is the American soldiers up there on the DMZ."

I wanted Nixon to attack Humphrey for capitulating to the antiwar wing of his party by putting at risk the lives of U.S. soldiers and Marines. Not only did that seem right, it seemed necessary. For with this speech, Humphrey was seeking to unite the antiwar movement and the Democratic establishment and there was a chance he would succeed. If he did we were in trouble. As Humphrey was trying to reunite his party, I argued, we have to drive a wedge right back through it—on the war issue.

Harlow, Ellsworth, Price, and Jim Keogh were there. None agreed with me. No one thought Nixon should make Humphrey's conversion to a unilateral bombing halt a major issue. Nixon was keeping his own options open. But Humphrey was closing the breach in the Democratic Party. On October 4 another Gallup poll came out. Our 15-point lead had been cut to 12. The poll had been completed in September. Greenspan fed the figures into his computer and the computer allocated the electoral votes. The count:

RN 461
HH 11
GW 66

Humphrey had DC, Hawaii, and Rhode Island. Wallace had the five states of the Deep South he would eventually carry, plus the Carolinas. Nixon had Texas and the upper South, almost the entire Northeast, all of the Midwest, and every state west of the Mississippi to the Pacific Ocean. Why rock the boat?

After Salt Lake the campaign belonged to Humphrey. The

hostile demonstrations ended and the antiwar crowd was now cheering his pledge to halt the bombing. "If You Mean It, We're With You!" read the placards. Donations began to pour in. Humphrey regained his old "happy warrior" persona, denouncing "Fearless Fosdick" and "Richard the Chicken-Hearted" for refusing to debate and declaring Nixon's moratorium on debating the war a cop-out.

Ed Muskie had been adopted by the press as a statesmanlike contrast to Agnew, who had made a series of gaffes—calling reporter Gene Oishi the "fat Jap," using "Polacks" for Polish-Americans, and, the unpardonable sin, charging Humphrey with being "squishy soft on Communism." Press howls of "McCarthyism" followed. The press had concluded that Agnew was not qualified for the presidency, and the Democrats ran brutal attack ads. One was a lengthy sound track of laughter that followed the phrase "Vice President Spiro Agnew!" A voice warned that this was no laughing matter.

Humphrey got yet another break with Wallace's October 3 announcement of his running mate—General Curtis LeMay, who had commanded the B-29s over Japan and had said of the firestorm ignited with incendiaries over Tokyo in March 1945, "We scorched and boiled and baked to death more people in Tokyo on that night of March 9–10 than went up in vapor in Hiroshima and Nagasaki combined." At his introductory press conference in Pittsburgh, LeMay was asked if he would use nuclear weapons to end the war in Vietnam. The general stepped right in it:

> We seem to have a phobia about nuclear weapons. . . . I think there are many times when it would be most efficient to use nuclear weapons. However, public opinion in this country and throughout the world throw up their hands in horror when you mention nuclear weapons, just because of the propaganda that's been fed to them.

LeMay went on to describe the evanescent effects of the atom bombs tested on Bikini Atoll in the Marshall Islands: "The fish are all back in the lagoons; the coconut trees are growing coconuts; the guava bushes have fruit on them; the birds are back. As a matter of fact, everything is about the same." Were it necessary to achieve victory in Vietnam, LeMay said, "I would use anything we could dream up . . . including nuclear weapons." He added a postscript: The sand crabs on Bikini Atoll, said LeMay, "were a little bit hot." Wallace interrupted to stop the bleeding. But the press had its story. From that day, the Wallace tide began to recede—and Humphrey would be the beneficiary.

Something else was going Humphrey's way. While some of us were jolted by the nightly network TV news that always seemed slanted against us, we did not know the degree. Media critic Edith Efron's *The New Twisters* in 1971 would report that during the 1968 campaign, the ratio of words spoken by network reporters and anchors "against" Nixon exceeded those "for" Nixon by 11–1 on one network, 65–1 on another, and 67–1 on the third. In October 1968, the televison networks became the "Fifth Column" of the Humphrey campaign.

The momentum had shifted and I could sense it. Yet we campaigned as before. Nixon stayed with the speech the country had heard. I recalled Eisenhower's observation about planning being essential but, "plans are useless." "No plan survives contact with the enemy," Von Moltke had said. We seemed to be staying with a preconceived plan, which Von Moltke had warned against, after it had begun visibly to fail. We had lost the maneuverability we had in 1966 and the primaries of '68.

Kevin Phillips wrote Garment a strategy memo: "Wallace, HHH, and the need for an RN Second Offensive."

The greatest mistake RN could make would be repetition of the HHH error of going against the ideological re-alignment thrust of his party. The Democrats are going to be the Left party—and a minority—and the GOP are going to be the Right-Center majority. The tack to take in this conservative year is hard-hitting conservatism.

Nixon wrote on the Phillips memo that it contained good items for speech inserts: "Buchanan should prepare." One item Nixon had marked for me to take note of was Phillips's recitation of scandals in LBJ's Job Corps—muggings, rapes, and "the cost of thousands of dollars per graduate. Jobs-Corpsmen were given expensive blazers while troops in Vietnam couldn't get green T-shirts. Punks should be drafted or put in a hard-work CCC-type outfit." But nothing came of it. We continued to move serenely along.

In early October, riding on a staff bus behind the candidate's car on Long Island, I felt like a player sitting on the bench as the tide was turning against his team. I told Haldeman I wanted to transfer to the Agnew plane. I liked Agnew, supported his selection, and felt I could be of help there.

And Agnew needed help. I had been at Mission Bay when the staff gave him a rapid-fire oral exam on the issues. It had not gone well. And Agnew knew it. Then he had run into the problem with gaffes. The press had come to believe he did not belong a heartbeat away. And there was another factor working against Agnew: The press corps covering him was not the first team and they were not covering the main event. The one way they could make the front page was if Agnew fouled up. They were looking for gaffes. And by now the stories about gaffes and the media's search for more had embittered Agnew's staff against the press. The press reciprocated the sentiment. It was as bad as Nixon and the press, 1960. Yet I still believed Agnew, who had an authoritative commanding air about him, could be an asset in the border states, where our adversary was Wallace.

When I joined Agnew in Annapolis, he was elated. But I

discovered quickly that his press relations were awful. When I first got on his plane and looked back at the press, all of whom were seated, every pair of eyes staring at me seemed so full of hostility and hatred I almost broke out laughing.

For a week I wrote speeches for Agnew, worked up jokes, quips, and lines he could use on demonstrators, prepared answers to tarmac questions. It was like the primaries all over again. I was engaged. Agnew and I got on famously and would forever remain friends. While out there with him, I kept in constant contact with the Nixon plane, asking which issues they wanted us to raise. Things were going well.

Then came the call from Haldeman. The Boss wanted me back. A Gallup poll had come out showing Humphrey had sliced our 12-point lead to 8. The race was 44–36. Humphrey was surging. Wallace had dropped 6 points, losing almost a third of his vote. He was down to 15. The Northern Catholics who had been out on the town with Wallace were leaving him. They were listening as the AFL-CIO was going all out to persuade its blue-collar troops not to waste their votes on an ex–governor of Alabama who was no friend of labor. The American working class was leaving Wallace—but not coming to us. They were going home to Humphrey.

Suddenly, we were facing the Dewey situation. With our strategy of relying on the repetition of our basic message, taking no risks, sitting on our lead, coasting to a victory just weeks away, Nixon was now seen as the front-runner, the favorite, almost the incumbent, not the challenger. Humphrey, lashing out exuberantly, demanding Nixon debate, taunting him for ducking the Vietnam issue, was the hot candidate, the surging candidate, the "Give-'em-hell, Harry!" come-from-behind candidate. Nixon had called me back because he wanted to take on Humphrey the way we took on Johnson in 1966, and because I had coauthored his law-and-order articles, speeches, excerpts, and statements for three years. And law and order was the issue on which Nixon wanted to reengage, not

Vietnam, where Johnson held all the cards and could play them at a time of his choosing.

As we set out on an all-day whistle-stop train tour of western Ohio, from Cincinnati to Toledo, Nixon told me he wanted a fresh statement at every stop, all hitting Humphrey hard where he was most vulnerable—from being a lapdog of Lyndon Johnson to a conscientious objector in the war on crime. In Cincinnati we used the Humphrey quote from our 1966 statement, "I could have led a pretty good revolt myself," calling it "adult delinquency not worthy of the Vice President of the United States. . . . There is no cause that justifies breaking the law. . . . [W]e will make sure that the wave of crime is not the wave of the future in the United States." At Dayton, Nixon said,

> Hubert Humphrey . . . takes a lackadaisical do-nothing approach to law and order. For four years Mr. Humphrey has sat on his hands and watched the United States become a nation where fifty percent of American women are afraid to walk within a mile of their homes at night. . . . Freedom from fear must be restored to the cities and towns of America, and one of the first requisites is the defeat of Hubert Humphrey in November.

At London, Ohio, Nixon said, "Whenever I begin to discuss the Supreme Court, Mr. Humphrey acts like we're in church. Mr. Humphrey's respectful silence [on Supreme Court nominees] may stem from the fact that he has spent four years in Obedience School." In Deshler, Nixon noted, "In the forty-five minutes that it takes to ride from Lima to Deshler, this is what has happened in America: There has been one murder, two rapes, forty-five major crimes of violence, countless robberies and auto thefts. . . ."

"It was indisputably Law and Order Day on the rails across Ohio," wrote Witcover. Echoed Walter Mears of AP, "Who gave

Buchanan the keys to the mimeograph machine?" Nixon had ordered up the red meat and I had prepared and delivered it. But the press reports from the train of the candidate tearing into Humphrey like the Nixon of old appalled the liberals in New York. "The media boys had apoplexy," wrote Witcover. "They wanted law and order dropped and Nixon to reach Wallace voters by campaigning for social security and the minimum wage." The struggle within the staff between those who thought that a fighting center-right Republican could win and those who believed Nixon should campaign as a Rockefeller-Lindsay-Hatfield Republican would last through the election and into the White House. At its root, the quarrel was over whether Nixon should build a new governing coalition by rallying the nation against the Liberal Establishment and the New Left. Or whether, as he said the morning of his victory, mentioning a placard he had seen that day in Deshler, he should set out to "Bring Us Together," a goal some of us had come to regard as the politics of nice and utterly utopian.

With the exception of Washington, the great Presidents had earned their greatness by standing out against and routing entrenched, hostile, and powerful adversaries—as Nixon would through a politics of conflict and confrontation, not conciliation and compromise. Under Ike, Republicans had held the White House, but the party had atrophied and shriveled. Goldwater may have reduced party ranks to levels unseen since Alf Landon's rout in 1936, but, as 1966 had revealed, this party was now young, strong, vibrant, and surging in confidence. What some of us saw and the liberals and moderates in our campaign did not, or would not concede, was that conservatism was the future. Rockefeller Republicanism was dead. This did not mean the American people wished to repeal the New Deal, but it did mean the nation had had enough of LBJ's Great Society liberalism and wished to be rid of the whole crowd that had imposed it on the country.

As the race tightened and his vice presidential nominee was being blamed, inside and outside the campaign, for potentially losing the election, Nixon went out of his way to encourage his lieutenant. In his news summary, I included excerpts of a column by William F. Buckley, which said of Agnew:

> Mr. Agnew is the only spontaneous thing in town, and I like that. His instincts are gloriously unprogrammed, and I like that, too. . . .
>
> There is a view and I share it, that in Mr. Agnew, Nixon found a high deposit of the best American ore lying around: toughness, sincerity, decent-mindedness, decisiveness—much of what, after a fair amount of exposure, went into making Harry Truman a relatively happy national memory.

Nixon scribbled at the top: "Buchanan: Wire to Buckley (copy to Agnew) 'Thanks for saying deeply what I believe about Agnew.'" Nixon was showing the kind of consideration for an embattled vice president few had shown him during the phony fund scandal of 1952.

MAN IN THE ARENA

As Humphrey continued to close the gap, rumors of a breakthrough in Paris percolated. And, on Thursday, October 31, Lyndon Johnson swept the campaign out of the headlines with a dramatic White House announcement.

> I have now ordered that all air, naval and artillery bombardment of North Vietnam cease as of eight A.M. Washington time, Friday morning. I have reached this decision . . . in the belief that this action can lead to progress towards a peaceful settlement of the Vietnamese war. . . . What we now expect . . .

are prompt, productive, serious and intensive negotiations in
an atmosphere that is conducive to progress.

Johnson had changed the debate five days before the election and
shoved his whole stack in for Humphrey. If the country believed
what appeared to be true—a deal to end the war might be at hand—
this could swing it. But the White House did not have all its ducks
in a row. Twenty-four hours later, headlines about a bombing halt
had been replaced. In the *New York Times*, the new headline read,
"Saigon Opposes Paris Talk Plans, Says It Cannot Attend Next
Week." If Saigon was not aboard, peace was not at hand. Suddenly
new questions arose: Have we been had? Who fouled this up? Are
we being played one last time by Lyndon Johnson?

Reports that Anna Chennault, widow of the Flying Tigers
General Claire Chennault, had contacted Saigon and told Marshal
Nguyen Van Thieu to sabotage the talks, as he would get a better
deal from Nixon, and that our staff knew and condoned this if we
did not orchestrate it, I did not believe then and do not believe now.
Humphrey did not believe it. Nixon would never have taken the
insane risk of opening a back channel through Mrs. Chennault to
Saigon to torpedo a peace agreement negotiated to end the war in
Vietnam. Such a revelation would not only have been ruinous to
Nixon's reputation, the revelation of it would have killed his candidacy or poisoned his presidency should he win.

The simplest explanation is often the right one. Saigon had to have
concluded that Nixon, with his reputation as an anti-Communist
since the 1940s, would be tougher on their Communist enemy than
a Democratic candidate who, a month before, had promised an
unconditional halt to all bombing of North Vietnam. Why would
Saigon want Humphrey, when it was apparent Humphrey had given
up on victory? On Saturday, November 2, my thirtieth birthday, I
memoed Nixon, "LBJ has committed a major diplomatic blunder."

Hanoi has played brilliantly on Johnson's desperate desire for peace and immediate progress in the talks. Johnson had a deadline—November 5—and Hanoi knew it; so Hanoi just waited and sure enough Johnson and Old Ave [Harriman] decided to take a gamble giving Hanoi what it wanted and screwing Saigon in the process.

Tomorrow, after TV tonight and the press tomorrow morning, everybody in the United States who is aware will know something has gone terribly wrong. . . . RN does not need to make this case today and he should not for the following reasons.

First, I said, the country did not yet know what we knew, and would not know for twenty-four hours. Second, President Johnson "is embattled . . . at war with Saigon . . . being shafted by his friends in Hanoi. The press is appalled; and the American people are shocked." There is "no need for a Nixon-Johnson Battle."

And as Johnson was now in near desperation, we would be wise not to provoke him and provide a target for his wrath. The "political timing" of the bombing halt is a legitimate issue, but why substitute an argument about politics when "the country's concern is going to be about what a horrible blunder the U.S. has committed, and what . . . does this mean in Vietnam. We must address ourselves to their concern not ours."

I urged Nixon to say nothing for eighteen hours. The unfolding story would turn the public toward suspicion of LBJ's motives and mishandling of the peace negotiations. Hence the story would turn against Humphrey. We should not get into the story, but get out of the way and let the story unfold. "I know of no statement or comment that has suffered from being held up for 18 hours—but I do know a hell of a lot of them that could have been improved or better forgotten if we had waited 18 hours," I concluded, with thoughts of "the Flying *Pueblo*" very much in mind.

November 2, 1968, was a memorable day, the day I not only turned thirty but also got a call from Sears that concentrated the mind wonderfully. He began, "We're down three in the final Harris poll, 43–40, and Michigan is gone." I was jolted. It all seemed to be slipping away. I went to Nixon's suite. We were staying that last weekend at the Ambassador in L.A., as we were doing our election eve telethon from there. When I entered, Nixon was sitting with Bebe watching the Oregon Ducks playing USC. I told him about Harris and Michigan. He nodded, and went back to watching the game.

That evening Shelley and Rose invited me to join them in the main suite. When I entered there was a balloon drop. The staff had arranged a surprise birthday party, a feature of which was a full edition of the *Nixon Elector*, our campaign newspaper, devoted to my thirtieth by editor Frank Leonard, with photos of me with Nixon, Dick Allen, Marty Anderson, and Haldeman and Ehrlichman.

ELECTION EVE

On the Monday before the election we got word out of Saigon that despite or more likely because of Johnson's bombing halt, Hanoi had begun to move convoys of trucks out onto the Ho Chi Minh Trail. Humphrey had accused Nixon of trying to "frighten the American people" with the charge and said he had talked to officials who denied it was true. Correspondent Burt Okuley of UPI, however, in Vietnam, validated what Nixon had said.

> Saigon UPI—U.S. reconnaissance pilots ranging over North Vietnam have detected numerous military truck convoys moving toward S. Vietnam since the bombing halt began last Friday, American military sources said Monday. . . .
>
> U.S. informants said trucks in the area (225 miles north of the DMZ) four days ago were stacked up in a massive jam.

The sources said it was not known whether the trucks were waiting for the bombing halt which started the same day or had stopped because the road was washed out.

In a last preelection memo, I urged Nixon to "nail him on this one," as voters went to the polls to choose the 37th President.

THE LAST TELETHON

Richard Nixon was in a good mood. He sat in his comfortable black swivel chair with the back that had been tightened, his legs crossed, his smile seeming less forced than usual, his voice and rhetoric pleasantly subdued. If camera four had been any closer it would have put out his eye.

He leaned into it as Bud Wilkinson read each question and responded in his most conversational tone. The substance was no different from what it had been all along, but the style was at its peak. The social security question was repeated at the beginning of each hour—on both shows—so that anyone who had just tuned in would be sure to hear that Richard Nixon did not intend to have senior citizens forming bread lines in the streets.

Thus did Joe McGinniss describe the last campaign appearance of 1968, a four-hour telethon in Los Angeles, on Monday, November 4, where Nixon took questions from across America phoned in to a bank of Nixon women volunteers, including Julie and Tricia. A studio audience was there to cheer the candidate on. As McGinniss wrote in *The Selling of the President*, which earned him a small fortune, in the final hours of that campaign Nixon was at the top of his game.

The producer of those four hours of national television, split by a one-hour intermission, was twenty-eight-year-old Roger Ailes, who limped around, as he had torn ligaments in his ankle from a rookie parachute jump. In a room offstage, as in the Oregon primary telethon, I would take in the questions called in to the Nixon volunteers, read and rewrite them, and dictate more precise questions to Rose, Shelley, and Marge Acker, who would type them up.

Then I put the questions in a tiny pile in the order they were to be asked and sent the packets out to Coach Wilkinson. Rewrite was essential, for the questions came in as "What about Vietnam?" or "Social Security?" I might rewrite it to say, "Is there truth to the charge that, if elected, you will change Social Security?" This gave Nixon an opportunity to rebut the charge and address his plan to index Social Security to protect benefits from being eaten up by inflation. Nixon told me he wanted the Social Security question asked twice each hour to knock down the Democratic charge that was so ruinous to Goldwater. We wanted to be certain that Nixon touched all of the critical issues and introduced a wide variety to keep it interesting. Coach Wilkinson would put the new packet on the bottom of his pile and ask the questions in the order in which he received them. Hence, I knew what questions were coming and in what order they were to come. Nixon did not.

Having prepared Nixon's briefing books for years, I noted that almost all the questions that came in during the telethon we had anticipated, and we had written answers with backup material. By now Nixon had dealt with these questions scores of times in a year of campaigning. Unlike Ronald Reagan, who would prepare for presidential press conferences by standing behind a podium in the White House theater as we fired questions at him, Nixon, from the day I went to work for him, would retreat to solitary confinement, study for hours the briefing book Q & A I had prepared, write notes on each page of the book, then emerge, sometimes after two days, to perform. Nixon was like an actor who not only studied his lines but rewrote them and decided how he would deliver them.

One understood why he had been an excellent student, why class-mates at Duke had called him "Iron Butt." Yet it paid off. Nixon's presidential press conferences may have descended into gladiatorial contests, but almost always they gave him a boost in the polls, as a nation sitting down to watch would take sides, and usually against the bear-baiters.

It was said the telethon was fixed. This is absurd. Nixon, over the course of the campaign, had held countless press conferences and press availabilities and taken questions on rope lines and from live audiences. I had kept him updated with Q & A based on the day's news and with Q & A from the Greenspan and Allen shops, crammed into a briefing book, on all issues foreign and domestic. Nixon's book was constantly updated, with issues regularly dropped and added and the whole book retyped every few weeks. There was virtually no question—political, national, or international—Nixon could be asked that he had not been asked before. Indeed, I sought out questions that would bring some freshness and spontaneity that would let Nixon roam. During the telethon we did, however, ensure he hit critical issues where the Democrats were attacking—Agnew's qualifications, Social Security, Vietnam, crime—again and again.

We were never apprehensive that Nixon would be caught flat-footed and fumble or fall into a gaffe. Intending no disrespect to the governor of Michigan, Richard Nixon was no George Romney. We looked on televised questioning of Nixon by his press adversaries as opportunities, his strongest format in the campaign and the White House. Among his finer performances in 1968 had been the one before the American Society of Newspaper Editors, where Nixon had opened himself up to questioning by the editors after Governor Rockefeller bored them with one of his ponderous speeches on more money for the cities. Nixon had stolen the show and reinforced the impression that this Nixon of '68 was not the candidate of '60 or of '62.

As for that final telethon, Nixon wrote after his presidency that going ahead with those four hours was "my best campaign decision. Had we not had that last telethon, I believe Humphrey would have squeaked through with a close win on Election Day."

ELECTION DAY, November 5, 1968, Nixon and staff boarded the *Tricia* and flew across America, as Americans went to the polls to choose the 37th President of the United States. When I awoke that morning in Los Angeles, however, I noted something odd. Both hands had broken out in hives that made them twice normal size. This had to be stress-related. My fear that morning was that we had lost it, that the Humphrey surge, the Wallace fade, the bombing halt, and the sense peace might be at hand may have cost us, in the last few days, the prize for which we had worked for years, a prize that had seemed assured just weeks before.

On the plane back, the writers were called up to the front. Nixon seemed relaxed, confident, fatalistic about the outcome. After the previous evening's jolting remark on the telethon about getting down to the "nut-cutting," he went into a disquisition on "sheep fries" and "lamb fries"—testicles, how they were obtained, and how delicious some folks thought they were. Landing in New York, we motorcaded to the Waldorf Astoria.

As the returns began to come in, giving us Tennessee and Kentucky, it appeared the outer South—Virginia, North Carolina, Florida—was coming our way. Wallace had been driven back into the Deep South. Early in the evening, Humphrey came on strong, winning Maine, Massachusetts, Rhode Island, Connecticut, New York, Pennsylvania, Michigan, and Minnesota. But once we left the Northeast and the industrial Midwest, and headed into the farm belt, the plains and mountain states, and the far West, there did not seem to be a sufficient number of states for Humphrey to cobble together the 270 electoral votes to make him president. As Teddy White wrote, "By midnight, it was quite clear that Richard

M. Nixon had won 202 electoral votes . . . and George Wallace had won 45 electoral votes in five Southern states, and between them Nixon and Wallace held 247 sure electoral votes." If Nixon won just 23 added electoral votes from a basket of states where he was the favorite, Humphrey was out of the running. The question of the night at the Waldorf now became: Will we get to 270 or fall short?

If Humphrey could win 225 electoral votes, then Nixon, though he might win both the popular and electoral vote totals, could be denied the presidency. For the issue would go to the House of Representatives, where the Democratic Party, despite the losses of '66, still held a 60-vote margin.

By 3 a.m., it appeared Ohio, Missouri, and California were going for Nixon. We did not need Illinois. Yet Cook County had not come in. We were told that friends in neighboring DuPage County were—memories of 1960 fresh—holding out Republican votes, so Daley would not know how many votes he needed to make up for his candidate. Rose's brother, an ex–FBI agent, was now the sheriff of Cook County, and there were reports in Chicago before the election that hundreds of FBI agents were flooding into the city. How much of this was true, I am unsure. Early Wednesday, fed up with the holdout in Chicago, John Mitchell called Mike Wallace at CBS to demand that Daley throw in his votes. Daley was short of what Humphrey needed, and threw them in. It didn't matter. Richard Nixon, without Illinois, was President of the United States.

Postscript

Nixon was the first President since Zachary Taylor in 1849 to take office without carrying either house of Congress. Not only was Capitol Hill firmly in the hands of the opposition, the federal bureaucracy was saturated with New Deal and Great Society Democrats. The Washington press corps largely loathed Nixon, with many bearing grudges dating to the Truman era. The Supreme Court of his old nemesis Earl Warren was at the pinnacle of its power. And the best and the brightest who had led America into Vietnam were deserting the cause they had once championed to join their children in protest of what they would soon discover was "Nixon's War."

Yet the years that followed that 1969 inaugural would be a time of extraordinary accomplishment. By spring of 1973, all U.S. troops were out of Vietnam, the POWs were home, every provincial capital was in Saigon's hands. Having mined Haiphong harbor and bombed Hanoi, Nixon had ended the war with honor, as he had promised. Americans had walked on the moon. Nixon had negotiated SALT I and the ABM treaty, the greatest arms-limitation treaties since the Washington Naval Agreement. He had ended decades of hostility between the United States and the People's Republic of China dating to Mao's revolution and the Korean War. He had put an end to the draft, signed into law the eighteen-year-old vote, put four justices on the Supreme Court, including Chief Justice Warren Burger and future chief justice William Rehnquist. He had created the Environmental Protection Agency, the Occupational Safety and Health Administration, the National Cancer Institute. Though routinely denounced for a "Southern Strategy," by the time he left office he had desegregated the public schools of the South and been rewarded in 1972 with the greatest landslide in modern history, winning 62 percent of the vote and 49 states, creating the New Majority that would dominate presidential politics until 1992. He would go on to rescue Israel from defeat in the Yom Kippur War, end Soviet domination of Egypt, and convert that largest of Arab nations into a de facto American ally for four decades, from Sadat through Mubarak.

Had Nixon stepped down in January 1973 he would be ranked as one of the great or near-great presidents. But loyalists at the Committee to Reelect the President had foolishly authorized a break-in to bug phones at the Democratic National Committee, and, about to be exposed, rushed to the White House, where a clumsy effort was made to contain the fallout. "A prime minister has to be a good butcher," Asquith had said. Nixon was not a good butcher. He was indecisive. He delayed and dissembled until what would have been a political embarrassment metastasized into a scandal that grew until August 1974, when the President of the United States with the largest landslide in the history of American politics was forced to resign his office. His enemies, repudiated and humiliated after the Democratic debacle of 1972, but still dominant in both houses of Congress, the bureaucracy, and the media, used the residual power of the capital to effect the first successful coup d'état in U.S. history. The first attempt, against Andrew Johnson for reaching his hand out to the defeated South, had failed by one vote.

Nixon was not without fault. I told him in San Clemente, "We gave them a sword and they ran it right though us." He would use the metaphor in his David Frost interviews.

In all of this, I was there, right from the beginning and right to the end, intimately involved in every battle of Nixon's White House years, as I was in those of his "wilderness years," described in this book. Those were the days of the largest mass demonstrations in U.S. history, the Great Silent Majority speech of 1969, the Agnew attack on the TV networks and national press, the secret bombing and invasion of Cambodia, the 1970 campaign against the "Radical Liberals," the Pentagon Papers, the opening to China, the rout of McGovern, the rise of the New Majority. Came then the Christmas Bombing, the end of the Vietnam War, the return of the POWs, John Dean's defection, the firing of Haldeman and Ehrlichman, the Watergate hearings, the resignation of Agnew and the Saturday Night Massacre, impeachment hearings, and discovery of the "smoking gun" tape at Camp David on August 3, 1974, that led to Nixon's resignation by week's end. But all that is the subject, the Lord willing, of another book.

Acknowledgments

THIS MEMOIR IS the fruit of recollections, refreshed and forti-
fied by half a dozen cabinet drawers of personal files from January
1966 to the final hours of the campaign of 1968 that gave Richard
Nixon the presidency. For half a century these files had remained
untouched. They contain thousands of clippings from those three
years, before the advent of the computer and word processor, with
individual files for the columnists, commentators, newspapers, and
magazines of that era, and Nixon staffers and opponents.

Within these cabinet drawers are perhaps a thousand memos
to and from "RN" and "DC," our code for the Boss. From these,
and what the Lord blessed me with, a good memory for anecdotes
and phrases—all buttressed by the two dozen books on which I
have drawn to reconfirm events, dates, comments, and quotes—*The
Greatest Comeback* emerged.

Special thanks go to my wife, Shelley, who was with Nixon
in his campaigns for president in 1960, for governor in 1962, and
for Goldwater in 1964, before I arrived at Nixon, Mudge from St.
Louis. Shelley has been the custodian of these files since we were
married, May 8, 1971, with the President and First Lady Pat Nixon
in attendance.

My gratitude, again, to my friend of three decades, Fredrica
Friedman, who first came to see me in Ronald Reagan's White

House and has been my ambassador to the publishing world and agent now for nine books.

Thanks, too, to my friend Dr. Frank Mintz, who has spent much of the last two years rereading, editing, and remarking upon my changing chapter drafts from his own experience as a scholar of history and observer and participant in the political events of the 1960s. My thanks also to Professor John David Briley of East Tennessee State University, who provided boxes of documents from the archives at the Nixon Library in Yorba Linda from those days that the Boss called his "wilderness years." Finally, my appreciation to Roger Scholl, my editor at Crown Forum, and Derek Reed, who aided in the photo search; to Jonathan Mavroydis at the Nixon Foundation; and to my friend from those Nixon comeback days, Dwight Chapin, for helping run down photographs from almost fifty years ago.

Appendix

Parks & Knox

MEMO TO RN
From Buchanan
July 24, 1967

① *The office must be a disaster (5 days to get a letter typed*
② *Better get Huston or someone to work*

✓

    Ron McCoy, who is supposed to be heading up our ____
Youth For Nixon operation, gave me a call---having exhausted
his recourse with the Nixon for President Operation. Here is
his problem. A) He has no money budgeted and B) He himself ad-
mits that he does not have the experience or background at nineteen to be running *the* organization. He says he could be fine
as a front man; but he needs somebody with experience guiding
him.

    As of right now, we have exactly zero in the Youth
Department he says, and it is not likely we will have anything
even by November unless we make a crash effort now.

    What he wants is both guidance and some dough to do some
of the mailings that he feels are necessary. T. Huston has talked
with him, he says, over the weekend, giving him some helpful advice.
My suggestion is that we get Huston to work full-time in the even-
ings with this kid, to show him what to do, to set him
up etc. But I think that this is going to take some dough; not
much but some. What is so disgusting about the current situation
is that it was predictable and predicted, and if we had done
this five months ago, we might be in good shape right
now.

                                     Buchanan

MEMO TO RN

From Buchanan

October 17, 1967

Handwritten annotations:
Pat —
① inform the local F.B.I. Chief
② Continue to see him — emphasizing "RN is tough but not doctrinaire..."

I mentioned some time ago that I ran into a Russian individual at a party who had requested an autographed copy of "Six Crises." They left a copy of the book at my home. I got Rose to drop "With Best Wishes, Richard Nixon" in it, got a call from the Russian Legation at the UN, met with a fellow named "Edward," the press secretary last night.

"Edward" was not like the first character who was a heavy drinker and not very bright. Edward is sharp, very knowledgeable in global affairs; he did some work at Columbia and a little at the Journalism School, 1962-3.

He spaces his scotches well; Buchanan stayed on draft beer. He is very interested in a number of things. Our conversation touched on these subjects.

What are RN's chances. On this I ran the party line by him, the same sort of thing that is running in the press about the necessity of winning the primaries and then, if we win them, the excelllent chances of victory at Miami. We ran ████████ briefly over the other candidates.

Foreign affairs. He is concerned about RN's tough policies on trade, on which he was surprisingly well versed. You will never get the European co-operation on this, he said. Also, he says the Russians will never tolerate economic or diplomatic pressures; also, as for Vietnam, the North Vietnamese will never ████ quit. They will fight to the death.

MANCHESTER  UNION LEADER   NEW HAMPSHIRE SUNDAY NEWS

"*There Is Nothing So Powerful As Truth*"

UNION LEADER CORPORATION
MANCHESTER, N. H. 03105
AREA CODE 603-625-5432

WILLIAM LOEB
PRESIDENT AND PUBLISHER

January 8, 1968

Honorable Richard M. Nixon
20 Broad Street
New York, New York

Pat
go up + have a chat
with Loeb

Dear Dick:

The attached editorial about George Wallace speaks for itself.
Nackey and I spent several hours with George when he was in New Hampshire
earlier this year. This fellow is no dope.

I neve never been able to make anybody in your camp, or in
Reagan's camp, understand that if Wallace runs as an independent, you might
just as well forget the Republican nomination--it will be worthless.

Now that the latest Gallup Poll has shown that Wallace would
take 12 per cent of the popular vote, most of; them from Republicans, I hope
you will realize the fact that in addition to gaining the nomination, the next
important thing is to stop Wallace from running. Find out what he wants and
give it to him. It would be the best political bargain you ever made.

Incidentally, Dick, take it easy on the pro-negro speeches.
Neither the popular vote nor justice is in that direction. You have no idea how
stirred up the people in the metropolitan cities are on this subject, especially
those in the north.

Driving into New York City from LaGuardia a short while ago,
the cab driver said to me, "I have always been a Democrat, but all Dick Nixon's
got to say is, 'I am going to enforce the laws of this nation equally without regard to race or color and I am going to stop treating the negro as if he had a
right to break laws and get away with it", and he has my vote.

Thank you for your Christmas card. As depicted on the card,
I thought the family looked very well.

NEW HAMPSHIRE'S LARGEST NEWSPAPER COVERING THE NEW HAMPSHIRE MARKET

Draft

MEMO TO RN

From Buchanan

October 23, 1967

In the timing and writing of the volunteer army thing, we should consider carefully, what the reaction will be in light of the fact that this was one of the anti-war ~~peaenkixx~~ peacenik's major gripes at that demonstration. <u>Will it be said</u> <u>that RN is giving these guys the means to avoid service---and will</u> <u>then our genuine position be lost in the ensuing discussion.</u>

Buchanan

MEMORANDUM

December 4, 1967

This memo substantially represents DC's views — Duplicate as is & distribute to staff who talk to Press

Dealing with the press is an imperfect science; but from experience of recent months some useful guidelines have emerged. These are but a few of them.

A) <u>No discussion of strategy at all is the best policy.</u>

Almost without exception, the stories that have come out about the DC strategy have damaged us in some quarter. As soon as the Times says we are thinking of running with a Lindsay, a Percy or a Volpe, we alienable others groups and other individuals, who either do not like Lindsay or Percy or Volpe or who see themselves in the job.

Stories that puport to say that RN is running in New Hampshire to defense Governor Reagan, or because he is concerned about leakage to Governor Rockefeller don't do a bit of good. They make the Unity candidated, the candidate who is not running against any Republican, look like the rest of the crowd which are running against each other.

Also, the provide grist for the mills of those who write regularly with the lead "Strategists ████ for former Vice President Richard Nixon are increasingly goncerned about the growing momentum of the _____ candidacy.

Any story that says how we are going to use TV, or whether brings out other stories that we are "concerned" about the use of tv, worreid about image etc. All this is "defensive" crap, damaging as far as we are concerned, and counter-productive in dealing with the loser thing.

RN's people ought to stop ████████ the excessive frankness and leveling with press guys which has been evident in the past and has done us no good. Let the press find our problems themselvez without us pointing out the way; let's not give them anything with which to hang us on.

URGENT

MEMO TO: Pat Buchanan

FROM: Bill Timmons

DATE: Friday, March 22, 1968

SUBJECT: Open Housing Bill before Congress

HELP, HELP, HELP !!

In the South we are in serious trouble over the ~~alleged~~
press reports that RN called leading members of the House to
urge adoption of the Senate version of the Civil Rights-Open
Housing legislation. This was carried in the NY Times, Washington
Post and , unfortunately, many southern newspapers. Not only are
"kooks" and diehard conservatives upset but so are members of
congress from the South who have stuck their necks out for our
candidate. A week from tomorrow is the South Carolina GOP State
Convention, and our guys will catch the devil if they are not
prepared. RN personally told me last fall that he was on record
against a national open housing law -- that it should be left up
to the states. Is there a U.S. News reprint or something else
we can use? Secondly, did he in fact call the leadership on this
matter?

HELP, HELP, HELP!

[handwritten: B.T.]

[handwritten: Just keep lid on as well as possible R.N. has only asked Ford et al to get a bill + remove the issue — he has not told them how to kill it]

[handwritten: NOT BROCK BUT THURMOND, WATSON, Thompson etc.]

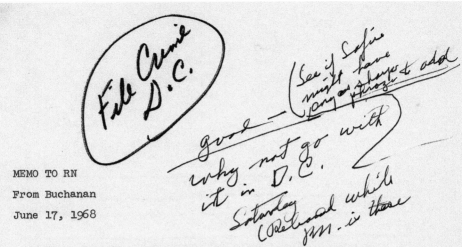

MEMO TO RN
From Buchanan
June 17, 1968

    Attached is a rough of a statement which Buchanan and
Bellmx prepared. It could serve as the basis of an editorial
soon, when we get a peg to hang it on. Would hate to see Rocky
make the pledge to "sweep crime from the streets of the American
capital."

                    Buchanan

Note---Hahn has been praised by WPost and WStar, and has went his
proposal (attached)all over the country---If NR's people are looking
sharply, they will find here something I think.

File RJB Personal

The New York Times -- Sunday, September 22, 1968

PRESIDENT'S HOPES FOR SUMMIT RECEDE

By Benjamin Welles

Washington, September 21 -- Senior United States officials have made it clear that the occupation of Czechoslovakia a month ago has rivtually eliminated President Johnson's hopes for a summit meeting with leaders of the Soviet Union.

The psychological effect throughout Western Europe would be grave, one official said recently, if Mr. Johnson were to go to Geneva at this time to talk disarmament with the Soviet leaders.

[handwritten:] Statement? ? ? ?

no

Shelby File RJB Personal

I have told L.B.J. (through Rusk) that a trip would be a mistake — If he does it — I will hit him on it — But I feel I should give him time to react

Partial Bibliography

Ambrose, Stephen E. *Nixon, Vol. 2: The Triumph of a Politician 1962–1972*. New York: Simon & Schuster, 1989.

Burke, Bob, and Ralph G. Thompson. Foreword by Henry Kissinger. *Bryce Harlow: Mr. Integrity*. Oklahoma City: Oklahoma Heritage Association, 2000.

Califano, Joseph A., Jr. *The Triumph and Tragedy of Lyndon Johnson: The White House Years*. New York: Simon & Schuster, 1991.

Chester, Lewis, Godfrey Hodgson, and Bruce Page. *An American Melodrama: The Presidential Campaign of 1968*. New York: Viking Press, 1969.

Garment, Leonard. *Crazy Rhythm: My Journey from Brooklyn, Jazz, and Wall Street to Nixon's White House, Watergate, and Beyond . . .* New York: Times Books, 1997.

Johnson, Lyndon Baines. *The Vantage Point: Perspectives of the Presidency, 1963–1969*. New York: Holt, Rinehart and Winston, 1971.

Mailer, Norman. *Miami and the Siege of Chicago*. New York: World, 1968.

Margolis, Jon. *The Last Innocent Year: America in 1964—The Beginning of the "Sixties."* New York: William Morrow, 1999.

Matthews, Christopher. *Kennedy and Nixon: The Rivalry That Shaped Postwar America*. New York: Simon & Schuster, 1996.

Mazo, Earl, and Stephen Hess. *Nixon: A Political Portrait*. New York: Harper & Row, 1968.

McGinniss, Joe. *The Selling of the President*. New York: Andre Deutsch, 1970.

Nixon, Richard. *RN: The Memoirs of Richard Nixon*. New York: Grosset & Dunlap, 1978.

Nixon, Richard M. *Six Crises*. Garden City, NY: Doubleday, 1962.

Oshinsky, David M. *A Conspiracy So Immense: The World of Joe McCarthy*. New York: The Free Press, 1983.

Patterson, James T. *The Eve of Destruction: How 1965 Transformed America.* New York: Basic Books, 2012.

Perlstein, Rick. *Nixonland: The Rise of a President and the Fracturing of America.* New York: Scribner, 2008.

Safire, William. *Before the Fall: An Inside View of the Pre-Watergate White House.* Garden City, NY: Doubleday, 1975.

Whalen, Richard J. *Catch the Falling Flag: A Republican's Challenge to His Party.* Boston: Houghton Mifflin, 1972.

White, Theodore H. *The Making of the President 1968.* New York: Atheneum, 1969.

Wicker, Tom. *One of Us: Richard Nixon and the American Dream.* New York: Random House, 1991.

Wilson, Woodrow. Arthur Bernon Tourtellot, ed. *Selections for Today.* New York: Duell, Sloan & Pearce, 1945.

Witcover, Jules. *The Resurrection of Richard Nixon.* New York: G. P. Putnam's Sons, 1970.

Witcover, Jules. *White Knight: The Rise of Spiro Agnew.* New York: Random House, 1972.

Witcover, Jules. *The Year the Dream Died: Revisiting 1968 in America.* Foreword by David Halberstam. New York: Grand Central Publishing, 1998.

INTERVIEWS

Janet S. Cramer with Paul S. Smith, February 9, 1977. Richard M. Nixon Project/The Life and Times of Richard M. Nixon. Fullerton, CA: California State University, Fullerton, n.d.

Ed Edwin with Earl Mazo, November 1971. Eisenhower Administration. New York: Oral History Research Office, Columbia University, 1973.

TRANSCRIPTS, TELEVISION PROGRAMMING

William F. Buckley. *Firing Line*: Discussion with Robert Novak, "Elections 1966 and 1968." Public Broadcasting System, n.d.

Howard K. Smith. *News and Comment*: "The Political Obituary of Richard M. Nixon." ABC Television: Sunday, November 11, 1962.

INDEX